LONGMANS' LINGUISTICS LIBRARY

A SHORT HISTORY OF LINGUISTICS

Also in Longmans' Linguistics Library

The Linguistic Sciences and Language Teaching
M. A. K. Halliday, Angus McIntosh and Peter Strevens

General Linguistics: *An Introductory Survey*
R. H. Robins

A Linguistic Study of the English Verb
F. R. Palmer

What *is* Language? *A New Approach to Linguistic Description*
Robert M. W. Dixon

In Memory of J. R. Firth
Editors: C. E. Bazell, J. C. Catford, M. A. K. Halliday and R. H. Robins

Patterns of Language: *Papers in General, Descriptive and
Applied Linguistics*
Angus McIntosh and M. A. K. Halliday

Selected Papers of J. R. Firth 1952–59
Editor: F. R. Palmer

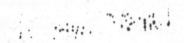

A Short
History of Linguistics

R. H. Robins
Professor of General Linguistics
in the University of London

 LONGMANS

LONGMANS, GREEN AND CO LTD
48 Grosvenor Street, London W.1

Associated companies, branches and representatives
throughout the world

First published 1967

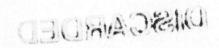

Made and printed in Great Britain
by William Clowes and Sons, Limited, London and Beccles

Preface

In this book I have attempted to give a brief account of the history of linguistic studies up to the present day. For the reasons stated in the first chapter, the narrative is organized around the history of linguistics in Europe, but it is my hope that due notice has been taken of the contributions that the subject has drawn from work originating outside the European continent.

The history of linguistics is now widely recognized as a field for teaching and research, and it has been incorporated into the syllabus of courses in linguistics in a number of universities in Great Britain and elsewhere. The interest currently being shown by linguists in past developments and in the earlier history of their subject is in itself a sign of the maturity of linguistics as an academic discipline, quite apart from any practical applications of linguistic science. It is my hope that the present book will go some part of the way towards fulfilling teachers' and students' needs in this field, both in deepening their appreciation of what has been done in the study of language and in suggesting profitable areas of further research.

In venturing on a book of this scope, one is at once made conscious of a number of difficulties. In the first place, no one person can achieve anything like equal familiarity with the entire range of linguistic work that such an undertaking requires of him. Secondly, the extent, the nature, and the present state of the source material varies widely from one period to another. There are lamentable gaps in our knowledge of some of the early pioneers of linguistics, while in the contemporary history of current trends the problem is an opposite one, that of trying to select from the great mass of published material that which is likely to be of permanent historical significance. Moreover, different periods vary greatly in the amount of basic research already undertaken; quite a lot has been written on the Greco-Roman era of linguistics, and a number of recent historical treatments have followed the inspiration of

Pedersen's important *Linguistic science in the nineteenth century*; Chomsky has recently drawn attention to some striking anticipations of present-day topics in the works of certain seventeenth-century writers; studies of mediaeval and Renaissance work within the various branches of knowledge comprised by general linguistics are now being taken in hand, but a great deal remains to be done before a really satisfactory full-scale historical treatment of the years linking western antiquity with the modern world can be envisaged.

If one looks outside Europe to the linguistic scholarship on which Europeans drew so heavily and so beneficially, the need for editions and commentaries is no less urgent. Much of Chinese, Arabic, and Indian linguistic work has been extensively studied already, but largely from the standpoint of its place in the cultural and literary history of the peoples themselves. Scholarly treatments that relate individual writings in these fields to current linguistic theory and practice will fill a considerable gap in our understanding of the world's cultural history.

For all these reasons, in addition to the inadequacy of the author's knowledge and abilities in relation to this self-imposed task, readers are likely to find substantial grounds for disagreement and disappointment with what is here written. But if this book should stimulate further detailed research into our sources for the history of linguistics, it will have achieved a part of its purpose.

In trying to cover so wide an area, one is made more than usually aware of one's debt to contemporary and to earlier scholars who have laboured in this field. This debt is partially acknowledged in the bibliographical references that follow each chapter. More personally, I am happy to express my thanks to colleagues in London and elsewhere whom I have consulted, and in particular to Professor David Abercrombie, for his painstaking help in reading and checking the text of this book and for his important comments and corrections, and to those who have been kind enough to read drafts of chapters dealing with topics in which they are far better qualified than I am: Dr. Theodora Bynon, Mrs. Vivian Salmon, and Mr. K. L. Speyer. The book is the better for their help and advice; I remain responsible for any remaining errors and blemishes. Finally, I have been greatly assisted by the kindness and patience of my wife, who read through the entire book in typescript, making numerous valuable suggestions on diverse points of detail.

London, 1967   R. H. ROBINS

Contents

'Pereant qui ante nos nostra dixerunt',
Aelius Donatus apud St. Jerome
(*To the devil with those who took the words out
of our mouths*)
'Alles Gescheidte ist schon gedacht worden,
man muss nur versuchen es noch einmal zu
denken', Goethe
(*Everything worthwhile has been thought of
already, one must just try and think of it once
more*)

One

Introduction

During the greater part of our lives, we accept our use and understanding of our native language without awareness, comment, or questioning. Memories of early childhood and experience in bringing up young children may cause us temporarily to ponder the complexity of every normal person's linguistic ability, and the learning of one or more foreign languages after mastering one's first or native tongue reveals just how much is involved in mankind's faculty of communication through language.

However, despite this general acceptance of the gift of articulate speech, most cultures in the world have engendered among certain of their members some realization of the scope and power of language. This linguistic self-consciousness may be first stimulated by contacts with foreign speakers, by the existence and recognition of dialect cleavage within a speech community, or by a particular orientation of man's inherent and disinterested curiosity about himself and the world around him. From this source springs 'folk linguistics', speculation or dogmatic pronouncement about the origin of language, or of one's own language, and its place in the life of the community. It may take the form of pejorative comments on other dialects and other languages; but many cultures contain aetiological myths purporting to describe the origin of language as a whole or, at least, of the favoured language of the people. The conception of language as a special gift of a god has been found in several diverse and unrelated cultures, and is itself significant of the reverence rightly accorded by reflective persons to this priceless human capability.[1]

In certain cultures, namely those that are for this and for other reasons credited with the title of civilizations, curiosity and awareness of one's environment have been able to grow into science, the systematic study of a given subject or range of phenomena, deliberately fostered and transmitted from one generation to another by persons recognized for their skill and knowledge in a particular activity of this sort; and all mankind owes a great debt to those cultures that have in one way or another fostered the growth of the sciences.

Among the sciences that arise in this fashion, folk linguistics has developed in different parts of the civilized world into linguistic science. The term *science* in the collocation *linguistic science* is used here deliberately, but not restrictively. Science in this context is not to be distinguished from the humanities, and the virtues of exactness and of intellectual self-discipline on the one hand, and of sensitivity and imagination on the other are all called into operation in any satisfactory study of language.

The sciences of man, which include linguistics, arise from the development of human self-awareness. But equally these sciences, or more strictly their practitioners, may become aware of themselves for what they are doing and for what they have done. When this scientific self-awareness includes an interest in the origin and past development of a science, we may recognize the birth of that specific discipline known as the history of science. In recent years the rapid and at times bewildering growth in linguistics as an academic subject, both in the numbers of scholars involved and in the range of their activities, has led to a corresponding growth in the interest of linguists in the past history of the subject. In part this may be due to the feeling that some understanding and appreciation of the problems and achievements of earlier generations may be a source of stability during a period of unprecedentedly swift changes in theory, procedures, and applications.

Linguistic science today, like other parts of human knowledge and learning, and like all aspects of human cultures, is the product of its past and the matrix of its future. Individuals are born, grow up, and live in an environment physically and culturally determined by its past; they participate in that environment, and some are instrumental in effecting changes in it. This is the basis of human history. Like a people and like an intellectual or moral conception, a science (in the widest sense) has its history. Scientists do not start from scratch in each generation, but they work within and on the basis of the situation which their science, and science in general, has inherited in their culture and in their age. Historical thinking about science or about anything else in human affairs consists in the study of the temporal sequences of persons and events, and the causal connections, influences, and trends, that may be discovered in them and may throw light on them.

It is tempting, and flattering to one's contemporaries, to see the history of a science as the progressive discovery of the truth and the attainment of the right methods. But this is a fallacy. The aims of a science vary in the course of its history, and the search for objective standards by which to judge the purposes of different periods is apt to be an elusive one. 'The facts' and 'the truth' are not laid down in advance, like the solution to a crossword puzzle, awaiting the completion of discovery. Scientists themselves do much to determine the range of facts, phenomena, and operations that fall within their purview, and they themselves set up and modify the conceptual framework within which they make what they regard as significant statements about them.

Brief historical sketches of a subject, such as are often included in introductory textbooks, inevitably look at the past through the eyes of the present, concentrating on those aspects of earlier work that seem either peculiarly relevant or, on the other side, shockingly irrelevant, to present-day approaches. This is quite proper, indeed it is almost inevitable, in such a short notice; but it carries with it the danger of evaluating all past work in a subject from the point of view in favour at the present, and of envisaging the history of a science as an advance, now steady, now temporarily interrupted or diverted, towards the predetermined goal of the present state of the science.

This does not mean that one should exclude the evaluation of past work against later achievements and against the present position in the same field, where there is reason to see therein a definite advance. Indeed, such comparisons may be rewarding, in that they show which aspects of a science were most favoured by particular circumstances and in particular periods and areas of civilization. What is needed is an attempt to discern the evolution of the past into the present and the changing states of the science in its changing cultural environments. One should strive to avoid the deliberate selection of only those parts of earlier work that can be brought into a special relationship with present-day interests.

If history is to be more than just an annalistic record of the past, some subjective judgment is inevitable in the ordering and in the interpretation of events; hence the classic statement that there can be no unbiased history. In the history of a science, and in the present case in the history of linguistics, there is the additional subjective element involved in determining what activities and aims on the part of earlier workers shall be deemed to fall within its sphere and so to belong to its history. In order not to impose the standards of linguistics today on the decision on what to admit as linguistic work from the past, we may agree to understand as part of the history of linguistics any systematic study directed towards some aspect or aspects of language envisaged as an interesting and worthy object of such study in its own right.

Changes and developments in a science are determined by a number of causes. Every science grows from its past, and the state reached in a previous generation provides the starting point for the next. But no science is carried on in a vacuum, without reference to or contact with other sciences and the general atmosphere in which learning of any sort is encouraged or tolerated in a culture. Scientists and men of learning are also men of their age and country, and they are participants in the culture within which they live and work. Besides its own past, the course of a science is also affected by the social context of its contemporary world and the intellectual premises dominant in it. Applications of the science, its uses for practical purposes and the expectations that others have of it, may be a very important determinant of the directions of its growth and changes. In linguistics, as elsewhere, attempted and projected applications, practical ends to be achieved, have often preceded the statement of the theoretical positions on which they implicitly depend.

Scientists are not all alike in ability, motivation, and inspiration. Every practitioner must learn his craft and master the state of his science as it is presented to him when he enters upon it; and if it is to continue, some must teach it in turn to others. Probably most scientists must be content to do no more than that, but every lively branch of knowledge attracts a few men of outstanding enterprise who are able to take some control of its direction and to respond positively to the challenges that the present inherits from the past. Such persons think more deeply and question accepted theory and practice more searchingly. If a culture is not to be entirely static they are a necessity, and in our own European history it is fortunate that ancient Greece of the classical age produced men of this character in hitherto unprecedented numbers and of unprecedented qualities, in so many spheres of human thought and activity.

When some lead, others follow; and leaders and innovators in a science, given favourable circumstances or making for themselves favourable circumstances, become the founders of schools, with disciples and followers continuing the exploitation of the lines of thought or practice developed by the founder or leader. Changes in scientific thinking and in scientific attitudes may arise from outside or from inside the science whose history is being traced. The existing state of a science, the starting point for any change, is the product both of external and internal factors. The general contemporary intellectual and social context, whether favouring stability or encouraging change, is largely external to the particular science itself, although each science and branch of learning is a part of the whole context along with all the others and along with the general cultural attitude towards learning.

When the dominant innovators in a science respond to the challenge of a situation that demands some change in its practice, this may take a number of forms, and rival schools may grow up around different leaders responding differently to a particular situation. These rivalries may be reinforced and perpetuated by the use of standard textbooks in the teaching of newcomers to the field. Any empirical science (and linguistics is an empirical science, since its data are observable) must be able to cope with its own phenomena, and once any observation is accepted as relevant its theory and modes of description and analysis must be able to handle it, and to handle it with scientific adequacy, of which exhaustiveness, consistency, and economy are canons. Fresh data, or the extension of a science to new but relevant fields, may require the further elaboration and articulation of existing theory along lines similar to those followed in the past and logically implied by them; it may, on the other hand, demand a radical recasting of existing theory and existing models of description. The Copernican heliocentric universe is a classic example of the recasting of existing theory when it was becoming incapable of handling economically some of the newly observed astronomical data. Equally well, the data considered relevant to a science and the methods of that science in dealing with the data may be fundamentally altered by the response that one or more of its leaders makes to what he accepts as the dominant situation in which he is working or to the practical and intellectual needs that he is persuaded it is to the task of his science to fulfil. Throughout the history of linguistics all these factors can be seen at work in different ages and among different groups, as the science experienced changes in its objectives, its methods, and its theoretical positions.

Interest in language and in practical linguistic problems led independently to linguistic science in more than one centre of civilization. Each had its own merits and its own achievements, and in the course of history each has come into contact with the European linguistic tradition and has contributed to it. In some important respects it is difficult to believe that European linguistics would be in the position it is today without the insights brought to it by linguistic work from outside Europe, in particular the work of the ancient Indian linguists on Sanskrit grammar and phonology. But since in the present age European science has become international science, and linguistics is no exception here, we can trace several streams of linguistic studies flowing into the European tradition and becoming part of it at different times, thus to constitute linguistic science as the world knows it today.

This statement may provide and justify the framework on which to organize a history of linguistics. To build it around the history of linguistics in Europe in no way implies a claim to European superiority in the linguistic field. Indeed, in much phonetic and phonological theory, and in certain aspects of grammatical analysis, European scholarship was manifestly inferior to that of the ancient Indians. But in the European tradition we are in a position to follow a continuous line of development from the origins of the subject in ancient Greece, whereas we know little of the origin and early stages that lie behind the mature Sanskrit work of the Indians. The practical and theoretical results of Greek linguistics were taken over by Rome (with so much else of Greek intellectual life), and passed on by Rome at the hands of the late Latin grammarians to the Middle Ages, to be received from them in turn by the modern world during and after the Renaissance, together with the vital contributions from outside Europe. At no stage is there a break that amounts to discontinuity in the European tradition of linguistics. Changes of theory, aims, methods, and concepts are repeatedly found, and they are the material of the history of linguistics; but each generation of European linguists has had at its disposal a knowledge of the existence and some of the work of its forerunners.

It is, therefore, reasonable to make the history of European linguistics the foundation for a history of linguistics as a whole. This procedure is not based on any evaluation of the relative merits of European and extra-European work, but it does determine the place at which linguists outside Europe receive attention. They and their achievements will be described at that period wherein they made their first significant impact on European linguistics, and thus entered the stream leading to world linguistics of the present day.

In the history of a science, as in more general historical studies, there is the constant temptation to discern and extract pervasive themes or patterns running through and manifested in the succession of events and activities. Where such themes may legitimately be revealed they can prove enlightening interpretations of the historian's narrative, and certain very broad correlations suggest themselves. For example, the failure of western antiquity to evolve an adequate theory of historical linguistics, despite the fascination shown for etymology, may be linked with the failure of ancient historians to envisage the fact of change as more than the revelation of what was innately present all the time in a political system or in a person's character;[2] and the all-embracing synthesis of language, thought, and objective reality involved in late mediaeval 'speculative grammar' appears as a facet of the synthesis of knowledge and learning within Catholic theology that characterized the scholastic age.

But at the present stage, at least, of our knowledge and research in much of the history of linguistics, our aims must be more modest. The importance of the history of a science is that it helps to place the present in perspective. Linguists today are not alone in their achievements, their disputes, and their problems. They are the heirs to more than two millennia of the wonder that the 'strangeness, beauty, and import of human speech'[3] has never failed to arouse among sensitive and enquiring minds.

FOR FURTHER CONSULTATION

H. ARENS, *Sprachwissenschaft: der Gang ihrer Entwicklung von der Antike bis zur Gegenwart*, Freiburg/Munich, 1955, covers the history of linguistics as a whole, principally through extracts from representative writers of each period linked by commentaries. Arens devotes most space to nineteenth-century comparative work and historical linguistics; but twentieth-century descriptive work is surveyed up to 1950.

A. BORST'S exhaustive *Der Turmbau von Babel*, Stuttgart, 1957–63, treats in great detail the history of men's ideas and beliefs in different parts of the world on the origin and diversity of languages and peoples in relation to current religious and philosophical opinions.

R. G. COLLINGWOOD, *The idea of history*, Oxford, 1946.

T. S. KUHN, *The structure of scientific revolutions*, Chicago, 1962.

C. SINCLAIR, *A short history of science*, Oxford, 1941.

P. A. VERBURG, *Taal en functionaliteit*, Wageningen, 1952, deals with the period from the Middle Ages to the beginning of the nineteenth century, examining the changing attitudes towards the functioning of language in human life.

NOTES

Bibliographical references to publications listed in the titles 'for further consultation' at the end of a chapter are given in the form of the author's name followed by the date of the work in question; other references are given in full in the first instance, but are repeated more briefly on repetition within a chapter.

1. cp. BORST, 1957–63, volume I.
2. cp. COLLINGWOOD, 1946, 42–5.
3. L. BLOOMFIELD, *Language*, London, 1935, vii.

Two

Greece

For the reasons given in the preceding chapter, it is sensible to begin the history of linguistic studies with the achievements of the ancient Greeks. This has to do, primarily, not with the merits of their work, which are very considerable, nor with the deficiencies in it that latter-day scholars, looking back from the privileged standpoint of those at the far end of a long tradition, may justifiably point out. It is simply that the Greek thinkers on language and on the problems raised by linguistic investigations initiated in Europe the studies that we can call linguistic science in its widest sense, and that this science was a continuing focus of interest from ancient Greece until the present day in an unbroken succession of scholarship, wherein each worker was conscious of and in some way reacting to the work of his predecessors.

The European tradition of linguistics has passed through several different stages, and has changed its main impetus and direction several times, being sensitive both to internal developments and to external situations. In the course of its history it has made contact with the major contributions of groups of linguistic scholars who started their labours outside the European tradition and developed their own insights independently of it. European linguistics has learned much from them. Indeed, without them present-day European linguistics (and this now inevitably means present-day linguistics in the world as a whole) would be poorer in content and less advanced in technique than we have the right to think it is. In starting from Greece and following the course of linguistic studies in Europe we can take in the work of scholars outside Europe at the point where it became known to Europeans and thereby entered and enriched the subject as the world knows it today.

2—S.H.O.L.

By the time at which we have any record of linguistic science in Greece, the beginning of the classical age in the fifth century B.C., the Greeks had been settled for many generations in the habitable parts of the Greek mainland, the western coastal areas of Asia Minor, the islands of the Aegean, the east coasts of Sicily, and a few places in south Italy and elsewhere. The settlement of Greece by the Greeks was the result of successive movements of invaders from the north coming down into Greece and spreading outwards from it. The last such invasion was the arrival of the Dorians, probably around the end of the second millennium, disrupting the earlier Greek civilization of the 'Mycenaean age' achieved by other groups of Greek-speakers who had settled the mainland and some of the islands in the preceding centuries.

It is, of course, not just in linguistics that the Greeks were the European pioneers. The intellectual life of Europe as a whole, its philosophical, moral, political, and aesthetic thought finds its origin in the work of Greek thinkers, and still today one can return again and again to what we have of Greek activity in the intellectual field for stimulus and encouragement. With the Greeks as with no other earlier or contemporary civilization modern man feels an undeniable kinship of the spirit. Just what circumstances, environmental, cultural, and biological, gave rise to this brilliant flowering of the human intellect in the Greece of the classical age we shall never know with certainty. We can only be thankful that it all happened.

The Greeks were not the first group of civilized men in the area that they entered. They learned much from established civilizations with which they came into contact in and around the eastern end of the Mediterranean and the 'fertile crescent' of Asia Minor, the cradle of civilized man in the west. But with the Greeks and in Greek civilization there developed for the first time in human history an insatiable demand for questioning the world around and the ways of men in the world. Among the Greeks there were those who insisted on enquiring into things that others failed to notice or in which they were uninterested. The Babylonians had made use of geometry for land surveying and of arithmetic and astronomy for the calendrical measurement of time, but in Greece we find astronomy, arithmetic, and geometry studied as abstract independent sciences for the first time, and built up on the basis of systematic observation and the establishment of postulates and principles. In taking notice of the Greek achievement in linguistics, Bloomfield remarks of their peculiar brilliance of intellect: 'The ancient Greeks had the gift of wondering at things that other people take for granted'.[1]

Among the factors that were observed in the preceding chapter as giving rise to an interest in language as part of human life, the Greeks of the classical age were already aware both of the existence of peoples speaking languages other than Greek and of dialectal divisions within the Greek-speaking population. There must have been considerable linguistic contacts between Greeks and non-Greeks in trade, diplomacy, and in much of everyday life in the Greek 'colonies', settlements of Greeks on the coastal fringes of non-Greek-speaking areas in Asia Minor and Italy. We know surprisingly little about this. Herodotus and others quote and discuss foreign words, Plato admits in the *Cratylus* dialogue the possibility of the foreign origin of part of the Greek vocabulary, and we know of the existence of bilingual speakers and of professional interpreters. But of serious interest in the languages themselves among the Greeks there is no evidence; and the Greek designation of alien speakers, *bárbaroi* (βάρβαροι), whence our word 'barbarian', to refer to people who speak unintelligibly, is probably indicative of their attitude.

Quite different was the Greek awareness of their own dialectal divisions. The Greek language in antiquity was more markedly divided into fairly sharply differentiated dialects than many other languages. This was due both to the settlement of the Greek-speaking areas by successive waves of invaders, and to the separation into relatively small and independent communities that the mountainous configuration of much of the Greek mainland and the scattered islands of the adjoining seas forced on them. But that these dialects were dialects of a single language and that the possession of this language united the Greeks as a whole people, despite the almost incessant wars waged between the different 'city states' of the Greek world, is attested by at least one historian; Herodotus, in his account of the major achievement of a temporarily united Greece against the invading Persians at the beginning of the fifth century B.C., puts into the mouths of the Greek delegates a statement that among the bonds of unity among the Greeks in resisting the barbarians was 'the whole Greek community, being of one blood and one tongue'.[2]

Not all the dialects were reduced to writing, but by the classical age the major dialects were, and we have inscriptional evidence of them, giving us a more detailed knowledge of the ancient Greek dialect situation than is available elsewhere in antiquity. Apart from the spoken dialects, educated Greeks were aware that the language of the Homeric poems, the Iliad and the Odyssey, was not precisely identifiable with any living dialect of the time. These poems held a special place in Greek education; they were publicly recited, and regarded and quoted in sources of moral precepts. 'Homeric scholarship', the establishment of acceptable texts of the poems and their critique, had begun in Athens during the sixth century.

The first achievement of linguistic scholarship in Greece, essentially part of 'applied linguistics' (to use later terminology), necessarily occurred before records appeared. Early in the first millennium B.C. an alphabetic system for writing the Greek language was developed, and this served as the basis for the Greek alphabet of classical Attic (Athenian) and the other literary dialects, and, together with the Roman alphabet, derived from a western Greek variety of the Greek alphabet, became the parent of the most widely diffused means of writing in the world today.[3] We now know that a writing system was developed twice in Greece independently. During the second millennium the Mycenae-ans made use of a syllabic writing system that included some logograms (symbols for individual words). This was formerly known as Linear B, and for long remained undeciphered. The interpretation of this script and the definite identification of the language it recorded as an early variety of Greek constituted one of the outstanding events of recent classical scholarship, with a profound effect on our linguistic and historical knowledge of early Greece.

However, during the dark ages accompanying the Dorian invasions the knowledge of writing was lost, and the Greek alphabet as we know it today was independently developed from an adaptation of the Phoenician script, itself a derivative of the Egyptian writing system. The original Egyptian form of writing, like that of ancient (and modern) China and of the Aztecs, was in the nature of a set of characters, signs or logograms, partly pictorially representative, standing for individual words or morphemes. From this a number of syllabic scripts were evolved in the Near East. When the Greeks made use of the Phoenician system, it was largely a set of consonant signs, the vowels being sup-plied by the reader from his sense of what was written. The Greeks cannot claim to have invented writing; but by devising an alphabet, in the modern sense of the term, separately representing all the distinctive segments, vowels as well as consonants, they can claim to have broken new ground in their application of linguistic science. Essentially what the Greeks did was to apply certain consonant signs of the Hebrew system standing for consonant sounds not used distinctively in Greek to represent the Greek vowel sounds. Thus Ɀ (*aleph*) standing for /ʔ(a)/ in Phoenician became the Greek letter *A* (*alpha*) standing for the vowel phoneme /a/. This very significant historical event is recorded mythically: Cadmus is said to have introduced writing from overseas, thus acknowledging the alien origins of the historical Greek alphabet.

Broadly the Greek alphabet was phonemic. It was not completely so, and no alphabet is; hence the need for phonemic transcriptions. In particular, the suprasegmental features of distinctive pitch (the accents) and of juncture, which were observed and described later, with the accents graphically represented, had no symbolization in the classical period. But the devising of an alphabet for the segmental phonemes of Greek depended on an unconscious phonemic analysis of the language (or of its individual dialects). We have little knowledge of the steps by which this was achieved, but the appearance in certain inscriptions of the letter ꟼ for /k/ before back vowels (from Phoenician φ standing for /q/ a distinct phoneme in that language) indicates a stage of incomplete phonemic analysis, since the varieties of velar position in Greek, being dependent on the nature of the adjacent vowels, are all allophones of one phoneme /k/, written κ in the classical alphabet.[4]

That the development and use of writing was the first piece of linguistic scholarship in Greece is attested by the history of the word *grammatikós* (γραμματικός); up to and including the time of Plato and Aristotle the word meant simply one who understood the use of letters, *grámmata* (γράμματα), and could read and write, and *téchnē grammatikḗ* (τέχνη γραμματική) was the skill of reading and writing.[5] The later extension of the meaning of this and of its formally associated terms follows the further development of linguistic science, specifically in the field of grammar, by later generations.

In the classical age of Greek literature and afterwards we can follow the progress of conscious linguistic speculation, as men reflected on the nature and the use of their language. Looking backward in history we may think ourselves to be tracing the growth of part of linguistic science towards a preconceived end; but from the point of view of each generation of thinkers we are seeing what those who came after did with what they found left by their predecessors, without any ultimate systematically organized subject in mind. The term *grammatikḗ* meant no more at first than the understanding of letters, and much of what one thinks of today as early linguistic enquiries fell under the general heading of *philosophía* (φιλοσοφία), itself covering a much wider field in ancient Greece than 'philosophy' does today, and initially embracing virtually the whole realm of human knowledge.

Observations on language, always with reference to the Greek language, are found in the records we have of the pre-Socratic philosophers, the fifth-century rhetoricians, Socrates, Plato, and Aristotle, though one must wait until the time of the Stoics for the separate recognition of linguistic studies within the much wider field of *philosophía*.

Our knowledge of the pre-Socratics and of the early rhetoricians is fragmentary and derived from secondary sources. From the end of the sixth century B.C., philosophers in Ionia and elsewhere ranged widely over astronomy, physics, mathematics, ethics, and metaphysics, and they included language within their purview. In the fifth century, the rhetoricians became well known in the Greek world, among them Gorgias from Sicily. These persons made a professional study of oratory, and some of them travelled about giving instruction for fees and writing books on their subject; they formed part of that body of itinerant purveyors of instruction of all kinds known as the Sophists.

Our knowledge of Socrates is also indirect. He left no writing himself, but his arguments and viewpoints are reported in some of the writings of Xenophon and in the more famous Dialogues of Plato, though in these latter it is always an open question how much of what we have is directly taken from Socrates and how much is the thought of Plato expressed as the speech of Socrates. Certainly Socrates stood for fearless criticism and for total freedom of speech; he went to his death for his ideals. In the somewhat totalitarian polity sketched out in Plato's *Republic* and put into Socrates's mouth he might soon himself have endured suppression or expulsion.

One dialogue, the *Cratylus*, is devoted to linguistic questions, though in some ways it is disappointing in its content; and references to language and its analysis are found in several other Platonic dialogues in which Socrates is the main speaker. Though Plato does not gather together his separate observations, he is credited with some part in initiating grammatical studies in Greece by the later writer Diogenes Laertius, who says that Plato 'first investigated the potentialities of grammar'.[6]

Aristotle (384–322 B.C.) knew the works of Plato, on which he developed his own thinking. His was probably the most remarkable intellect in antiquity; almost all fields of human knowledge then recognized fell within his scope. His writings range from ethics, politics, and

logic, to physics, biology, and natural history, and in a survey of the
forms of life he in some ways anticipated the nineteenth-century
evolutionary tree model of the living universe.[7]

As with the works of Plato, we must assemble Aristotle's linguistic
doctrine from statements scattered among several works on rhetoric
and logic, where they appear incidentally and in other contexts. This
makes it difficult to state Aristotle's position on any detail with exactitude
and certain questions are likely to remain controversial. Nevertheless
the outlines of Aristotle's linguistics are fairly clear, and it may be seen
that his work marks a development from the positions reached by Plato.

The Aristotelian age marked the end of an era in Greek history.
Aristotle had been appointed tutor to the young Alexander of Macedon,
and, if his political teaching is reflected in his political writing, he
preached to his pupil the merits of the small independent Greek 'city
state' such as had been the typical polity for several centuries. But
Alexander's conquests, that brought all Asia Minor and Egypt as well
as the Greek homeland under Macedonian control, altered the Greek
world irreversibly. Though his empire was divided among his successors, who were often at war with each other, Greek administration and
Greek ideas spread over the eastern Mediterranean area, and Asia
Minor, and a variety of the Attic dialect known as *koinè* (*diálektos*)
(κοινή (διάλεκτος)), or common dialect, became a standard language
for government, trade, and education over the whole area, gradually
displacing the local dialects of earlier periods.

Among the philosophical schools that grew up in Athens after
Aristotle, the most important in the history of linguistics is the Stoic
school. The Stoics, founded by Zeno (*c.* 300 B.C.), worked in a number
of fields in which Aristotle had worked, but in certain aspects of
philosophy and rhetoric they developed their own methods and
doctrines.

Under the Stoics linguistics achieved a defined place within the
overall context of philosophy, and linguistic questions were expressly
treated in separate works devoted to aspects of language, and treated in
an orderly manner. The works themselves are not extant; we know of
them from later writers. The position of language in the Stoic system
can be summarized in three quotations: 'First comes the impresssion,
then the mind, making use of speech, expresses in words the experience
produced by the impression'; 'All things are discerned through dialectic
studies'; 'Most people are agreed that it is proper to begin the study of
dialectic from that part of it dealing with speech'.[8]

The Stoics formalized the dichotomy between form and meaning, distinguishing in language 'the signifier' and 'the signified', in terms strikingly reminiscent of de Saussure's *signifiant* and *signifié*. The relevant texts are hard to interpret, but it seems that 'the signified' was not just a mental impression, but something produced in the hearer's mind by an utterance through his knowledge of the language, somewhat akin to the Saussurean union of sound and thought by the operation of *la langue*.[9]

They gave separate treatment to phonetics, grammar, and etymology, to which they devoted considerable attention; but their most notable contribution, as is the case with the whole of western linguistics during antiquity, was in the field of grammar, in which a progressive development through more than one stage of theory and terminology can be traced.

The Stoic school was founded in what is called the Hellenistic age, the post-Alexandrian age, whose characteristics were mentioned above. Linguistically this period, more than the earlier centuries, was marked by increasingly close contacts between Greek-speakers and speakers of other languages (the first translation of the Old Testament into Greek, the Septuagint, was carried out in this age); it was also characterized by the divergence of current spoken Greek, the *koiné*, from the language of the Athenian classical authors, the literary standard, apart from Homer, of all educated Greeks. Some have held that the attention paid to linguistic questions by the Stoics and the insight that they showed in analysing the semantics of the Greek verbal tense system (pp. 29-30, below) may be attributed in part to the fact that Zeno, their founder, was himself a bilingual whose first language was a Semitic one and who had learned Greek in later life.

Up to this period the context in which linguistics had developed had been philosophical, and in particular logical, enquiries; the linguistic science of the Stoics formed a part, though a distinct and articulated part, of their general philosophical system. But from this time on another motivation made itself felt in ancient linguistics, the study of literary style; firstly, there was a concern for 'correct' Greek pronunciation and grammar, that is classical Greek as against much of the current *koiné* and the changes caused by the large-scale acquisition of Greek by previous speakers of other languages; and secondly, in the widespread study of classical literature and of the works of Homer, commentaries on the language and the content were required by many readers within the newly Hellenized world. To the Hellenistic period

belong a number of glossaries of different non-Attic dialects, evidence
of the systematic study of the differences between varieties of Greek
that had a representative writing system. Greek literary scholarship was
deliberately fostered by several of the Macedonian rulers who succeeded
Alexander; they endowed libraries and maintained men of learning, in
part to justify the political power over the Greek world that had fallen
to them.

The written accent marks of Greek writing date from the Hellenistic
age, as guides to the correct pronunciation of words, and the description
of accentual and junctural features graphically represented by word
boundaries and punctuation marks, under the general heading of prosodies, *prosōdíai* (προσῳδίαι), was part of the movement in favour of
correctness, or Hellenism, *Hellēnismós* ('Ελληνισμός), as it was called.
Homeric scholarship reached an advanced stage during the Hellenistic
age, and a number of important grammarians engaged in linguistic research were best known for their work in the establishment of correct
Homeric texts and their exegesis.

Having taken notice of the principal scholars concerned in the first
stages of Greek linguistics, we may return to consider the main lines on
which their work was organized and developed. Once again, we should
try to see this not as a series of tentative anticipations of what we know
became the culmination of Greek linguistic thought, but as successive
movements from the positions reached as lines of thinking and modes of
statement were tested, extended to new material, and adapted in the
light of experience.

From the outset it is found that questions about language, concentrated entirely on the Greek language, were considered within the terms
of two somewhat interrelated controversies. These were the rival claims
made on behalf of nature, *phýsis* (φύσις), as against convention, *nómos*
(νόμος) or *thésis* (θέσις), in the first place, and of regularity or analogy,
analogía (ἀναλογία), as against irregularity or anomaly, *anōmalía*
(ἀνωμαλία), in the second, in the control of man's speech and our
proper understanding of its working. These two dichotomies represent
opposing viewpoints, one being favoured by some and the other by
others, rather than continuous formalized debates with rigidly distinguished adherents in permanent argument.

The *phýsis-nómos* question seems to have been the earlier controversy;
the one between the analogists and the anomalists persisted throughout
antiquity, though its relevance became less as time wore on. Both put
linguistic questions within the context of wider ranging arguments,

and each side could draw on obvious support from the facts of the case.

A principal topic of discussion among the pre-Socratic philosophers and among the later Sophists, and one that appears in several dialogues of Plato, was to what extent accepted standards, institutions, and judgments of what is right and wrong, just and unjust, and so on, were grounded in the nature of things and to what extent they were essentially the products of a tacit convention or even of explicit legislation. The theme of the *Cratylus* is a debate on the origin of language and on the relations between words and their meanings: are they based on a natural affinity between word form and word meaning or are they the result of convention and agreement?[10] Both views are given due consideration in the mouths of the participants, without a definite conclusion being reached. The naturalist argument leaned as it must on the weight of onomatopoeia in a vocabulary and on a more general sound symbolism in the phonological structure of some words, and a good deal of play was made with the fanciful and impossible etymologies of some Greek words by which it was hoped to trace them back to an allegedly 'natural' source, since it was admitted on the naturalist side that time had wrought changes in the 'first' forms of words.[11] The conventionalists pointed out that vocabulary can be changed at will and that the language is equally efficient once the change has been accepted.[12]

In itself the nature-convention discussion does not seem properly framed or very fruitful as far as language is concerned. Language is a universal capability of every normal human being, and in terms of total complexity, orderliness, and cultural adequacy there are no valid means of grading languages in a scale or of picking out alleged survivals of primitivity. In this sense the capability of communicating by speech (de Saussure's *langage*) is natural. But a wider acquaintance than the early Greeks envisaged with different languages shows how limited a role onomatopoeia and sound symbolism play and that in the greater part of the vocabulary of any given language (*langue*) the arbitrary and conventional status of the relation between form and meaning prevails (*l'arbitraire du signe*), though the convention is tacit, not explicit, like the social contract adduced as the basis of social organization. Speculation on whether in its origin language was far more onomatopoeic than in any known period remains and will remain largely unverifiable speculation, and was rightly subject to the sarcastic criticism of Max Müller in the last century.[13]

Historically the importance of the controversy is due to its place in the early development of linguistic theory and to the stimulus it provided to more detailed examination of the Greek language. In maintaining and in criticizing each side of the argument people were led to examine more closely the structures and the meanings of words and the formal patterns that words exhibited. In such examinations lies the beginning of precise linguistic analysis.

Later scholars took up more definite positions than we find in Plato. Aristotle firmly adopted a conventionalist point of view: 'Language is by convention, since no names arise naturally.'[14] Onomatopoeia need not invalidate this, since onomatopoeic forms vary from language to language and are always cast within the phonology of the particular language. Aristotle's view of language is summed up at the beginning of the *De interpretatione*: 'Speech is the representation of the experiences of the mind, and writing is the representation of speech.'[15]

Epicurus (341–270) took up a middle position, holding that word forms arose naturally but were modified by convention. More importantly in the history of linguistics, the Stoics favoured the natural status of language, again relying heavily on onomatopoeia and sound symbolism: 'In the opinion of the Stoics names are naturally formed, the first sounds imitating the things which they name.'[16] This attitude fitted well with their more general emphasis on nature as the guide to man's proper life; and in their etymology much weight was placed on the 'original forms' or 'first sounds' of words, *prõtai phõnaí* (πρῶται φωναί), which were said to have been onomatopoeic but later to have suffered changes of various kinds.[17]

These opposing views of Aristotle and the Stoics are important since they lead to the second linguistic controversy of antiquity, analogy versus anomaly. This was not set out formally, with the opposing arguments marshalled against each other, before the extended treatment accorded to the question by the first-century B.C. Latin writer Varro; and one must not envisage the two views as the exclusive tenets of permanent opponents locked in continuous conflict, but rather as two attitudes to language, each in itself reasonably justified by part of the evidence and each favoured by some individuals groups.

It seems clear that Aristotle favoured analogy and the Stoics favoured anomaly as the dominant theme in language. Later analogists tended to concentrate on linguistic questions for the purposes of literary criticism and the maintenance of standards of correctness (*Hellēnismós*); Stoic interests were more broadly based. The division may have been sharpened by the rivalry of Alexandria and Pergamum under Macedonian rule as two main centres of learning, Alexandria dominated by analogists and Pergamum by Stoics. Chrysippus, the Stoic, wrote a treatise on linguistic anomaly.[18]

Once more it may be felt that the controversy was expressed in terms that one would not resort to today; but, like the nature-convention argument, it was part of the context within which the detailed investigation of Greek and Latin grammar took place, and a lack of historical sympathy is perhaps shown by those who would dismiss it, as Classen did, as not worth so much as a yawn.[19]

Broadly, the controversy turned on the extent to which orderliness and especially proportional regularity held sway in the Greek language, and by implication in language as a whole, and to what extent irregularities, 'anomalies', characterized it. The regularities looked for by the analogists were those of formal paradigms wherein words of the same grammatical status had the same morphological terminations and accentual structure, and those involving the relations between form and meaning, whereby words that were comparable morphologically could be expected to bear comparable, 'analogical', meanings, and *vice versa*. These sorts of analogies lie at the heart of morphology, and without them paradigms of different word classes, and their subclasses (declensions and conjugations in Latin and Greek), in which repetitive patterns are summarized, would not be discoverable. They are moreover the basis of any attempted semantic labelling of grammatical categories such as singular and plural and the nominal cases. To this extent, as the later grammarian Dionysius Thrax pointed out, the morphological component of grammar largely consists of 'the working out of analogy'.[20]

Analogical arguments were sometimes used to prefer one word form over another as correct Greek and to establish the proper text of a Homeric line.[21] Some analogists went further than this and tried to reform Greek irregular paradigms in the interests of analogical regularity (a process that in some respects took place of its own accord in the passage from classical Attic through the *koiné* and Byzantine Greek to the modern language); the forms *Zeós* (Ζεός), *Zeí* (Ζεί), *Zéa* (Ζέα), etc. were suggested in place of the actual but 'anomalous' forms *Zēnós*, etc. as the oblique cases of the word *Zeús* (Ζεύς). Such attitudes were attacked by Sextus Empiricus, writing in the second century A.D. when grammarians were identified with the analogists, who challenged their whole work, accusing them of fabricating more unknown 'analogical' forms such as *kýōnos* (κύωνος), instead of *kynós* (κυνός), from *kýōn* (κύων), dog; and a later Latin writer was led to protest that to speak Latin and to speak grammatically were now two different things.[22]

While it may now be seen that the entire basis of an economical description of Greek morphology rested on the recognition and systematization of formal analogies, the anomalists had no lack of counter-examples with which to maintain their thesis. Most nominal and verbal paradigmatic classes admit exceptions, irregular members, which cannot be expurgated from the languages at the behest of grammarians. Proportional semantic relations between formal categories and their generic meanings are upset by such anomalies as single cities being designated by formally plural nouns (*Athênai* ('Αθῆναι), Athens; *Thêbai* (Θῆβαι), Thebes), and positive states or attributes like immortality being referred to by negatively prefixed words (*athánatos* (ἀθάνατος); Latin *immortālis*). Sextus, in a genial attack on grammarians as a class, makes much of the semantic anomalies of gender, pointing not only to the masculine and feminine genders of nouns denoting inanimates and abstractions and the use of a single masculine or feminine (and sometimes a neuter) noun to refer to both sexes of an animate, but also to dialectal variation between the genders of some nouns.[23]

The anomalist case appeared at first more cogent when no adequate distinction was made between inflection and derivation within grammatical word form variations. It is a characteristic of Greek and indeed of most languages that the inflexional paradigms are much more regular and apply to entire classes of stems, whereas the incidence of derivational formations is more irregular. Almost all Greek nouns had forms for five cases, singular and plural, but derivational suffixes were restricted to specific noun stems; thus we find *patér* (πατήρ), father, and *pátrios* (πάτριος), paternal, but no corresponding form **métrios* (μήτριος) with *mētēr* (μήτηρ), mother. Likewise English derives nouns from adjectives by such varied formations as *true, truth, happy, happiness, hot, heat, high, height*, and *possible, possibility*, and some speakers would hesitate between *suitableness* and *suitability*.

In rejecting an equation of one word, one meaning, the Stoic anomalists showed an important insight into the semantic structure of language: word meanings do not exist in isolation, and they may differ according to the collocation in which they are used. Augustine, setting out Stoic views, points to the different meanings of Latin *aciēs* when collocated with *mīlitum* (soldiers), line of battle, *ferrī* (sword), sharp edge of the blade, and *oculōrum* (eyes), keenness of vision.[24]

The consonance of the analogical attitude to language with Aristotle's general philosophical position is not hard to illustrate. Proportionality (*análogon, analogía*) appears in several places in his works as a guiding principle in conduct and in reasoning. It was moreover logically associated with the conventionalist view of language, which he espoused, since the more regularity there is to be found in any arbitrary, conventional system of communication, the more efficient it will be.

The Stoics, however, regarded language as a natural human capability to be accepted as it was, with all its characteristic irregularity. They took a broader view of what was good Greek (*Hellēnismós*) than the analogists,[25] and were interested in linguistic questions not principally as grammatical and textual critics; they were philosophers for whom language served as the expression of thought and feeling and for whom literature held deeper meanings and insights veiled in myth and allegory (the Greek word *allēgorikôs* (ἀλληγορικῶς), allegorically, is first known to have been used by the Stoic Cleanthes[26]).

While Aristotelian methods characterized all post-Aristotelian linguistic description in antiquity, one sees in the contrasting tendencies of the Stoic philosophers and the Alexandrian literary critics the opposition between philosophical and literary considerations as the determining factors in the development of linguistics. With the later full development of Greek grammar, literary interests predominated, but throughout antiquity and the Middle Ages this conflict of principle, now tacit, now explicitly argued, can be observed as a recurrent feature of the history of linguistic thought and practice.

The three main aspects of linguistic study that received specific attention among early Greek scholars were etymology, phonetics (pronunciation), and grammar. In the first, despite a lot of enthusiasm, little of value was achieved; interest in etymological research was stimulated by the nature-convention controversy over the origin of language, but a proper conception of linguistic change and the factors involved in it largely escaped the western world in ancient times. From the start etymological investigation was directed towards attempts at tracing the forms of words back to the forms of other words by which the meaning of the former could, it was thought, be explained. This produced the absurd etymologies proposed in all seriousness, some of which appear in Plato's *Cratylus*, for example *ánthrōpos* (ἄνθρωπος), man, from *anathrôn hà ópōpen* ('ἀναθρῶν ἃ ὄπωπεν), looking up at what he has seen, and *Poseidôn* (Ποσειδῶν) from *posì desmós* (ποσὶ δεσμός), restraint to the feet (presumably in walking through water, Poseidon being the god of the sea).

Similar efforts continued to disfigure etymological scholarship throughout antiquity and the Middle Ages. It is a pity that failure in this field is better known than the undoubted and important success elsewhere achieved, particularly in grammar, and that the level of the ancient world's etymological work has sometimes been quite unjustly taken to be typical of Greco-Roman linguistics as a whole.

More progress was made in phonetics. Some articulatory classifications were attempted, the syllable was introduced as a structural unit of phonological description, and by the time of the Stoics a rudimentary picture was grasped of speech as the effect of articulatory interference with egressive air from the lungs. Only Greek was studied. Foreign words were written as best they could be with the Greek letters, but no scholarly concern was evinced over alien sounds or alien sound systems. The descriptive framework for Greek phonetics was the Greek alphabet, and statements took the form of accounts of the pronunciation of the letters in it.

One objection to such a letter-based approach to phonetics is that the recognition of allophonic differences within the Greek phonemes was obstructed; commentators refer to different conjoint realizations of vowels with different accents and with and without aspiration and length, but they make no mention of different qualities of vowel sounds themselves though such differences must have accompanied different segmental and suprasegmental environments.[27] Nor were the phonetic differences between the dialects described except those differences that were represented by different spellings. More seriously, an improper analogy was accepted between the relation of discrete letters to a text and that of allegedly discrete sounds to a spoken utterance. This fallacy was not challenged, and it appears explicitly in Priscian at the end of the classical period, writing on Latin: 'Just as atoms come together and produce every corporeal thing, so likewise do speech sounds compose articulate speech as it were some bodily entity'.[28] The relations are otherwise: letters actually do compose written sentences; speech may be analysed into speech sounds.

Plato made a number of distinctions among classes of segmental phonemes in Greek, grouping together vowels in contrast to consonants and distinguishing within them between continuants and stops, the latter not being pronounceable without an adjacent vowel sound.[29] He was also aware of accentual differences between words having similar sequences of segments, or letters; he compared *Diì phílos* (Διì φίλος), a friend to God, with the name *Díphilos* (Δίφιλος) in respect of their different pitch sequences.[30]

Further advances were made in phonetics by the Stoics, who recognized the study of speech sounds as a distinct part of the study of language. They distinguished three aspects of a written letter: its phonetic value, e.g. [a], its written shape, e.g. α, and the name by which it was designated, e.g. *alpha*.[31] These three properties of letters continued to be distinguished throughout antiquity, their Latin names being *potestās* (power), *figūra* (shape), and *nōmen* (name).

The Stoics studied the syllabic structures of the Greek language, and made the threefold distinction between sound sequences actually occurring as meaningful parts of discourse, sound sequences which could occur according to the rules of syllable formation but in fact do not (e.g. *blítyri* (βλίτυρι)), and sequences excluded as being phonologically impossible in the language.[32]

A number of precise and correct observations on the phonetics of Greek were made by ancient scholars, and they are of great value in reconstructing the pronunciation of Greek (and so are the phonetic statements of the later Latin grammarians); but several serious omissions of factual observation as well as a lack of adequate descriptive theory remain, and in the history of phonetics Greco-Roman work is not of prime significance. In particular, their classifications and descriptions were couched mainly in impressionistic acoustic terms, for which they had no adequate technical terminology, rather than in terms of articulations such as were used more successfully by the ancient Indians and the Arabs (pp. 141–3, 98–9, below). Nineteenth-century phonetics, which saw such rapid progress in this aspect of linguistics, owed its main inspiration to the descriptive techniques of the Indians and to the observational methodology of the empirical tradition of the preceding three centuries.

It was in the field of grammar that the Greek (and the Roman) world did its best work. In this we not only see the purposeful and fruitful building of later generations on their predecessors' results, but we know of authoritative books written on Greek and on Latin grammar, several of which are extant, and the grammatical descriptions provided in them were maintained by a continuous tradition through the Middle Ages and the modern world to become the basis of the standard grammars of these languages today. Moreover the theories, categories, and terminology evolved by ancient scholars in relation to the grammar of their own languages have become part of the general grammatical equipment of descriptive linguists of our own day.

The framework of grammatical description in western antiquity was the word and paradigm model.[33] Despite the richness of classical morphology, a theory of the morpheme was not achieved, and classical grammatical statements exhibit the strengths and the weaknesses of a word based morphology. As Greek phonology was based on the pronunciation of the letters of the Greek alphabet, so Greek grammar concentrated on the written language, mostly the Attic Greek of the classical authors, though always with a proper attention to its implication of utterance in reading aloud.

A word based grammar involves three main procedures: the identification of the word as an isolable linguistic entity, the establishment of a set of word classes to distinguish and classify the words in the language, and the working out of adequate grammatical categories to describe and analyse the morphology of words entering into paradigms of associated forms and the syntactic relations obtaining between words in the construction of sentences.

Though there are general grammatical arguments in favour of treating syntactic relations as the central component of grammar (they are, for example, dealt with in earlier rules than those covering word morphology in a generative grammar), in the history of western grammatical theory morphology appears to have been formalized first; our first extant description of Greek morphology antedates our first extant description of Greek syntax by two centuries, and the latter is based on the former in its statements.

Logically one might argue that in working out a word based grammar one should proceed first with the formal identification of the word unit, then with the classes of words, and finally with the categories relevant to them. This, in fact, is the order of treatment in Dionysius Thrax's Greek grammar. Historically, however, we find what were later to be part of the system of grammatical categories discussed first, sporadically by the fifth-century Sophists. Protagoras considered the nominal category of gender in Greek, and is reported to have wished *mênis* (μῆνις), anger, and *pélex* (πήληξ), helmet, to be masculine instead of feminine, presumably on the grounds of a semantic association with male characteristics and activities rather than with female.[34] Socrates may himself have discussed this category, as Aristophanes makes fun of him in his comedy *The Clouds* for suggesting new formally feminine

3—S.H.O.L.

words like *alektrýaina* (ἀλεκτρύαινα), hen, instead of the use of *alektryón* (ἀλεκτρυών) in both the masculine and feminine genders for 'cock' and 'hen', and for worrying about words like *kárdopos* (κάρδοπος), trough, one of the few second declension nouns ending in -*os* that were feminine.[35]

Protagoras also set out the different types of sentence in which a general semantic function was associated with a certain grammatical structure, e.g. wish, question, statement, and command.[36] This lay within the field of rhetoric, but it provided the material for more formal syntactic analysis of sentence structures by later generations.

Plato and Aristotle make scattered references to grammar, but do not deal with it consecutively or as a specific topic. Plato, however, is said to have been the first to take the subject seriously, as in his dialogues we encounter a fundamental division of the Greek sentence into a nominal and a verbal component, *ónoma* and *rhêma* (ὄνομα, ῥῆμα), which remained the primary grammatical distinction underlying syntactic analysis and word classification in all future linguistic description.[37]

Aristotle maintained this distinction, but added a third class of syntactic component, the *sýndesmoi* (σύνδεσμοι), a class covering what were later to be distinguished as conjunctions (and probably prepositions, though this is not apparent from the examples cited), the article, and pronouns.[38] This tripartite analysis of the sentence was probably intended to distinguish the components of the declarative statement, *apophantikòs lógos* (ἀποφαντικὸς λόγος), in which as a logician Aristotle was most interested and which he took as basic. Aristotle additionally gave a formal definition of the word as a linguistic unit: a component of the sentence, *méros lógou* (μέρος λόγου), having a meaning of its own but not further divisible into meaningful units.[39] Plato had not explicitly stated whether his *ónoma* and *rhêma* referred to words or to phrases or to both. Aristotle's definition is remarkably like Meillet's 'association of a given meaning with a given group of sounds capable of grammatical employment'[40]; in fact neither is wholly adequate, since both exclude the morpheme from consideration, which itself is always 'capable of grammatical employment' and often enough carries an isolable meaning. The sentence (*lógos*) involved more for Aristotle at the semantic level, since unlike the isolated word it affirmed or denied a predicate, or made an existential statement.[41] He further defined the *rhêma* as additionally (i.e. unlike the *ónoma*) indicating a time reference and as representing the predicate.[42] This second part of the definition allowed him, like Plato, to include adjectives such as *leukós* (λευκός), white, and *díkaios* (δίκαιος), just, among the *rhḗmata*,[43] since they frequently serve in Greek as predicates (*leukòs ho híppos* (λευκὸς ὁ ἵππος), the horse is white), and, with the copula *estí* (ἐστί), is, 'understood', and always available for insertion, it could be said that they carry (present) time reference as well. For this reason the translation of *ónoma* and *rhḗma* by *noun* and *verb* at this stage in the development of Greek grammatical theory may be misleading.

Aristotle, like Protagoras, recognized the category of gender in nouns and listed typical gender marking terminations,[44] but other formal differences in word shapes are treated under the category of *ptôsis* (πτῶσις). In Aristotelian usage this term covers a number of grammatically relevant alterations of a descriptively basic form of a word; oblique cases of nouns, comparative and superlative forms of adjectives, deadjectival adverbs in *-ōs*, like *dikaíōs* (δικαίως), justly, verbal tenses other than the present, and perhaps some other verbal inflections are all *ptôseis*, either of the *ónoma* or of the *rhḗma*.[45]

It is easy to see the inadequacy of Plato's and Aristotle's grammatical frames of reference; but what is more significant is to notice the first stage, taken by them, in forging a technical metalanguage for the description and analysis of Greek, from the lexical resources of the language, which had not hitherto been required to serve in this way. *Ónoma*, on its way to becoming the translation of English *noun*, had originally meant 'name', and *rhḗma*, 'predicate', later 'verb', had been used to mean 'saying' or 'proverb'[46]; *ptôsis*, literally 'fall', of which the technical etymology is obscure, was used by Aristotle as a logical term as well as a very general grammatical term.[47] This term was to have a very long history; its restriction in meaning to that of English *case*, Latin *cāsus*, was one of the distinctive advances in theory made by the Stoic grammarians.[48]

Successive generations of Stoic philosophers achieved a great deal in grammar; some scholars indeed would say that grammar in the modern sense only began with them, but the work that has just been surveyed provided them with their starting point. The Stoics, whose philosophical attitude led them to pay great attention to language, are known to have written books wholly on linguistic topics, including some on syntax, though we do not know their exact content.[49] These Stoic writings do not survive, but from later authors we can get a fair picture of their theory, though several questions of detail remain unanswered and perhaps unanswerable.

Stoic grammar remained as part of Greek linguistic scholarship among members of the Stoic schools, but in the historical tradition of linguistics in Greece and Rome it may be viewed rather as a stage in the growth of Greek grammatical theory to be superseded by Alexandrian work. It is, however, important to take note of the main outlines of the Stoic achievement.

The Aristotelian system was further articulated by the Stoics in two directions: the number of word classes was increased, and more precise definitions and additional grammatical categories were introduced to cover the morphology and part of the syntax of these classes. Later writers saw the developing word class system as the progressive subdivision of the previous one; [50] it seems that the Stoics proceeded in three stages. Firstly, among Aristotle's *sýndesmoi* the inflected members (later pronoun and article) were separated jointly as *árthra* (ἄρθρα) from the invariant uninflected members, to which alone the term *sýndesmos* was applied (the later preposition and conjunction); secondly, Aristotle's *ónoma* was divided into proper noun, to which the term *ónoma* was applied, and common noun, *prosēgoríā* (προσηγορία); and, thirdly, from within this the class of adverbs was split off and named *mesótēs* (μεσότης), literally 'those in the middle', perhaps because they belonged syntactically with verbs but were mostly associated morphologically with noun stems.

Of these Stoic classes all were taken over by later writers except for the *prosēgoríā*, which was reunited with the *ónoma* as a single class under a single definition, *prosēgoríā* being recognized within it as a subclass only. The Stoics defined the distinction between their two classes of noun semantically by reference to individual quality ('being Socrates') as against general quality ('being a horse'). This is logically important, but it is not a morphological distinction, and attempts to assign separate paradigms to common and proper nouns are not borne out by the facts of Greek, though a more delicate syntactic analysis may provide a formal basis for a subclass of proper nouns. [51]

Case in its modern usage as an inflectional category of nouns and other words inflected like them was the creation of the Stoics; thereafter *klísis* (κλίσις) was used generically of grammatical word form variation. By restricting *ptôsis* to nouns and words likewise inflected, the Stoics were able to make case inflection the *fundamentum divisionis* between *ónoma* and *rhêma*, which it remained, with the result that Greek (and Latin) adjectives formed part of the noun class membership henceforth, and between their *árthra* (case inflected) and their *sýndesmoi* (uninflected). Within the category they extended the use of the term to cover all the forms of case inflected words, and divided them into *ptôsis eutheîa* (εὐθεῖα) or *orthé* (ὀρθή), nominative (Latin *cāsus rectus*), and the *ptóseis plágiai* (πλάγιαι), oblique cases (in Greek the accusative, genitive and dative). The position of the vocative in the Stoic system is uncertain. It was seen that the nominative, as the subject case, in concord of number with the finite verb, contrasted with the three oblique cases, all of which construct with verbs in different syntactic relations and with prepositions, and the genitive with other nouns as well.

The restriction of *ptôsis* to nominal words both required separate terminology for the verbal categories and provided criteria for its use. Active transitive verbs (*rhémata orthá*), passives (*hyptía* (ὑπτία)), and 'neutral' (intransitive) verbs (*oudétera* (οὐδέτερα)) were each defined by their constructing, respectively, with an oblique case (usually the accusative), with *hypó* (ὑπό) and the genitive, and with neither.[52] The partially common terminology, *ptôsis orthé* and *rhêma orthón*, was not accidental; the syntax of active and passive verbs in the classical languages were closely linked with differences of case.[53] Other verbal categories and distinctions appeared in the Stoic system, but their most important contribution to the analysis of the Greek verb was the abstraction of the temporal and aspectual meanings inherent in the tense forms.

The indication of time, recognized by Aristotle, is only part of the semantic function of the Greek verbal tenses. Two dimensions are involved, time reference, and completion as against incompletion or continuity. Four tenses can be arranged in relation to these two categorial distinctions like this:

Aspect \ Time	present	past
incomplete	Present	Imperfect
complete	Perfect	Pluperfect

The future (*méllōn* (μέλλων)) and the aorist (*aóristos* (ἀόριστος)) fall outside this symmetrical system, and for this reason they were regarded as indeterminate, *méllōn* with reference to the future and *aóristos* with reference to the past; the morphological similarity of stem in many future and aorist forms may have reinforced this semantic interpretation.[54] The Greek future perfect was regarded as a feature largely peculiar to the Attic dialect and not much used in that.[55]

That any overall semantic analysis can be given of the inflexions of all the verbs in a language is a naive and unwarrantable assumption, as recent studies in English grammar have shown.[56] Different lexical classes of verbs have different semantic functions statable of their inflected forms, and ancient Greek can have been no exception to this. None the less, the Stoic tense system marked a very considerable insight into the forms and functions of the Greek verb.

Stoic linguistic work continued among the members of the Stoic philosophical schools; but in the history of linguistics, the changes made by Alexandrian scholars in the Stoic positions brought the subject, more particularly in its grammatical aspects, to the state in which the later Latin grammarians and through them the European tradition took it over.

Unlike the Stoics, the Alexandrians were predominantly interested in language as a part of literary studies, and were adherents of the analogist position. They applied analogist principles to textual emendation and to the determination of standards of acceptability (*Hellēnismós*). Homeric studies received special attention in Alexandria, and one of the most famous Alexandrians, Aristarchus (second century B.C.), has been considered a founder of scientific Homeric scholarship; he is also credited with a number of developments in grammar, and was the teacher of Dionysius Thrax (*c.* 100 B.C.), who appears as the author of the first surviving explicit description of the Greek language.

Thrax's *Téchnē grammatikḗ* (τέχνη γραμματική), as it is called, runs to fifteen pages and twenty-five sections, and comprises a summary account of the structure of Greek. Its only major omission is any statement of Greek syntax, although the word class system and the morphological analysis that are set out in it formed the basis of later syntactic statements. Basically it was an Alexandrian work, but Thrax was obviously aware of Stoic linguistic studies and some traces of Stoic influence have been detected in it.

Some doubts on the authenticity of the text as we have it were raised in later antiquity and have been revived in modern times,[57] and there are certain difficulties over this question, though the majority of scholars have accepted it as the work of Dionysius Thrax, and its genuineness will be assumed here. Certainly the stage in Greek grammatical thought that it represents appears to have been reached at this time and to have been assumed by later grammarians.

In fact the description given by Thrax was regarded as definitive. It was translated into Armenian and Syriac early in the Christian era, and was the subject of a considerable amount of comment and exegesis from Byzantine critics, or scholiasts. It remained a standard work for thirteen centuries, and a modern writer has declared that almost every textbook of English grammar bears evidence of a debt to Thrax.[58] Its orderliness, brevity, and explicitness make it well worth the serious study of anyone with a knowledge of ancient Greek, whether from the point of view of general linguistics or from that of classical scholarship, and a brief notice of its main features is appropriate in any history of linguistics.[59]

The *Téchnē* begins with an exposition of the context of grammatical studies as this was seen by the Alexandrians. He writes: 'Grammar is the practical knowledge of the general usages of poets and prose writers. It has six parts: first, accurate reading (aloud) with due regard to the prosodies; second, explanation of the literary expressions in the works; third, the provision of notes on phraseology and subject matter; fourth, the discovery of etymologies; fifth, the working out of analogical regularities; sixth, the appreciation of literary compositions, which is the noblest part of grammar.'[60]

We see that his attitude was observational; the material was drawn from the written texts of accepted authors, and their usage justifies his descriptive statements. Such an empirical attitude finds many supporters today, but some later commentators had their feelings hurt by his use of *empeiríā* (ἐμπειρία), practical knowledge; and drawing on an accepted scale of accomplishments from *peîra* (πεῖρα), skill, the lowest, through *empeiríā* and *téchnē*, skill, to *epistémē* (ἐπιστήμη), understanding, the highest, they complained that he had cheapened the subject he professed.[61]

We see further how grammar in the strict sense was part of a wider scheme of propaedeutic studies leading to a proper appreciation of classical Greek literature. Only the fifth division, the working out of regularities in the language, or of analogy, covers what both then and later was regarded as the central province of grammar, and this is the only division that actually receives detailed development in the text. The first extant formulation of Greek grammar, and the pattern for centuries of later work can thus be seen as a product of the analogist-anomalist argument.

The description begins with an account of the phonetic values of the letters of the Greek alphabet. Letters, *grámmata* (γράμματα), are de-

fined as elements, *stoicheîa* (στοιχεῖα), a term already in use for the
ultimate constituents of the physical world,[62] and specified linguistically by a writer of about 20 B.C. as the primary and indivisible elements
of articulated speech,[63] a definition which, given the ancient failure properly to distinguish letter and speech sound, bears comparison with
early definitions of the phoneme in our own century. Such had been
the framework for Greek phonetic and phonological studies hitherto,
and Thrax draws heavily on the work of his predecessors. He confines
himself to the description of the segmental phonemes and the distinction of length in vowels and in syllables, despite his mention of prosodic
features, a subject taken up by later commentators. Little of permanent
linguistic interest is to be found in these sections, though they provide
valuable evidence for the reconstruction of ancient Greek pronunciation. The treatment is determined by Thrax's starting with the letters;
the descriptions are presumably of the phonetic characteristics of the
phonemes represented by the letters. Allophonic differences are not
mentioned by Thrax, but a later commentator, referring to the threefold distinction of sound, shape, and name (p. 24, above), already made
by the Stoics, pointed out that there was more than one pronunciation
to a single letter shape.[64] In both classical Attic and in Hellenistic
Greek the written vowel letter sequences *ei* (ει) and *ou* (ου) almost
certainly represented long monophthongs, [eː] (later [iː]) and [oː] (later
[uː]),[65] but no mention of this is made by Thrax. A scholiast, however,
later explained that *ei* (ει) and the 'subscript diphthongs', in which the
letter *i* was written below the other vowel letter, ᾳ, ῃ, and ῳ, had a
pronunciation of the same quality as that indicated by the simple letters
ε, α, η, and ω.[66]

Thrax identified the consonantal triads of Greek, *p, ph, b, t, th, d*, and
k, kh, g, as sharing the same sets of articulatory distinctions. He differentiated the aspirated and unaspirated members as 'rough' (*daséa*
(δασέα)) and 'smooth' or 'bare' (*psīlá* (ψιλά)), thus linking the differ-
entiating feature with the difference between aspirated and unaspirated
vocalic onset, as in *heîs* (εἷς), one, and *eis* (εἰς), into. Mysteriously he
referred to the voiced members of the triads as 'middle' (*mésa* (μέσα)).
The exact meaning of this term is uncertain, but it seems clear that like
the rest of antiquity in the west he and his later commentators had not
understood the articulatory basis of the voice-voiceless contrast. The
term *mediae* (*litterae*), the Latin translation of Thrax's *mésa* (*grámmata*),
lingered on in some nineteenth-century writings in reference to voiced
consonants; and the present-day, apparently phonaesthetic, designation

'liquid' for [l] and [r] types of sound can be traced back to Thrax's use of *hygrá* (ὑγρά), liquid, to refer to Greek *l* (λ), *r* (ρ), *m* (μ), and *n* (ν).

Alexandrian scholars had devised the graphic marks, in general use today in the writing of classical Greek, for the three distinctive Greek accents or pitches: acute (high) ´, grave (low) `, and circumflex (high falling to low) ^. These were listed by Thrax without comment or explanation, but further elaboration is to be found in the observations of the scholiasts.[67]

Passing to the strictly grammatical sections Thrax makes the two basic units of description the sentence (*lógos* (λόγος)), the upper limit of grammatical description, and the word (*léxis* (λέξις)), in western antiquity the minimal unit of grammatical description.[68] The sentence is defined notionally as 'expressing a complete thought'.[69] The term *méros lógou* (μέρος λόγου), whence the modern 'part of speech', recurs in the listing of the different grammatical classes of words. It had been first used by Plato, so far as is known, where it stands for constituents of the sentence; only with the growth in the numbers of classes of words distinguished by Greek linguists did the expression take on its later meaning of 'word class'.

Thrax distinguished eight word classes, whose number, with one change necessitated by the absence of an article word in Latin, remained constant to the end of the Middle Ages in the grammatical description of Greek and Latin, and with very marked influence on the grammatical analysis of several modern European languages. His word class system was regarded as one of his chief claims on the memory of posterity.[70] The Stoic common and proper nouns were reunited into the single *ónoma* class, the participle (*metochế* (μετοχή)) was separated from the verb to become a word class in its own right, and the Stoic *sýndesmos* and *árthron* were each split into *sýndesmos*, conjunction, and *próthesis* (πρόθεσις), preposition, and into *árthron*, article, and *antōnymiā* (ἀντωνυμία), pronoun, respectively. The adverb was renamed *epírrhēma* (ἐπίρρημα), in place of the Stoic *mesótēs*. The eight class names are worth quoting with their definitions as an example of Thrax's conciseness of terminology and his application to linguistics of Aristotelian methods of classification:

> *ónoma* (noun): a part of speech inflected for case, signifying a person or a thing,
> *rhêma* (verb): a part of speech without case inflection, but inflected

for tense, person, and number, signifying an activity or process performed or undergone,

   metochḗ (participle): a part of speech sharing the features of the verb and the noun,

   árthron (article): a part of speech inflected for case and preposed or postposed to nouns,[71]

   antōnymíā (pronoun): a part of speech substitutable for a noun and marked for person,

   próthesis (preposition): a part of speech placed before other words in composition and in syntax,

   epírrhēma (adverb): a part of speech without inflection, in modification of or in addition to a verb,

   sýndesmos (conjunction): a part of speech binding together the discourse and filling gaps in its interpretation.[72]

It will be seen that refinements in diagnostic criteria were used by the Alexandrians to give a greater number of discriminations; some of the features involved had been noted by the Stoics but not formalized by them as the basis of separate word classes. Two principal discrepancies are apparent between the Dionysian system and that of current presentations of Greek grammar. Firstly, the separate recognition of the participle, which aroused comment in antiquity since all participial roots were verbal roots, and *vice versa*, was due to the high place accorded since the time of the Stoics to case inflexion as a *fundamentum divisionis*. The two primary parts of speech, noun and verb, are differentiated by this feature and its absence, but the participle is both case inflected and tense inflected, and shares (*metéchei* (μετέχει), 'partakes' (Latin *participat*)), in the syntactic relations contracted by both nouns and verbs. Secondly, the adjective, whose morphology and syntax were more similar to those of nouns in both Greek and Latin, was included in the *ónoma* (noun) class. This allocation is reflected in the terms *noun substantive* and *noun adjective* still occasionally encountered in current use.

Each defined word class is followed by a statement of the categories applicable to it. Thrax's term for these is *parepómena* (παρεπόμενα), consequential attributes, and the use of this word can be compared to Aristotle's use of *symbebēkóta* (συμβεβηκότα), accidents, in logic.[73] The *parepómena* refer collectively to grammatically relevant differences in the forms of words, and include both inflectional and derivational categories. The five *parepómena* which apply to the noun class will serve as illustrations:

1. *Génos* (γένος), gender: masculine, feminine, or neuter.
2. *Eîdos* (εἶδος), type: primary or derived. The adjective *gaiéios* (γαιήιος), of the earth, is given as an example of a derived noun, and referred to the primary noun *gê* (also *gaîa*), earth. Among other subclasses of derived nouns are listed adjectival comparative and superlative forms (e.g. *andreióteros* (ἀνδρειότερος), braver, and *andreiótatos* (ἀνδρειότατος), bravest). Thus the forms that could have served as one criterion for distinguishing adjectives as a separate class were themselves assigned their own specific place within the noun class.
3. *Schêma* (σχῆμα), form: simple or compound, according to whether the roots of more than one noun could be identified within a single noun stem. Examples are given from proper nouns; *Mémnōn* (Μέμνων) is simple, *Philódēmos* (Φιλόδημος) is compound (*philo* + *démos*).
4. *Arithmós* (ἀριθμός), number: singular, dual, or plural. The distinct dual forms of both nouns and verbs, inherited from Indoeuropean, had a limited use in classical times and ultimately disappeared.
5. *Ptôsis* (πτῶσις), case: nominative, vocative, accusative, genitive, or dative. The five cases of the Greek noun (and adjective) are listed, and named by reference to part of their semantic function (e.g. *dotiké* (δοτική), dative ('giving to')). It is interesting to notice that the Latin *cāsus accūsātīvus*, our *accusative case* arises from a mistranslation of the Greek *aitiātikè ptôsis* (αἰτιατικὴ πτῶσις), the object case, referring to the recipient of some action caused to happen (*aitíā* (αἰτία), cause). Varro, who was responsible for the Latin term, appears to have been misled by the other meaning of *aitíā*, accusation or charge.[74]

The *parepómena* of the verb are mood, voice, type, form, number, person, tense, and conjugation. Thrax's systematization of the Greek tenses differs somewhat from that of the Stoics. Three basic time references are distinguished: present, past, and future. Of these, past time alone is assigned more than one tense form, four in fact: imperfect, perfect, pluperfect, and aorist. The six tenses are further linked into three pairs:

present	imperfect
perfect	pluperfect
aorist	future.

The first two links (*syngeneîai* (συγγενεῖαι)) of Thrax are the same as
linked pairs of tenses within the aspects of completion and incompletion set up by the Stoics, though the terminology of the two schools
differs in part, and the aorist and future were also associated by the
Stoics as being both indeterminate tenses. Morphologically the forms
of regular Greek verbs show proportional correspondences (*analogíai*),
the first pair being built on the present stem, the second on the perfect
(reduplicated) stem, and the third each having a 'sigmatic' (-*s*-) stem,
though the two were probably not etymologically connected.[75] Despite
the similarities between the two systems, Thrax's failure to give proper
recognition to the aspectual dimension in the semantic structure of the
Greek tenses must be considered a definite loss of insight.

The five inflected word classes are defined and described first; the
last three, uninflected or invariable word classes, are distinguished on
syntactic grounds, though their syntactic functions are not further
dealt with. The adverb is designated *epírrhēma* (whence the Latin
adverbium, and English *adverb*) from its principal syntactic association
with verbs (Thrax and those following him seem to have ignored the
possibility of its immediate constituency with members of any other
word class, though this is quite common in Greek). The Stoic term
mesótēs, no longer in use for the whole class, appears in Thrax's description as the name for a subclass of adverbs, namely those formed
deadjectivally with the suffix -*ōs*.

Later work in Greek grammar took the form of developments from
the linguistic description summarized in Thrax's *Téchnē* and of comments on specific passages in it. Its main omission from the standpoint
of modern linguistics was the absence of any sections on syntax, although the term *sýntaxis* (σύνταξις) was employed and syntactic analysis was partly presupposed in some definitions given in the *Téchnē*.
Syntax was dealt with extensively by Apollonius Dyscolus writing in
Alexandria in the second century A.D. He wrote a large number of
books, only a few of which survive, and it would appear that despite
earlier writings on Greek syntax his was the first attempt at a comprehensive theory of syntax systematically applied to the Greek language.
His importance together with that of Thrax was realized by his successors, and the great Latin grammarian, Priscian, some three centuries
later referred to him as 'the greatest authority on grammar', and
explicitly imposed Apollonian methods on his own full-scale description
of the Latin language.[76]

Apollonius worked with the material supplied by the *Téchnē* and the syntactical observations of earlier writers, many deriving from rhetorical studies. He made use of the same set of eight word classes as those given in the *Téchnē*, but he redefined some of them, more particularly to make greater use of philosophical terminology and to establish a common class meaning for each word class.[77] He defined the pronoun not merely as a noun substitute as Thrax had done, but additionally as standing for substance (*ousíā* (οὐσία)) without qualities, a statement repeated by Priscian and of considerable importance later in mediaeval linguistic thought.[78]

Though he worked on the basis of the morphological description of Greek set down by the Alexandrian school, his general outlook on linguistic matters was more mentalist than theirs and owed much to Stoic influences. He sharply distinguished form and meaning (*schêma* (σχῆμα) and *énnoia* (ἔννοια) in his terminology), and assigned grammatical structure to the side of meaning, in statements markedly similar to some found among writers of 'general grammar' today.[79]

Just as the nominal and verbal constituents of the Greek sentence were the first to be recognized as distinct and were always regarded as the most fundamental division in the grammar of the language, Apollonius expressly built his syntactic description on the relations of the noun and the verb to each other and of the remaining classes of words to these two.[80] In describing these relations he relied on the cases of nominally inflected words in their different interconnections with each other and with verbs, and on the three classes of verbs, active (transitive), passive, and neutral (intransitive), with their separate relationships to the nominal case forms. One finds under the active verbs the statement that they designate an action 'passing over to something or someone else', whence the Latin *verbum transitīvum* and English *transitive verb* may be said to originate.[81]

These developments foreshadow the distinction of subject and object and of later concepts such as government (rection) and dependency. Such however do not appear to have been part of Apollonius's descriptive apparatus. He devotes considerable attention to concordial relations (*katallēlótēs* (καταλληλότης), *akolouthiā* (ἀκολουθία)), which hold, for example, between a finite verb form and a nominative case noun or pronoun in respect of number and person, but not between a finite verb and an oblique case form.[82] Of more abstract syntactic relations, such as can be established for all languages and not merely those morphologically similar to Latin and Greek, he mentions the relationship of constituent structuring (*paralambánesthai* (παραλαμβάνεσθαι) to be taken together) to refer to the construction of participle and main verb in a sentence, or of noun or pronoun and verb.[83] Substitution (*anthypágesthai* (ἀνθυπάγεσθαι)) occurs when a word of one class, e.g. a pronoun, can be used in place of one of another class, e.g. a noun.[84] In his use of *symparalambánesthai* (συμπαραλαμβάνεσθαι), 'to be taken along in addition', something like the modern concepts of immediate constituency and hierarchical ranking seems to be envisaged, as in his analysis of the sentence *tachỳ elthòn paidíon ốnēsen hēmâs* (ταχὺ ἐλθὸν παιδίον ὤνησεν ἡμᾶς), quickly coming up, the boy helped us, in which the adverb *tachý*, quickly, is immediately associated with the participle *elthón*, having come, which in turn is associated with the main verb *ốnēsen*, (he) helped.[85]

However a good deal of Apollonius's discussion of grammatical questions was directed not so much towards the extension of the framework of description available at the time as to attempts at explaining particular features of Greek constructions. Thus the fact that two verbs meaning 'to love', phileîn (φιλεῖν) and *erân* (ἐρᾶν), take respectively the accusative and genitive case is referred for explanation to the more passionate and therefore less controlled nature of the love involved in *erân*[86]; and the true explanation of the peculiar Greek concord of singular verb with a neuter plural subject noun (*gráphei tà paidía* (γράφει τὰ παιδία), the boys are writing) quite escaped him, arising, in fact, as is now known, historically in the origin of the nominative neuter plural case ending from a singular collective.[87]

Apollonius's son, Herodian, is best known for his work on Greek accentuation and punctuation, covering the field of the *prosōdíai* referred to by Dionysius Thrax. The *prosōdíai* were described in more detail by later scholiasts and came to include the distinctive pitch levels symbolized by the accent marks on written words, length and shortness in vowels and quantity in syllables, aspiration and non-aspiration of vocalic onset at the beginning of words ('rough' and 'smooth breathings'), and such junctural phenomena as vowel elision, pitch changes in word compounding, and word boundary markers of the type that could distinguish *estì Náxios* (ἐστὶ Νάξιος), he is a Naxian, from *estìn áxios* (ἐστὶν ἄξιος), he is worthy (perhaps comparable with the features available to keep apart English *a notion* from *an ocean*). It is interesting to see the Greek word *prosōdíā* covering very much the range of phonetic phenomena to which the term *prosody* has been applied in recent Firthian phonological analysis.[88]

The *analogíai* of Thrax's morphology found their ultimate consummation in the lists of nominal and verbal inflections, known as canons (*kánones* (κάνονες)), on which later paradigms were modelled. The best known is the complete set of all the theoretically available forms of the verb *týptein* (τύπτειν), to hit, of which, however, in classical Greek only a limited number were actually in use.

Byzantine scholars continued the study of the Greek case system, and a semantic analysis of the cases by Maximus Planudes (*c.* 1260–1310), highly praised by Hjelmslev in his study of this category, was one of the linguistic insights carried back to Renaissance Europe from Byzantium at the end of the Middle Ages, and became influential in the development of theories of case in modern Europe.[89]

These later developments all belong to a post-classical age. By general recognition the literature of the post-Hellenistic eras never approached the standard of the classical epochs of Greece, in variety, spontaneity, or profundity. In the Byzantine period, theological controversies apart, literary studies were largely concentrated on the past, and in this respect linguistic scholarship was a proper product of the times. The descriptions, analyses, and explanations of the grammarians and the commentators formed part of a wider body of learning devoted to the study of earlier literary works. This was an age of dictionaries, glossaries, and commentaries, of working over past originals rather than of new creation.

It is not difficult to detect omissions and misrepresentations in that part of Greek grammar summarized by Dionysius Thrax and in the later contributions of Apollonius Dyscolus and his successors. While this criticism may seem at first sight flattering to modern scholarship, it is much less appropriate than is some sympathetic reflection on the very great achievements of successive generations of Greek scholars in devising and systematizing a formal terminology for the description of the classical Greek language as it was written and read aloud (and they set their sights no higher), a terminology which, through the medium of translation and adaptation to Latin, became the foundation for nearly two thousand years of grammatical theory and the teaching and study of the Greek and Latin languages. From the resources of a language not previously required to embody precise metalinguistic statements the Greeks had hammered out, through stages that we are able in great part to retrace, a detailed and articulated technical vocabulary for grammatical description.

The Greek triumph in intellectual civilization is to have done so much in so many fields; their work in logic, ethics, politics, rhetoric, and mathematics, to mention only some subjects, comes to mind at once. Their achievement in that part of linguistics in which they were strongest, namely grammatical theory and grammatical description, is strong enough to deserve and to sustain critical examination. It is also such as to inspire our gratitude and admiration.

FOR FURTHER CONSULTATION

H. ARENS, *Sprachwissenschaft: der Gang ihrer Entwicklung von der Antike bis zur Gegenwart*, Freiburg/Munich, 1955, 1–28.

K. BARWICK, 'Probleme der stoischen Sprachlehre und Rhetorik', *Abhandlungen der sächsischen Akademie der Wissenschaften zu Leipzig, philologisch-historische Klasse* 49.3 (1957).

F. H. COLSON, 'The analogist and anomalist controversy', *Classical quarterly* 13 (1919), 24–36.

E. EGGER, *Apollonius Dyscole: essai sur l'histoire des théories grammaticales dans l'antiquité*, Paris, 1854.

H. KOLLER, 'Die Anfänge der griechischen Grammatik', *Glotta* 37 (1958), 5–40.

L. LERSCH, *Die Sprachphilosophie der Alten*, Bonn, 1838–41.

M. POHLENZ, 'Die Begründung der abendländischen Sprachlehre durch die Stoa', *Nachrichten von der Gesellschaft der Wissenschaften zu Göttingen, philologisch-historische Klasse Fachgruppe I Altertumswissenschaft*, N. F. 3.6 (1939).

R. H. ROBINS, *Ancient and mediaeval grammatical theory in Europe*, London, 1951, chapter 1.

——, 'Dionysius Thrax and the western grammatical tradition', *TPS* 1957, 67–106.

——, 'The development of the word class system of the European grammatical tradition', *Foundations of language* 2 (1966), 3–19.

J. E. SANDYS, *History of classical scholarship* (third edition), Cambridge, 1921, volume 1.

H. STEINTHAL, *Geschichte der Sprachwissenschaft bei den Griechen und Römern* (second edition), Berlin, 1890.

NOTES

1. L. BLOOMFIELD, *Language*, London, 1935, 4.
2. HERODOTUS 8.144.2: τὸ Ἑλληνικόν, ἐὸν ὅμαιμόν τε καὶ ὁμόγλωσσον.
3. C. D. BUCK, *Comparative grammar of Greek and Latin*, Chicago, 1933, 68–78.
4. BUCK, op. cit., 68–74; *The Greek dialects*, Chicago, 1928, 16.
5. e.g. PLATO, *Theaetetus* 207 B, *Philebus* 17 B, 18 D.
6. DIOGENES LAERTIUS 3.25: πρῶτος ἐθεώρησε τῆς γραμματικῆς τὴν δύναμιν.

7. W. D. ROSS: *Aristotle*, London, 1923, 116–17; C. SINGER, *A short history of science*, Oxford, 1941, 40–1.

8. DIOGENES 7.49: προηγεῖται ἡ φαντασία, εἶθ' ἡ διάνοια ἐκλαλητικὴ ὑπάρχουσα, ὃ πάσχει ὑπὸ τῆς φαντασίας τοῦτο ἐκφέρει λόγῳ. id. 7.83: πάντα τὰ πράγματα διὰ τῆς ἐν λόγοις θεωρίας ὁρᾶσθαι. id. 7.55: τῆς διαλεκτικῆς θεωρίας συμφώνως δοκεῖ τοῖς πλείστοις ἀπὸ τοῦ περὶ φωνῆς ἐνάρχεσθαι τόπου.

9. DIOGENES 7.62 (τὸ σημαῖνον and τὸ σημαινόμενον); STEINTHAL, 1890, volume 1, 286–90; BARWICK, 1957, chapter 1; F. DE SAUSSURE, *Cours de linguistique générale* (fourth edition), Paris, 1949, 156–7.

10. PLATO, *Cratylus*, 384 D.

11. ibid., 399 C, 414 C, 421 D, 423 B, 426 C–427 D.

12. ibid., 384 D.

13. *Lectures on the science of language*, London, 1862, lecture 9.

14. ARISTOTLE, *De interpretatione* 2: κατὰ συνθήκην, ὅτι φύσει τῶν ὀνομάτων οὐδέν ἐστιν (cp. 4).

15. ibid., 1: ἔστι μὲν οὖν τὰ ἐν τῇ φωνῇ τῶν ἐν τῇ ψυχῇ παθημάτων σύμβολα, καὶ τὰ γραφόμενα τῶν ἐν τῇ φωνῇ.

16. ORIGEN, *Contra Celsum* 1.24: ὡς νομίζουσιν οἱ ἀπὸ τῆς Στοᾶς φύσει [ἐστὶ τὰ ὀνόματα] μιμουμένων τῶν πρώτων φωνῶν τὰ πράγματα.

17. ibid., 1.24; BARWICK, 1957, chapter 4.

18. DIOGENES 7.192.

19. J. CLASSEN, *De grammaticae Graecae primordiis*, Bonn, 1829, 80.

20. I. BEKKER, *Anecdota Graeca*, Berlin, 1816, volume 2, 629: ἀναλογίας ἐκλογισμός.

21. cp. COLSON, 1919.

22. SEXTUS EMPIRICUS, *Adversus grammaticos* 195; QUINTILIAN, *Institutio oratoria* 1.6.27.

23. SEXTUS, op. cit., 148–53.

24. STEINTHAL, 1890, volume 1, 360.

25. DIOGENES 7.59.

26. SANDYS, 1921, 149.

27. BEKKER, *Anecdota Graeca*, volume 2, 774–5.

28. PRISCIAN 1.2.4: Sicut enim illa (sc. elementa mundi) coeuntia omne perficiunt corpus, sic etiam haec (sc. elementa vocis) literalem vocem quasi corpus aliquod componunt.

29. *Cratylus* 424 C; *Theaetetus* 203 B.

30. *Cratylus* 399 A–B.

31. DIOGENES 7.56; BEKKER, *Anecdota Graeca*, volume 2, 773.

32. DIOGENES 7.57.

33. cp. C. F. HOCKETT, 'Two models of grammatical description', *Word* 10 (1954), 210–34.

34. ARISTOTLE, *De sophisticis elenchis* 14.

4—S.H.O.L·

35. ARISTOPHANES, *Clouds* 660–80.

36. DIOGENES 9.53–4.

37. *Cratylus* 399 B, 425 A; *Sophistes* 262 A-263 D.

38. *Rhetorica* 3.5, 3.12.

39. *De interpretatione* 2–3.

40. A. MEILLET, *Linguistique historique et linguistique générale*, Paris, 1948, 30.

41. *De interpretatione* 3–6.

42. op. cit. 3: ῥῆμα δέ ἐστι τὸ προσσημαῖνον χρόνον ... καὶ ἔστιν ἀεὶ τῶν καθ' ἑτέρου λεγομένων σημεῖον.

43. op. cit. 1; 10; cp. PLATO, *Cratylus*, 399 B.

44. *De sophisticis elenchis* 14.

45. *De interpretatione* 2, 3; *Topica* 5.7, 1.15.

46. PLATO, *Protagoras* 342 E, 343 A–B.

47. *Analytica priora* 42 b, 30; *Analytica posteriora*, 94 a 12.

48. L. HJELMSLEV, *La catégorie des cas*, Aarhus, 1935, 1–70.

49. J. VON ARNIM, *Stoicorum veterum fragmenta*, Leipzig, 1905–24, volume 2, 206 a; DIOGENES 7.192.

50. e.g. DIONYSIUS OF HALICARNASSUS, *De compositione verborum* 2.

51. DIOGENES 7.57–8; BEKKER, *Anecdota Graeca*, volume 2, 842; cp. BLOOMFIELD, *Language*, 205.

52. DIOGENES 7.64; STEINTHAL, 1890, volume 1, 299.

53. HJELMSLEV, *Cas*, 7.

54. BEKKER, *Anecdota Graeca*, volume 2, 890–1; STEINTHAL, 1890, volume 1, 307–17; BARWICK, 1957, 51–3.

55. BEKKER, op. cit., 891–2.

56. cp. F. R. PALMER, *A linguistic study of the English verb*, London, 1965. On Greek, cp. J. LYONS, *Structural semantics* (Publications of the Philological Society 20 (1963)), 111–19.

57. V. DI BENEDETTO, 'Dionisio Trace e la Techne a lui attribuita', *Annali della scuola normale superiore di Pisa*, serie 2, 27 (1958), 169–210 and 28 (1959), 87–118.

58. P. B. R. FORBES, 'Greek pioneers in philology and grammar', *Classical review* 47 (1933), 112.

59. Text in BEKKER, *Anecdota Graeca*, volume 2, 627–43 (together with the comments by later scholiasts); also in G. UHLIG, *Dionysii Thracis ars grammatica*, Leipzig, 1883.

60. γραμματική ἐστιν ἐμπειρία τῶν παρὰ ποιηταῖς τε καὶ συγγραφεῦσιν ὡς ἐπὶ τὸ πολὺ λεγομένων. μέρη δὲ αὐτῆς εἰσὶν ἕξ· πρῶτον ἀνάγνωσις ἐντριβὴς κατὰ προσῳδίαν, δεύτερον ἐξήγησις κατὰ τοὺς ἐνυπάρχοντας ποιητικοὺς τρόπους τρίτον γλωσσῶν τε καὶ ἱστοριῶν πρόχειρος ἀπόδοσις, τέταρτον ἐτυμολογίας εὕρεσις, πέμπτον ἀναλογίας ἐκλογισμός, ἕκτον κρίσις ποιημάτων, ὃ δὴ κάλλιστόν ἐστι πάντων τῶν ἐν τῇ τέχνῃ.

61. BEKKER, op. cit., 656, 732.

62. e.g. PLATO, *Theaetetus* 201 E; ARISTOTLE, *Metaphysics*, 983 b 12, 1014 a 26–9.

63. DIONYSIUS OF HALICARNASSUS, *De compositione verborum* 14, 1–2: ἀρχαὶ τῆς ἀνθρωπίνης καὶ ἐνάρθρου φωνῆς, αἱ μηκέτι δεχόμεναι διαίρεσιν.

64. BEKKER, op. cit., 774.

65. BUCK, *Comparative grammar*, § 89, 92; E. H. STURTEVANT, *The pronunciation of Greek and Latin*, Philadelphia, 1940, § 29, 41.

66. BEKKER, op. cit., 804.

67. BEKKER, op. cit., 754–7; STURTEVANT, op. cit., chapter 4.

68. λέξις ἐστὶ μέρος τοῦ κατὰ σύνταξιν λόγου ἐλάχιστον.

69. λέξεως σύνθεσις διάνοιαν αὐτοτελῆ δηλοῦσα.

70. BEKKER, op. cit., 676: ὁ Θρᾷξ Διονύσιος, ὁ περὶ τῶν ὀκτὼ μερῶν τοῦ λόγου διδάξας ἡμᾶς.

71. Thrax included the relative pronoun, ὅς, ἥ, ὅ, in the class of *árthron*. The position of relative clauses normally following their antecedent noun and the similar morphology of the article and the relative pronoun allowed him to refer to this as a postposed article.

72. ὄνομά ἐστι μέρος λόγου πτωτικόν, σῶμα ἢ πρᾶγμα σημαῖνον.

    ῥῆμά ἐστι λέξις ἄπτωτος, ἐπιδεκτικὴ χρόνων τε καὶ προσώπων καὶ ἀριθμῶν, ἐνέργειαν ἢ πάθος παριστῶσα.

    μετοχή ἐστι λέξις μετέχουσα τῆς τῶν ῥημάτων καὶ τῆς τῶν ὀνομάτων ἰδιότητος.

    ἄρθρον ἐστὶ μέρος λόγου πτωτικὸν προτασσόμενον καὶ ὑποτασσόμενον τῆς κλίσεως τῶν ὀνομάτων.

    ἀντωνυμία ἐστὶ λέξις ἀντὶ ὀνόματος παραλαμβανομένη, προσώπων ὡρισμένων δηλωτική.

    πρόθεσίς ἐστι λέξις προτιθεμένη πάντων τῶν τοῦ λόγου μερῶν ἔν τε συνθέσει καὶ συντάξει.

    ἐπίρρημά ἐστι μέρος λόγου ἄκλιτον, κατὰ ῥήματος λεγόμενον ἢ ἐπιλεγόμενον ῥήματι.

    σύνδεσμός ἐστι λέξις συνδέουσα διάνοιαν μετὰ τάξεως καὶ τὸ τῆς ἑρμηνείας κεχηνὸς πληροῦσα.

73. e.g., *De sophisticis elenchis* 168 b 28–31, *Topica* 117 a 7, 128 a 38, 131 a 27. The Latin grammarians translated *parepómena* by *accidentia*.

74. *De lingua Latina* 8.66–7.

75. BUCK, *Comparative grammar*, § 389.

76. PRISCIAN 11.1.1: Maximum auctor artis grammaticae.

77. e.g. *Syntax* 1.5.

78. *De pronomine* 33 b; PRISCIAN 13.6.29, 13.6.31.

79. *De adverbio*, BEKKER, *Anecdota Graeca*, volume 2, 529; *Syntax* 1.5: ἕκαστον αὐτῶν ἐξ ἰδίας ἐννοίας ἀνάγεται. *De pronomine* 85 a: οὐ φωναῖς μεμέρισται τὰ τοῦ λόγου μέρη, σημαινομένοις δέ.

44   CHAPTER TWO

80. *Syntax* 1.3: τὰ ὑπόλοιπα τῶν μερῶν τοῦ λόγου ἀνάγεται πρὸς τὴν τοῦ ῥήματος καὶ τοῦ ὀνόματος σύνταξιν.
81. ibid. 3.31: ἡ ἐνέργεια ὡς πρὸς ὑποκέιμενόν τι διαβιβάζεται.
82. ibid. 3.6.
83. ibid. 1.3, 2.10–11.
84. ibid. 1.3, 2.14, 3.19, 3.32.
85. ibid. 1.3, 1.9; cp. STEINTHAL, 1890, volume 2, 342.
86. ibid. 3.32: τὸ ἐρᾶν ὁμολογεῖ τὸ προσδιατίθεσθαι ὑπὸ τοῦ ἐρωμένου. ('Being in love admits to being affected by one's beloved', and therefore the verb properly constructs with the genitive case, the case used of the agent in passive sentences.)
87. BUCK, *Comparative grammar*, § 240; J. WRIGHT, *Comparative grammar of the Greek language*, London, 1912, § 326.
88. ROBINS, 1957, 81–3.
89. HJELMSLEV, *Cas*, 12.

Three

Rome

In passing from Greece to Rome we enter a very different world. One rightly speaks of the Greco-Roman era as a period of unified civilization around the Mediterranean area, but the respective roles of Greece and Rome were dissimilar and complementary. Without the other, the contribution of either to European civilization would have been less significant and less productive.

The Romans had for long enjoyed contact with Greek material culture and intellectual ideas, through the Greek settlements in the south of Italy; and they had learned writing from the western Greeks. But it was during the third and second centuries B.C. that the Greek world fell progressively within the control of Rome, by now the mistress of the whole of Italy. The expansion of Roman rule was almost complete by the Christian era, and the Roman Empire, as it now was, had achieved a relatively permanent position, which, with fairly small-scale changes in Britain and on the northern and eastern frontiers, remained free of serious wars for a further two hundred years. The second half of this period earned Gibbon's well-known encomium: 'If a man were called to fix the period in the history of the world during which the condition of the human race was most happy and prosperous, he would, without hesitation, name that which elapsed from the death of Domitian to the accession of Commodus'.[1]

In taking over the Hellenistic world, the Romans brought within their sway the Jewish people and the land of the Old and New Testaments. The intellectual background of Greece and Judaea and the polical unity and freedom of intercourse provided by Roman stability were the conditions in which Christianity arose and spread, to become in the fourth century A.D. the state religion of the Roman Empire. To these three peoples, the Greeks, the Romans, and the Jews, modern Europe and much of the entire modern world owe the origins of their intellectual, moral, political and religious civilization.

From their earliest contacts the Romans cheerfully acknowledged the superior intellectual and artistic achievements of the Greeks. Linguistically this was reflected in the different common languages of the eastern and the western provinces. In the western half of the empire, where no contact had been made with a recognized civilization, Latin became the language of administration, business, law, learning, and social advancement. Ultimately spoken Latin (by no means identical with classical literary Latin) displaced the former languages of most of the western provinces, and became in the course of linguistic evolution the modern Romance, or Neo-Latin, languages of contemporary Europe. In the east, however, already largely under Greek administration since the Hellenistic period, Greek retained the position it had already reached; Roman officials often learned and used Greek in the course of their duties, and Greek literature and philosophy were highly respected. Ultimately this linguistic division was politically recognized in the splitting of the Roman Empire into the Western and the Eastern Empires, with the new eastern capital at Constantinople (Byzantium) enduring as the head of the Byzantine dominions through much trial and tribulation up to the beginning of the western Renaissance.

The accepted view of the relation between Roman rule and Greek civilization was probably well represented in Vergil's famous summary of Rome's place and duty: let others (i.e. the Greeks) excel if they will in the arts, while Rome keeps the peace of the world.[2]

During the years in which Rome ruled the western civilized world, there must have been contacts between speakers of Latin and speakers of other languages at all levels and in all places. Interpreters must have been in great demand, and the teaching and learning of Latin (and, in the eastern provinces, of Greek) must have been a concern for all manner of persons both in private households and in organized schools. Translations were numerous. The first translation of the Old Testament into Greek (the Septuagint) was the work of Jewish scholars of the Hellenistic age, and from the third century B.C. Greek literature was systematically translated into Latin. So much did the prestige of Greek writing prevail, that Latin poetry abandoned its native metres and was composed during the classical period and after in metres learned from the Greek poets. This adaptation to Latin of Greek metres found its culmination in the magnificent hexameters of Vergil and the perfected elegiacs of Ovid. It is surprising that we know so little of the details of all this linguistic activity, and that so little writing on the various aspects of linguistic contacts is either preserved for us or known to have existed. The Romans were aware of multilingualism as an achievement. Aulus Gellius tells of the remarkable king Mithridates of Pontus (120–63 B.C.), who was able to converse with any of his subjects, who fell into more than twenty different speech communities.[3]

In linguistic science the Roman experience was no exception to the general condition of their relations with Greek intellectual work. Roman linguistics was largely the application of Greek thought, Greek controversies, and Greek categories to the Latin language. The relatively similar basic structures of the two languages, together with the unity of civilization achieved in the Greco-Roman world, facilitated this metalinguistic transfer.

The introduction of linguistic studies into Rome is credited to one of those picturesque anecdotes that lighten the historian's narrative. Crates, a Stoic philosopher and grammarian, came to Rome on a political delegation in the middle of the second century B.C., and while sightseeing fell on an open drain and was detained in bed with a broken leg. He passed the time while recovering in giving lectures on literary themes to an appreciative audience.

It is probable that Crates as a Stoic introduced mainly Stoic doctrine in his teaching; but Greek thinkers and Greek learning entered the Roman world increasingly in this period, and by the time of Varro (116–27 B.C.), both Alexandrian and Stoic opinions on language were known and discussed. Varro is the first serious Latin writer on linguistic questions of whom we have any records. He was a polymath, ranging in his interests through agriculture, senatorial procedure, and Roman antiquities. The number of his writings was celebrated by his contemporaries, and his *De lingua Latina*, wherein he expounded his linguistic opinions, comprised twenty-five volumes, of which books 5 to 10 and some fragments of the others survive.

One major feature of Varro's linguistic work is his lengthy exposition and formalization of the opposing views in the analogy-anomaly controversy (pp. 19–22, above), and a good deal of his description and analysis of Latin appears in his treatment of this problem. He is, in fact, one of the main sources for its details, and it has been claimed that he misrepresented it as a matter of permanent academic attack and counter-attack, rather than as the more probable co-existence of opposite tendencies or attitudes.[4]

Varro's style has been criticized as unattractive, but on linguistic questions he was probably the most original of all the Latin scholars. He was much influenced by Stoic thought, including that of his own teacher Stilo; but he was equally familiar with Alexandrian doctrine, and a fragment purporting to preserve his definition of grammar, 'the systematic knowledge of the usage of the majority of poets, historians, and orators',[5] looks very much like a direct copy of Thrax's definition (p. 31, above). On the other hand he appears to have used his Greek predecessors and contemporaries rather than merely to have applied them with the minimum of change to Latin, and his statements and conclusions are supported by argument and exposition, and by the independent investigation of earlier stages of the Latin language. He was much admired and quoted by later writers on linguistics, though in the main stream of linguistic theory his treatment of Latin grammar did not bring to bear the influence on the mediaeval successors to antiquity that more derivative scholars such as Priscian did, who set themselves to describe Latin within the framework already fixed for Greek by Thrax's *Téchnē* and the syntactic works of Apollonius.

In the evaluation of Varro's work on language we are hampered by the fact that only six of the twenty-five books of the *De lingua Latina* survive. We have his threefold division of linguistic studies, into etymology, morphology, and syntax,[6] and the material to judge the first and second.

Varro envisaged language developing from an original limited set of primal words, imposed on things so as to refer to them, and acting productively as the source of large numbers of other words through subsequent changes in letters, or in phonetic form (the two modes of description came to the same thing for him).[7] These letter changes take place in the course of years, and earlier forms, such as *duellum* for classical *bellum*, war, are cited as instances. At the same time meanings change, as, for example, the meaning of *hostis*, once 'stranger', but in Varro's time, and in classical and later Latin, 'enemy'.[8] These etymological statements are supported by modern scholarship, but a great deal of his etymology suffers from the same weakness and lack of comprehension that characterized Greek work in this field. *Anas*, duck from *nāre*, to swim, *vītis*, vine, from *vīs*, strength, and *cūra*, care, from *cor ūrere*, to burn the heart, are sadly typical both of his work and of Latin etymological studies in general.[9]

A fundamental ignorance of linguistic history is seen in Varro's references to Greek. Similarities in word forms bearing comparable meanings in Latin and Greek were obvious. Some were the product of historical loans at various periods once the two communities had made indirect and then direct contacts; others were the joint descendants of earlier Indo-european forms whose existence can be inferred and whose shapes can to some extent be 'reconstructed' by the methods of comparative and historical linguistics. But of this, Varro, like the rest of antiquity, had no conception. All such words were jointly regarded by him as direct loans from Greek, whose place in the immediate history of Latin was misrepresented and exaggerated as a result of the Romans' consciousness of their cultural debt to Greece and mythological associations of Greek heroes in the story of the founding of Rome.

In his conception of vocabulary growing from alterations made to the forms of primal words, Varro united two separate considerations, historical etymology and the synchronic formation of derivations and inflexions. Certain canonical members of paradigmatically associated word series were said to be primal, all the others resulting from 'declension' (*dēclīnātiō*), formal processes of change.[10] Derivational prefixes are given particular attention in book 6, chapter 38.

One must regret Varro's failure to distinguish these two dimensions of linguistic study, because, as with other linguists in antiquity, his synchronic descriptive observations were much more informative and perceptive than his attempts at historical etymology. As an example of an apparent awareness of the distinction, one may note his statement that, within Latin, *equitātus* cavalry, and *eques* (stem *equit-*), horseman, can be associated with and descriptively referred back to *equus*, horse, but that no further explanation on the same lines is possible for *equus*.[11] Within Latin it is primal, and any explanation of its form and its meaning involve diachronic research into earlier stages of the Indo-european family and cognate forms in languages other than Latin.

In the field of word form variations from a single root, both derivational and inflexional, Varro rehearsed the arguments for and against analogy and anomaly, citing Latin examples of regularity and of irregularity. Sensibly enough he concluded that both principles must be recognized and accepted in the word formations of a language and in the meanings associated with them.[12] In discussing the limits of strict regularity in the formation of words he noticed the pragmatic nature of

language, with its vocabulary more differentiated in culturally important areas than in others. Thus *equus*, horse, and *equa*, mare, had separate forms for the male and female animal because the sex difference
was important to the speakers, but *corvus*, raven, did not, because in
them the difference is not important to men; once this was true of doves,
formerly all designated by the feminine noun *columba*, but since they
were domesticated a separate, analogical, masculine form *columbus* was
created.[13] Varro further recognized the possibilities open to the individual, particularly in poetic diction, of variations (anomalies) beyond
those sanctioned by majority usage, a conception not remote from the
Saussurean interpretation of *langue* and *parole*.

One of Varro's most penetrating observations in this context was the
distinction between derivational and inflexional formation, a distinction
not commonly made in antiquity. One of the characteristic features of
inflexions is their very great generality; inflexional paradigms contain
few omissions and are mostly the same for all speakers of a single
dialect or of an acknowledged standard language. This part of morphology Varro called 'natural word form variation' (*dēclīnātiō nātūrālis*),
because, given a word and its inflexional class, we can infer all its other
forms.[14] By contrast, synchronic derivations vary in use and acceptability from person to person and from one word root to another (cp.
p. 21, above); from *ovis*, sheep, and *sūs*, pig, are formed *ovīle*, sheepfold, and *suīle*, pigsty, but *bovīle* is not acceptable to Varro from *bōs*,
ox, although Cato is said to have used the form (the normal Latin word
for ox-stall was *būbīle*).[15] The facultative and less ordered state of this
part of morphology, which gives a language much of its flexibility, was
distinguished by Varro in his use of the term 'spontaneous word form
variation' (*dēclīnātiō voluntāria*).

Varro showed himself likewise original in his proposed morphological classification of Latin words. His use in this of the morphological categories shows how he understood and made use of his Greek
sources without deliberately copying their conclusions. He recognized,
as they had done, case and tense as the primary distinguishing categories of inflected words in the classical languages, and set up a quadripartite system of four inflexionally contrasting classes:

Those with case inflexion,	nouns (including adjectives),
those with tense inflexion,	verbs,
those with case and tense inflexion,	participles,
those with neither,	adverbs.

These four classes were further categorized as forms which, respectively, named, made statements, joined (i.e. shared in the syntax of nouns and verbs), and supported (constructed with verbs as their subordinate members).[16] In the passages dealing with these classes the adverbial examples are all morphologically derived forms like *doctē*, learnedly, and *lectē*, choicely. His definition would apply equally well to the underived and monomorphemic adverbs of Latin, like *mox*, soon, and *crās*, tomorrow, but these are referred to elsewhere among the uninflected, invariable or 'barren' (*sterīle*) words.[17] A full classification of the invariable words of Latin would require the distinction of syntactically defined subclasses such as Thrax used for Greek and the later Latin grammarians took over for Latin; but from his examples it seems clear that what was of prime interest to Varro was the range of grammatically different words that could be formed on a single common root (e.g. *legō*, I choose, I read, *lector*, reader, *legēns*, reading, one who reads, and *lectē*, choicely).

In his treatment of the verbal category of tense, Varro displayed his sympathy with Stoic doctrine, in which two semantic functions were distinguished within the forms of the tense paradigms, time reference and aspect (p. 29, above). In his analysis of the six indicative tenses, active and passive, the aspectual division, incomplete-complete, was the more fundamental for him, as each aspect regularly shared the same stem form, and in the passive voice the completive aspect tenses consisted of two words, though Varro claims that erroneously most people only considered the time reference dimension:[18]

Active Time	past		present		future	
Aspect						
incomplete	*discēbam*	I was learning	*discō*	I learn	*discam*	I shall learn
complete	*didiceram*	I had learned	*didicī*	I have learned	*didicerō*	I shall have learned
Passive						
incomplete	*amābar*	I was loved	*amor*	I am loved	*amābor*	I shall be loved
complete	*amātus eram*	I had been loved	*amātus sum*	I have been loved	*amātus erō*	I shall have been loved

(The Latin future perfect was in more common use than the corresponding Greek (Attic) future perfect.)

Varro put the Latin 'perfect' tense forms *didicī*, etc., in the present completive place, corresponding to the place of the Greek perfect tense forms. In what we have or know of his writings he does not appear to have allowed for one of the major differences between the Greek and Latin tense paradigms, namely that in the Latin 'perfect' tense there was a syncretism of simple past meaning ('I did'), and perfect meaning ('I have done'), corresponding to the Greek aorist and perfect respectively. The Latin 'perfect' tense forms belong in both aspectual categories, a point clearly made later by Priscian in his exposition of a similar analysis of the Latin verbal tenses.[19]

If the difference in use and meaning between the Greek and Latin perfect tense forms seems to have escaped Varro's attention, the more obvious contrast between the five term case system of Greek and the six term system of Latin forced itself on him, as it did on anyone else who learned both languages. Latin formally distinguished an ablative case; 'by whom an action is performed' is the gloss given by Varro.[20] It shared a number of the meanings and syntactic functions of the Greek genitive and dative case forms. For this reason the ablative was called the 'Latin case' or the 'sixth case'.[21] Varro took the nominative forms as the canonical word forms, from which the oblique cases were developed, and, like his Greek predecessors, he contented himself with fixing on one typical meaning or relationship as definitive for each case (his apparent mistranslation of the Greek *aitiātikè ptôsis* by *cāsus accūsātīvus* has already been mentioned, p. 35, above).

Varro was probably the most independent and original writer on linguistic topics among the Romans.[22] After him we can follow discussions of existing questions by several authors with no great claim on our attention. Among others Julius Caesar is reported to have turned his mind to the analogy-anomaly debate while crossing the Alps on a campaign.[23] Thereafter the controversy gradually faded away. Priscian used *analogia* to mean the regular inflexion of inflected words, without mentioning *anōmalia*; the term *anōmalia* (whence English *anomalous*=irregular, as a technical term sometimes used in grammar) appeared occasionally among the late grammarians.[24]

Varro's ideas on the classification of Latin words have been noticed; but the word class system that was established in the Latin tradition enshrined in the works of Priscian and the late Latin grammarians was much closer to the one given in Thrax's *Téchnē*. The number of classes remained at eight, with one change. A class of words corresponding to the Greek (definite) article *ho, hē, tó*, the, did not exist in classical

Latin; the definite articles of the Romance languages developed later from weakened forms of the demonstrative pronoun *ille, illa, illud*, that. The Greek relative pronoun was morphologically similar to the article and classed with it by Thrax and Apollonius.[25] In Latin the relative pronoun, *quī, quae, quod*, who, which, was morphologically akin to the interrogative pronoun *quis, quid*, who?, which?, and both were classed together either with the noun or the pronoun class.[26]

In place of the article the Latin grammarians recognized the inter-jection as a separate word class, instead of treating it as a subclass of adverbs as Thrax and Apollonius had done.[27] Priscian regarded its separate status as common practice among Latin scholars, but the first writer who is known to have dealt with it in this way was Remmius Palaemon, a grammatical and literary scholar of the first century A.D., who defined it as having no statable meaning but indicating emotion.[28] Priscian laid more stress on its syntactic independence in sentence structure.

Quintilian was Palaemon's pupil; he wrote extensively on education, and in his *Institutio oratoria*, wherein he expounded his opinions, he dealt briefly with grammar, regarding it as a propaedeutic to the full and proper appreciation of literature in a liberal education, in terms very similar to those used by Thrax at the beginning of the *Téchnē* (p. 31, above). In a matter of detail, Quintilian discussed the analysis of the Latin case system, a topic always prominent in the minds of Latin scholars who had studied Greek. He suggested isolating the instrumental use of the ablative (*gladiō*, with a sword) as a seventh case, since it has nothing in common semantically with the other meanings of the ablative.[29] Separate instrumental case forms are found in Sanskrit, and may be inferred for unitary Indo-european, though the Greeks and Romans knew nothing of this. It was (and is) common practice to name the cases by reference to one of their meanings (dative 'giving', ablative 'taking away', etc.), but their formal identity as members of a six term paradigm rested on their meaning, or more generally, their meanings, and their syntactic functions being associated with a morphologically distinct form in at least some of the members of the case inflected word classes. Priscian saw this, and in view of the absence of any morphological feature distinguishing the instrumental use of the ablative case forms from their other uses, he reproved such an addition to the descriptive grammar of Latin as redundant (*supervacuum*).[30]

The work of Varro, Quintilian, and others during the classical age of Rome shows the process of absorption of Greek linguistic theory, controversies, and categories, in their application to the Latin language. But Latin linguistic scholarship is best known for the formalization of descriptive Latin grammar, to become the basis of all education in later antiquity and the Middle Ages and the traditional schooling of the modern world. The Latin grammars of the present day are the direct descendants of the compilations of the later Latin grammarians, as the most cursory examination of Priscian's *Institutiones grammaticae* will show.

Priscian's grammar (*c.* A.D. 500), comprising eighteen books and running to nearly a thousand pages as published today may be taken as representative of their work. Quite a number of writers of Latin grammars, working in different parts of the Roman Empire, are known to us from the first century A.D. onward.[31] Of them Donatus (fourth century) and Priscian are the best known. Though they differ on several points of detail, on the whole all these grammarians set out and follow the same basic system of grammatical description. For the most part they show little originality, doing their best to apply the terminology and categories of the Greek grammarians to the Latin language. The Greek technical terms were given fixed translations with the nearest available Latin word: *ónoma, nōmen, antōnymíā, prōnōmen, sýndesmos, coniunctiō*, etc. In this procedure they had been encouraged by Didymus, a voluminous Alexandrian scholar of the second half of the first century B.C., who stated that every feature of Greek grammar could be found in Latin.[32] He followed the Stoic word class system which included the article and the personal pronouns in one class (p. 28, above), so that the absence of a word form corresponding to the Greek article did not upset his classification.[33] Among the Latin grammarians, Macrobius (*c.* A.D. 400) gave an account of the 'differences and likenesses' of the Greek and the Latin verb,[34] but it amounted to little more than a parallel listing of the forms, without any penetrating investigation of the verbal systems of the two languages.

The succession of Latin grammarians through whom the accepted grammatical description of the language was brought to completion and handed on to the Middle Ages spanned the first five centuries of the Christian era. This period covered the *pax Romana* and the unitary Greco-Roman civilization of the Mediterranean that lasted during the first two centuries, the breaking of the imperial peace in the third century, and the final shattering of the western provinces, including Italy, by invasion from beyond the earlier frontiers of the empire. Historically these centuries witnessed two events of permanent significance in the life of the civilized world. In the first place, Christianity, which, from a secular standpoint, started as the religion of a small deviant sect of Jewish zealots, spread and extended its influence through the length and breadth of the empire, until, in the fourth century, after surviving repeated persecutions and attempts at its suppression, it was recognized as the official religion of the state. Its subsequent dominance of European thought and of all branches of learning for the next thousand years was now assured, and neither doctrinal schisms nor heresies, nor the lapse of an emperor into apostasy could seriously check or halt its progress. As Christianity gained the upper hand and attracted to itself men of learning, the scholarship of the period shows the struggle between the old declining pagan standards of classical antiquity and the rising generations of Christian apologists, philosophers, and historians, interpreting and adapting the heritage of the past in the light of their own conceptions and requirements.

The second event was a less gradual one, the splitting of the Roman world into two halves, east and west. After a century of civil turmoil and barbarian pressure, Rome ceased under Diocletian (284–305) to be the administrative capital of the empire, and his later successor Constantine transferred his government to a new city, built on the old Byzantium and named Constantinople after him. By the end of the fourth century the empire was formally divided into an eastern and a western realm, each governed by its own emperor; the division roughly corresponded to the separation of the old Hellenized area conquered by Rome but remaining Greek in culture and language, and the provinces raised from barbarism by Roman influence and Roman letters. Constantinople, assailed from the west and from the east, continued for a thousand years as the head of the Eastern (Byzantine) Empire, until it fell to the Turks in 1453. During and after the break-up of the Western Empire, Rome endured as the capital city of the Roman Church, while Christianity in the east gradually evolved in other directions to become the Eastern Orthodox Church.

Culturally one sees as the years pass on from the so-called 'Silver Age' (late first century A.D.) a decline in liberal attitudes, a gradual exhaustion of older themes, and a loss of vigour in developing new ones. Save only in the rising Christian communities, scholarship was backward-looking, taking the form of erudition devoted to the acknowledged standards of the past. This was an era of commentaries, epitomes, and dictionaries. The Latin grammarians, whose outlook was similar to that of the Alexandrian Greek scholars, like them directed their attention to the language of classical literature, for the study of which grammar served as the introduction and foundation. The changes taking place in the spoken and the non-literary written Latin around them aroused little interest; their works are liberally exemplified with texts, all drawn from the prose and verse writers of classical Latin and their ante-classical predecessors Plautus and Terence.

How different accepted written Latin was becoming can be seen by comparing the grammar and style of St. Jerome's fourth century trans-lation of the Bible (the Vulgate), wherein several grammatical features of the Romance languages are anticipated, with the Latin preserved and described by the grammarians, one of whom, Donatus, second only to Priscian in reputation, was in fact St. Jerome's teacher.

The nature and the achievement of the late Latin grammarians can best be appreciated through a consideration of the work of their greatest representative, Priscian, who taught Latin grammar in Con-stantinople in the second half of the fifth century. Though he drew much from his Latin predecessors, his aim, like theirs, was to transfer as far as he could the grammatical system of Thrax's *Téchnē* and of Apollonius's writings to Latin. His admiration for Greek linguistic scholarship and his dependence on Apollonius and his son Herodian, in particular, 'the greatest authorities on grammar', are made clear in his introductory paragraphs and throughout his grammar.[35]

Priscian worked systematically through his subject, the description of the language of classical Latin literature. Pronunciation and syllable structure are covered by a description of the letters (*litterae*), defined as the smallest parts of articulate speech, of which the properties are *nōmen*, the name of the letter, *figūra*, its written shape, and *potestās*, its phonetic value.[36] All this had already been set out for Greek (p. 24, above), and the phonetic descriptions of the letters as pronounced seg-ments and of the syllable structures carry little of linguistic interest except for their partial evidence of the pronunciation of the Latin language.

From phonetics Priscian passes to morphology, defining the word (*dictiō*) and the sentence (*ōrātiō*) in the same terms that Thrax had used, as the minimum unit of sentence structure and the expression of a complete thought, respectively.[37] As with the rest of western antiquity, Priscian's grammatical model is word and paradigm, and he expressly denied any linguistic significance to divisions, in what would now be called morphemic analysis, below the word.[38] On one of his rare entries into this field he misrepresented the morphemic composition of words containing the negative prefix *in-* (*indoctus*, untaught, etc.), by identifying it with the preposition *in*, in, into.[39] These two morphemes, *in-*, negative, and *in-*, the prefixal use of the preposition, are in contrast in the two words *invīsus*, unseen, and *invīsus*, hated (literally, looked (askance) at).

After a brief review of earlier theories of Greek linguists, Priscian set out the classical system of eight word classes laid down by Thrax and Apollonius, with the omission of the article and the separate recognition of the interjection, already mentioned. Each class of words is defined, and described by reference to its relevant formal categories (accidents (*accidentia*), whence the later *accidence* for the morphology of a language), and all are copiously illustrated with examples from classical texts. All this takes up sixteen of the eighteen books, the last two being devoted to syntax. Priscian seems to have addressed himself to readers already knowing Greek, as Greek examples are widely used and comparisons with Greek are drawn at various points, and the last hundred pages (18.20.157 ff.) are wholly taken up with the comparison of different constructions in the two languages. Though Constantinople was a Greek-speaking city in a Greek-speaking area, Latin was declared the official language when the new city was founded as the capital of the Eastern Empire; great numbers of speakers of Greek as a first language must have needed Latin teaching from then on.

The eight parts of speech (word classes) in Priscian's grammar may be compared with those in Dionysius Thrax's *Téchnē*. Reference to extant definitions in Apollonius and Priscian's expressed reliance on him allow us to infer that Priscian's definitions are substantially those of Apollonius, as is his statement that each separate class is known by its semantic content.[40]

> *nōmen* (noun, including words now classed as adjectives): the property of the noun is to indicate a substance and a quality, and it assigns a common or a particular quality to every body or thing.[41]
>
> *verbum* (verb): the property of a verb is to indicate an action or a being acted on; it has tense and mood forms, but is not case inflected.[42]
>
> *participium* (participle): a class of words always derivationally referable to verbs, sharing the categories of verbs and nouns (tenses and cases), and therefore distinct from both.[43]. This definition is in line with the Greek treatment of these words (p. 34, above).
>
> *prōnōmen* (pronoun): the property of the pronoun is its substitutability for proper nouns and its specifiability as to person (first,

second, or third).[44] The limitation to proper nouns, at least as far as third person pronouns are concerned, contradicts the facts of Latin. Elsewhere Priscian repeats Apollonius's statement that a specific property of the pronoun is to indicate substance without quality,[45] a way of interpreting the lack of lexical restriction on the nouns which may be referred to anaphorically by pronouns.

adverbium (adverb): the property of the adverb is to be used in construction with a verb, to which it is syntactically and semantically subordinate.[46]

praepositiō (preposition): the property of the preposition is to be used as a separate word before case inflected words and in composition before both case-inflected and non-case-inflected words.[47] Priscian, like Thrax, identified the first part of words like *prōconsul*, proconsul, and *intercurrere*, to mingle with, as prepositions.

interiectiō (interjection): a class of words syntactically independent of verbs, and indicating a feeling or a state of mind.[48]

coniunctiō (conjunction): the property of conjunctions is to join syntactically two or more members of any other word class, indicating a relationship between them.[49]

In reviewing Priscian's work as a whole, one notices that in the context in which he was writing and in the form in which he cast his description of Latin, no definition of grammar itself was found necessary. Where other late Latin grammarians defined the term, they did no more than abbreviate the definition given at the beginning of Thrax's *Téchnē*. It is clear that the place of grammar, and of linguistic studies in general, in education was the same as had been precisely and deliberately set out by Thrax and summarily repeated by Quintilian. Priscian's omission is an indication of the long continuity of the conditions and objectives taken for granted during these centuries.

Priscian organized the morphological description of the forms of nouns and verbs, and of the other inflected words, by setting up canonical or basic forms, in nouns the nominative singular and in verbs the first person singular present indicative active; from these he proceeded to the other forms by a series of letter changes, the letter being for him, as for the rest of western antiquity, both the minimal graphic unit and the minimal phonological unit. The steps involved in these changes bear no relation to morphemic analysis, and are of the type that found no favour at all in recent descriptive linguistics, though under the influence of the generative grammarians somewhat similar process terminologies are now being suggested.[50]

The accidents or categories in which Priscian classed the formally different word shapes of the inflected or variable words included both derivational and inflexional sets, Priscian following the practice of the Greeks in not distinguishing between them. Varro's important insight was disregarded. But Priscian was clearly informed on the theory of the establishment of categories and of the use of semantic labels to identify them. Verbs were defined by reference to action or being acted on, but he pointed out that on a deeper consideration (*sī quis altius consīderet*) such a definition would require considerable qualification; and case names were taken, for the most part, from just one relatively frequent use among a number of uses applicable to the particular case named.[51] This is probably more prudent, if less exciting, than the insistent search for a common or basic meaning uniting all the semantic functions associated with each single set of morphologically identified case forms. The status of the six cases of Latin nouns is shown to rest, not on the actually different case forms of any one noun or one declension of nouns, but on semantic and syntactic functions systematically correlated with differences in morphological shape at some point in the declensional paradigms of the noun class as a whole; the many-one relations found in Latin (as in other languages) between forms and uses and between uses and forms are properly allowed for in the analysis.[52]

In describing the morphology of the Latin verb, Priscian adopted the system set out by Thrax for the Greek verb (p. 35, above), distinguishing present, past, and future, with a fourfold semantic division of the past into imperfect, perfect, plain past (aorist), and pluperfect, and recognizing the syncretism of perfect and aorist meanings in the Latin perfect tense forms.[53] Except for the recognition of the full grammatical status of the Latin perfect tense forms, Priscian's analysis, based on that given in the *Téchnē*, is manifestly inferior to the one set out by Varro under Stoic influence. The distinction between incomplete and complete aspect, correlating with differences in stem form, on which Varro laid great stress, is concealed, although Priscian recognized the morphological difference between the two stem forms underlying the six tenses.[54] Strangely, Priscian seems to have misunderstood the use and meaning of the Latin future perfect, calling it the future subjunctive, though the first person singular form by which he cited it (e.g. *scripserō*, I shall have written) is precisely the form which differentiates its paradigm from the perfect subjunctive paradigm (*scripserim*, I wrote) and, indeed, from any subjunctive verb form, none of which show a first person termination in -ō. This seems all the more surprising because the corresponding forms in Greek, e.g. *tetýpsomai* (τετύψομαι), I shall have been beaten, are correctly identified.[55] Possibly his reason was that his Greek predecessors had excluded the future perfect from their schematization of the tenses, in that this tense was not much used in Greek, and was felt to be an Atticism (p. 30, above). A like dependence on the Greek categorial framework probably led him to recognize both a subjunctive mood (subordinating) and an optative mood (independent, expressing a wish) in the Latin verb, although Latin, unlike Greek, nowhere distinguishes these two mood forms morphologically, as Priscian in fact admits, thus confounding his earlier explicit recognition of the status of a formal grammatical category (p. 59, above).[56]

Despite such apparent misrepresentations, due primarily to an excessive trust in a point for point applicability of Thrax's and Apollonius's systematization of Greek to the Latin language, Priscian's morphology is detailed, orderly, and in most places definitive. His treatment of syntax in the last two books is much less so, and a number of the organizing features that we find in modern grammars of Latin are lacking in his account; they were added by mediaeval and postmediaeval scholars on to the foundation of Priscianic morphology. Confidence in Priscian's syntactic theory is hardly increased by reading his assertion that the word order, most common in Latin, nominative case noun or pronoun (subject) followed by verb is the natural one, because the substance is prior to the action it performs[57]; such are the dangers of philosophizing on an inadequate basis of empirical fact.

In the syntactic description of Latin, Priscian classified verbs on the same lines as had been worked out for Greek by the Greek grammarians, into active (transitive), passive, and neutral (intransitive), with due notice of the deponent verbs, passive in morphological form but active or intransitive in meaning and syntax and without corresponding passive tenses.[58] Transitive verbs are those colligating with an oblique case (*laudō tē*, I praise you, *noceō tibi*, I injure you, *egeō miserantis*, I need someone to pity me); and the absence of concord between oblique case forms and finite verbs is noted.[59] But the terms subject and object were not in use in Priscian's time as grammatical terms, though the use of *subiectum* to designate the logical subject of a proposition was common. Priscian made mention of the ablative absolute construction, though the actual name of this construction is a later invention; he gave an account and examples of exactly this use of the ablative case: *mē vidente puerum cecīdistī*, while I saw it you beat the boy, and *Augustō imperātōre Alexandria prōvincia facta est*, when Augustus was emperor Alexandria was made a province.[60]

Of the systematic analysis of Latin syntactic structures Priscian had little to say. The relation of subordination was recognized as the primary syntactic function of the relative pronoun, *quī, quae, quod*, and of similar words used to downgrade or relate a verb or a whole clause to another, main, verb or clause.[61] The concept of subordination was employed in distinguishing nouns (and pronouns used in their place) and verbs from all other words, in that these latter were generally used only in syntactically subordinate relations to nouns or verbs, these two classes of word being able by themselves to constitute complete sentences of the favourite, productive, type in Latin.[62] But in the sub-classification of the Latin conjunctions, the primary grammatical distinction between subordinating and coordinating conjunctions was left unmentioned, the coordinating *tamen*, however, being classed with the subordinating *quamquam* and *quamsī*, although.[63]

Once again it must be said that it is all too easy to exercise hindsight and to point out the errors and omissions of one's predecessors. It is both more fair and more profitable to realize the extent of Priscian's achievement in compiling his extensive, detailed, and comprehensive description of the Latin language of the classical authors, which was to serve as the basis of grammatical theory for eight centuries and as the foundation of Latin teaching up to the present day. Such additions and corrections, particularly in the field of syntax, as later generations needed to make could be incorporated in the frame of reference that Priscian had employed and expounded.

Any division of linguistics (or of any other science) into sharply differentiated periods is a misrepresentation of the gradual passage of discoveries, theories, and attitudes that characterizes the greater part of man's intellectual history. But it is reasonable to close an account of Roman linguistic scholarship with Priscian. In his detailed (if in places misguided) fitting of Greek theory and analysis to the Latin language he represents the culmination of the expressed intentions of most Roman scholars once Greek linguistic work had come to their notice. And this was wholly consonant with the general Roman attitude in intellectual and artistic fields towards 'captive Greece' who 'made captive her uncivilized captor and taught rustic Latium the finer arts'.[64]

Priscian's work is more than the end of an era; it is also the bridge between antiquity and the Middle Ages in linguistic scholarship. By far the most widely used grammar, Priscian's *Institutiones grammaticae* ran to no fewer than one thousand manuscripts, and formed the basis of mediaeval Latin grammar and the foundation of mediaeval linguistic philosophy, which must be considered in the next chapter. Priscian's grammar was the fruit of a long period of Greco-Roman unity. This unity had already been broken by the time he wrote, and in the centuries following, the Latin west was to be shattered beyond recognition. In the confusion of these times, the grammarians, their studies and their teaching, have been identified as one of the main defences of the classical heritage in the darkness of the Dark Ages.[65]

FOR FURTHER CONSULTATION

H. ARENS, *Sprachwissenschaft: der Gang ihrer Entwicklung von der Antike bis zur Gegenwart*, Freiburg/Munich, 1955, 28–9.

R. R. BOLGAR, *The classical heritage and its beneficiaries*, Cambridge, 1954.

J. COLLART, *Varron grammairien latin*, Paris, 1954.

D. FEHLING, 'Varro und die grammatische Lehre von der Analogie und der Flexion', *Glotta* 35 (1956), 214–70, 36 (1958), 48–100.

L. LERSCH, *Die Sprachphilosophie der Alten*, Bonn, 1838–41.

H. NETTLESHIP, 'The study of grammar among the Romans in the first century A.D.', *Journal of philology* 15 (1886), 189–214.

R. H. ROBINS, *Ancient and mediaeval grammatical theory in Europe*, London, 1951, chapter 2.

J. E. SANDYS, *History of classical scholarship* (third edition), Cambridge, 1921, volume 1.

H. STEINTHAL, *Geschichte der Sprachwissenschaft bei den Griechen und Römern* (second edition), Berlin, 1890.

NOTES

1. E. GIBBON, *The decline and fall of the Roman Empire* (ed. J. B. BURY), London, 1909, volume 1, 85–6.

2. VERGIL, *Aeneid* 6, 851–3:
   Tu regere imperio populos, Romane, memento
   (hae tibi erunt artes), pacisque imponere morem,
   parcere subiectis et debellare superbos.

3. *Noctes Atticae* 17.17.2; H. S. GEHMAN, *The interpreters of foreign languages among the ancients*, Lancaster, Pa., 1914.

4. FEHLING, 1956–58.

5. H. FUNAIOLI, *Grammaticorum Romanorum fragmenta*, Leipzig, 1907, 265: Ars grammatica scientia est eorum quae a poetis historicis oratoribusque dicuntur ex parte maiore.

6. *De lingua Latina* 8.1.
7. ibid. 8.5.
8. ibid. 5.3, 5.73.
9. ibid. 5.37, 5.78, 6.46.
10. ibid. 6.37–8, 8.3.
11. ibid. 7.4.
12. ibid. 9.3, 10.74.
13. ibid. 9.56.
14. ibid. 8.21–2, 9.35, 10.16.
15. ibid. 8.54; CHARISIUS, *Ars grammaticae* I (KEIL, *Grammatici* I, Leipzig, 1857, 104).
16. VARRO, op. cit., 6.36, 8.44, 10.17.
17. ibid. 8.9–10.
18. ibid. 9.96–7, 10.48.
19. PRISCIAN 8.10.54.
20. VARRO, op. cit., 8.16.
21. ibid. 10.62.
22. On Varro's linguistic theory in relation to modern linguistics, cp. D. T. LANGENDOEN, 'A note on the linguistic theory of M. Terentius Varro', *Foundations of language* 2 (1966), 33–6.
23. SUETONIUS, *Caesar*, 56; GELLIUS, *Noctes Atticae* 1.10.4.
24. PRISCIAN, *Institutio de nomine pronomine et verbo* 38, *Institutiones grammaticae* 5.7.38; PROBUS, *Instituta artium* (H. KEIL, *Grammatici Latini*, Leipzig, 1864, volume 4), 48.
25. DIONYSIUS THRAX, *Téchnē*, § 20 (I. BEKKER, *Anecdota Graeca* 2, Berlin, 1816, 640); APOLLONIUS DYSCOLUS, *Syntax* 1.43.
26. As noun, PRISCIAN 2.4.18, 2.6.30, 13.3.11; as pronoun, PROBUS, *Instituta* (KEIL, *Grammatici* 4), 133.
27. APOLLONIUS, *De adverbio*, BEKKER, *Anecdota Graeca* 2, 531.
28. CHARISIUS, *Ars grammaticae* 2.16 (KEIL, *Grammatici* I (1857), 238): Nihil docibile habent, significant tamen adfectum animi.
29. QUINTILIAN, *Institutio oratoria* 1.4.26.
30. PRISCIAN 5.14.79.
31. Their works are published in the eight volumes of H. KEIL, *Grammatici Latini*, Leipzig, 1855–1923.
32. PRISCIAN 8.17.96; *De figuris numerorum* 9.
33. PRISCIAN 11.1.1.
34. *De differentiis et societatibus Graeci Latinique verbi*, KEIL, *Grammatici* 5, Leipzig, 1923, 595–655.
35. 'Artis grammaticae maximi auctores', dedicatory preface 1–2, 6.1.1, 11.1.1.
36. 1.2.3, 1.3.7–8.
37. 2.3.14: Dictio est pars minima orationis constructae; 2.4.15: Oratio est ordinatio dictionum congrua, sententiam perfectam demonstrans.

38. 2.3.14.
39. 17.16.104.
40. 2.4.17.
41. 2.4.18: Proprium est nominis substantiam et qualitatem significare; 2.5.22; Nomen est pars orationis, quae unicuique subiectorum corporum seu rerum communem vel propriam qualitatem distribuit.
42. 2.4.18: Proprium est verbi actionem sive passionem . . . significare; 8.1.1.: Verbum est pars orationis cum temporibus et modis, sine casu, agendi vel patiendi significativum.
43. 2.4.18: Participium iure separatur a verbo, quod et casus habet, quibus caret verbum, et genera ad similitudinem nominum, nec modos habet, quos continet verbum; 11.2.8: Participium est pars orationis, quae pro verbo accipitur, ex quo et derivatur naturaliter, genus et casum habens ad similitudinem nominis et accidentia verbo absque discretione personarum et modorum.

The problems arising from the peculiar position of the participle among the word classes, under the classification system prevailing in antiquity, are discussed in 11.1.1–11.2.8.

44. 2.4.18: Proprium est pronominis pro aliquo nomine proprio poni et certas significare personas; 12.1.1: Pronomen est pars orationis, quae pro nomine proprio uniuscuiusque accipitur personasque finitas recipit.
45. 13.6.29: Substantiam significat sine aliqua certa qualitate (cp. 13.6.31).
46. 2.4.20: Proprium est adverbii cum verbo poni nec sine eo perfectam significationem posse habere; 15.1.1: Adverbium est pars orationis indeclinabilis, cuius significatio verbis adicitur.
47. 2.4.20: Praepositionis proprium est separatim quidem per appositionem casualibus praeponi . . . coniunctim vero per compositionem tam cum habentibus casus quam cum non habentibus; 14.1.1: Est praepositio pars orationis indeclinabilis, quae praeponitur aliis partibus vel appositione vel compositione.
48. 15.7.40: Videtur affectum habere in se verbi et plenam motus animi significationem, etiamsi non addatur verbum, demonstrare.
49. 2.4.21: Proprium est coniunctionis diversa nomina vel quascumque dictiones casuales vel diversa verba vel adverbia coniungere; 16.1.1: Coniunctio est pars orationis indeclinabilis, coniunctiva aliarum partium orationis, quibus consignificat, vim vel ordinationem demonstrans.
50. cp. P. H. MATTHEWS, 'The inflectional component of a word-and-paradigm grammar', *Journal of linguistics* 1 (1965), 139–71.
51. 8.2.7; 5.13.73.
52. 17.25.182–6.
53. 8.8.38; 8.10.51–8.

54. 8.10.55.
55. 8.8.38.
56. 18.8.76; 18.10.79; 18.10.82.
57. 17.16.105–6.
58. 8.2.7–8; 8.3.14.
59. 17.15.93; 17.21.153–4.
60. 18.2.30.
61. 17.5.30.
62. 17.2.12–13.
63. 16.1.1; 16.2.10.
64. HORACE, *Epistles* 2.1.156–7:
    Graecia capta ferum victorem cepit et artes
    Intulit agresti Latio.
65. F. LOT, *La fin du monde antique et le début du moyen âge*, Paris, 1951,
    189.

Four

The Middle Ages

'The Middle Ages' is a term used to designate and characterize the period of European history between the breakdown of the Roman Empire as a unitary area of civilization and administration, and the sequence of events and cultural changes known as the Renaissance and generally taken as the opening phase of the modern world. Periodization of this sort is a descriptive convenience for the historian rather than a precise record of the facts; the 'decline and fall' of the Roman Empire, and the revival of learning, the rise of humanism and nationalism, religious reformation, and the other features collectively regarded as characterizing and constituting the Renaissance are not events that can be located at particular points in time; they summarize a multitude of events of historical significance and, perhaps of more importance, changes of attitude and of ways of behaving, that took place gradually and at different times in different places, but together served to mark off the European situation after them as recognizably and irreversibly altered from what had preceded. Any date taken symbolically as the start or as the finish of the Middle Ages must be arbitrary, and, if taken at all literally, misleading.

'Middle', of course, would have no meaning for anyone living in the mediaeval period; the term springs from the sense of Renaissance men that, among other achievements, they were again linking hands with the bright civilization and humanism of the classical era across the gulf of intervening darkness and barbarism.[1] In this sweeping generalization, people of the first years of modern Europe exaggerated the blackness of mediaeval times and undervalued the cultural and intellectual activities and products of the Middle Ages. But a decline there undoubtedly was over a wide field of human life during the centuries immediately following the collapse of Rome.

The first six centuries following the dissolution of the western Roman Empire are often distinguished, as the 'Dark Ages', from the later mediaeval period between about 1100 and the Renaissance, during which the flowering of mediaeval civilization recovered much of the ground lost in the turmoil of earlier years.[2]

During this time the Eastern Empire fared better. Though its territory was attacked from different sides and reduced in area, a continuity of Greek thought and learning coexisted with the spread of official Christianity, which gradually attained the status of the separate Eastern Church. No sharp break in organized life and civilization occurred such as was suffered by the west, and in matters of scholarship, Greek philosophy and Greek literature were never lost, although little of original merit was achieved outside theology, and the ancient Greek authors were subjects of continuous commentary and exegesis. Byzantine scholars wrote explications and notes on the work of Dionysius Thrax, and research continued on the theory of grammatical cases (cp. p. 39, above).

The Roman Empire in the west, already under pressure from barbarian invasions over the frontiers that had been nearly stable from Augustus (27 B.C.–A.D. 14) to Marcus Aurelius (161–80), failed to stand the strain, and its territory passed into the hands of various tribes, mostly Germanic. In 410 Rome suffered the humiliation of being sacked by the Visigoths, and in 476 the last of the emperors in the west, poor Romulus Augustulus, was summarily deposed by a German mercenary, Odovacar, and Italy passed seventeen years later into the Ostrogothic kingdom under Theodoric.

The causes of the collapse of the empire of the 'eternal city' have been the focus of earnest enquiry from the time when, with the sack of Rome in his memory, Augustine sought for a Christian interpretation of secular history in *The city of God* (*Civitas Dei*). Certainly from the end of the second century A.D. external pressures on the frontiers were more severe than hitherto, and certainly, too, one can point to grave weaknesses of character and wrong decisions on the part of those called upon to face those pressures. Civil fighting, invasions, and later wars between the Eastern Empire and the successors to the western emperors cumulatively caused an absolute fall in standards of life, security, and liberal civilization such as had been enjoyed in the first two centuries of the Christian era. Two events may be thought symbolic: the fortification of Rome under Aurelian (270–5), and the destruction of the aqueducts supplying water to the city during the sixth century wars waged by Justinian in his attempts to reconquer the former territory of the old Roman Empire. These calamitous years were, probably, marked by no greater an amount of misdirection, shortsightedness, and obstinacy in the pursuit of impracticable and undesirable ends than that which disfigured the first half of the twentieth century; but our unhappy predecessors had not the uncovenanted advantages of modern technology to repair the results of wanton destruction.

But one must not overpaint the darkness. Many of the Germanic tribes had adopted Christianity, and were anxious to consider themselves part of the Roman Empire and indeed to defend their newly acquired territory against much more savage tribes, whose pressure had first impelled them across the imperial frontiers. The Latin of the western provinces survived every Germanic invader, whose speech left only a few lexical items in the modern Romance languages that are the descendants of the spoken Latin of those regions.

In the west, much of classical literature was irreparably lost; for some centuries the study and even the knowledge of Greek was greatly reduced, and in the Dark Ages much of Greek philosophy that was available was in the form of Latin translations of selected works. In the disturbance of the times and the collapse of pagan authority and standards, the Church grew in prestige as a refuge and as a patron of learning and education, possessing, in the Papacy and bishoprics, centres of secular power. The most formative literature of the period was Christian literature of various types, and with the closure of the philosophical schools of Athens by Justinian in 529, such learning as continued in both east and west was under clerical patronage and often clerically inspired.

A great debt is owed for the preservation of a continuity of education and learning to the monasteries, abbeys, churches, and, later, universities, that were founded during the early Middle Ages. In institutions dominated by Christian clerics, pagan literature, that is to say the classical literature of antiquity, was bound to be suspect, and there are instances of deliberate hostility to these authors and the language in which they wrote, as contrasted with the later, more nearly colloquial, Latin of the Vulgate and of church usage. Already Jerome had experienced feelings of guilt at his too great interest in Cicero and the classics at the expense of holy scripture, and Pope Gregory the Great (590–610) declared his contempt for the rules of Donatus in application to the language of divine inspiration; a French abbot of the ninth century was careful to draw the examples he used in his lectures on grammar from the scriptures to avoid clerical displeasure.[3] But in a number of places of learning ancient literature continued to be studied, ancient manuscripts were copied and preserved, and grammatical theory was taught.

Latin remained the language of learning, and its authority was increased by its use as the language of patristic literature and of the services and the administration of the western (Roman) Church. This alone ensured the language a high place, and linguistic studies in the early years of the Middle Ages were largely represented by studies in Latin grammar. Mediaeval education was built on the foundation of the 'Seven liberal arts'; grammar, dialectic (logic), and rhetoric formed the first part, or *trivium*, music, arithmetic, geometry, and astronomy the second part, or *quadrivium*. A jingle summarizes their functions:

Gram loquitur; dia vēra docet; rhet verba colōrat;
Mūs canit; ar numerat; ge ponderat; ast colit astra.[4]

The division into the *trivium* and *quadrivium* and these terms were the work of Boethius (*c.* A.D. 500), a Roman scholar and statesman, who among his many writings made a number of Latin translations from the works of Aristotle, which formed a good part of the restricted amount of Greek literature available in the west in the early Middle Ages.

Grammar was thus the foundation of mediaeval scholarship, both as a liberal art itself and as a necessity for reading and writing Latin correctly. All these studies were subordinate to theology, the study of the Christian faith and Christian doctrine; but as an example of the persistence of cultural themes, one can trace the organization of the seven arts back into the classical period. Varro is known to have written *Disciplinae*, an encyclopaedia on subjects of education, that included the seven arts, together with medicine and architecture. This was the model for Augustine's survey of the seven arts (in which he substituted philosophy for astronomy),[5] and around the same time Martianus Capella (fifth century A.D.) wrote an account of the seven arts in the form of an allegory of the marriage of Mercury and Philologia, at which the seven bridesmaids were Grammar, Logic, Rhetoric, Geometry, Arithmetic, Astronomy, and Music. Capella's style has been found tedious, but the book became a standard school text. Cassiodorus, who was one of those most responsible for organizing monastic life around the study and preservation of both classical and Christian literature, also set out the seven liberal arts in the course of his *Institutiones* (*c.* 550).

Such was the context in which grammar was studied and taught in the first centuries after the collapse of the western Roman Empire. The work itself was in the main practical and normative; Priscian and Donatus were the principal authorities and their theory and systematization were little altered. Further writing took the form of numerous commentaries and glosses; in other fields this linguistic scholarship was supported by etymological and lexicographical work such as is well known from the pen of Isidore of Seville (seventh century).

Christianity has from its earliest days been conceived as a world religion, and missionary activity has been held to be an important part of the work of the Church in most denominations. The contacts between Christians and non-Christians from the beginning involved linguistic work of a practical nature, and have through the course of history contributed significantly to the growth and development of linguistic science. St. Jerome, responsible for the Latin translation of the Bible (the Vulgate), devoted one of his letters to a discussion of the theory of translation, justifying a rendering of sense for sense rather than of word for word.[6] Such knowledge as we have of the Gothic language comes to us from the translation of parts of the New Testament into that language by Ulfilas in the fourth century; and the alphabet in use today for Russian and some other Slavic languages is the descendant of one devised in the ninth century by St. Cyril of the Eastern Church and Empire, who adapted the Greek alphabet for the use of Christianized Slavs.

Though a good amount of Latin teaching must have gone on throughout the period of Rome's ascendancy, little is known of the methods. Christian missionary work and the founding of monasteries and churches in foreign lands gave a new impetus and inspiration to the teaching of Latin grammar, and the status enjoyed by the Roman Church in Christianized Europe, and by Latin, its official language, gave, equally, a desire to be taught.

In England Bede and Alcuin wrote grammars of Latin in the seventh and eighth centuries. An example of a specifically didactic grammar of Latin is Aelfric's *Latin grammar* and *Colloquium* (Latin conversation book), and his Latin-Old English glossary that accompanied it. These were composed around 1000 for English children speaking Old English (Anglo-Saxon). Aelfric was abbot of Eynsham in Oxfordshire; he wrote a practical manual addressed to schoolboys, and he based his prescription on the works of Priscian and Donatus. Rather significantly, he told his readers that his book would be equally suitable as an introduction to (Old) English grammar.[7] Though he was aware of differences between the two languages, as in the matter of gender distribution between lexically equivalent nouns and the lack of exact correspondence between their two case systems,[8] he did not question or discuss the applicability of the Priscianic system to Old English, and as his was one of the first known grammars specifically directed at English-speaking learners, it may be taken as setting the seal on several centuries of Latin-inspired English grammar.

After the conversion of Ireland in the fifth century, Latin scholarship flourished to an important extent during the first millennium in centres of learning founded by the Church. Until the Scandinavian invasions of the ninth century, Ireland was in the forefront of Christian civilization, and Irish churchmen played an important part in the spread of Christianity and literacy on the continent of Europe. Latin grammar was studied in Ireland through the works of Donatus, Priscian, and Isidore, and this linguistic learning merged with the native bardic tradition to produce the grammatical and poetic teaching of the mediaeval bardic tracts, which indeed continued down to the seventeenth century. The technical terminology of Irish linguistic scholarship shows a combination of borrowing and adaptation of Latin terms with a parallel development of technical terms from native Irish words; this latter component included terminology devised to cover the features of the initial mutations, of great importance in the phonology and grammar of the Celtic languages, but not found in Latin (or elsewhere in Indo-european). A ninth-century manuscript of glosses on Priscian shows the partial assimilation of his terminology and descriptions into the Irish language; and the *Auraicept na n-Éces* (the poets', or scholars', primer) parts of which probably go back to the seventh century, also exemplifies the mingling in Ireland of the Latin and the native linguistic traditions; this work was studied down to the eleventh and twelfth centuries.[9]

In the history of linguistic science, the second part of the Middle Ages, from around 1100 to the close of the period, is the more significant. This was the period of scholastic philosophy, in which linguistic studies had an important place and in which a very considerable amount of linguistic work was carried on. This same era is also marked by the flowering of mediaeval architecture (the so-called 'Gothic') and literature, and the founding of several of the earliest universities of Europe.

The movements of whole populations had now ceased, and the ascendancy of the Roman Church, strengthened by the foundation of the Dominican and Franciscan Orders, provided a central authority which, despite controversies and antagonisms, united all men's cultural activities as part of the service of God, and subordinated all intellectual pursuits to the study of the faith.

Hitherto linguistic work had been almost wholly paedagogical in its aims and largely derivative in its doctrine, being applied to the teaching of Latin in accordance with the compilations of Donatus and Priscian. Such purely didactic work went on throughout the scholastic period. Several manuals of Latin grammar were published in verse, as an aid to the students' memory. One such is the *Doctrinale* of Alexander of Villedieu, written about 1200, and running to 2645 lines of rather barbarous hexameters.[10] It would seem that the Latin taught in the schools where this manual was in use was nearer the Latin serving as the mediaeval *lingua franca* of educated life than the language of the classical authors who had served Priscian as his material.

The *Doctrinale* is severely practical, and it remained a popular and prescribed textbook throughout the mediaeval period, and in some schools long afterwards, though in general it fell into the disfavour that mediaeval grammar of all sorts encountered in the renewed classicism of the Renaissance.[11]

Linguistic descriptions of other languages appeared during this period, serving the ends of literacy, popular literature, and educational standards. Irish work in this field has been noticed above; a Welsh grammar is known from the thirteenth century, and its source is said to go back to the tenth.[12]

One of the most striking examples of practical work in this period was the *First grammatical treatise*, by an unknown Icelandic scholar of the twelfth century, who showed a remarkable originality and independence of thought. The text takes its rather inappropriate title from the position it occupied in the original manuscript, and the author is in consequence identified simply as the 'First Grammarian'.[13] He was, in fact, primarily interested in spelling reform, in improving the use of an alphabet derived from the Latin alphabet for the writing of the Icelandic language of his day. He was well versed in the work of the Latin grammarians, notably in the work of Donatus; but it is in his treatment of orthographic problems that he displayed an understanding of the principles implicit in phonological analysis and in its application such as was rare in this period of the history of linguistics. Besides this,

his observations on the pronunciation of the language, which are in themselves valuable evidence for this stage of Icelandic, show him to have been a phonetician beyond the rank of any known European contemporary.

His short text points to the inadequacies of the existing Icelandic alphabet then in use, and, some eight hundred years in advance, antici-pates several parts of Prague phonological theory (p. 205, below) and the exploitation of the phoneme concept to a remarkable extent. The Icelandic of his time maintained the potentiality of thirty-six distinc-tive vowel segments, nine vocalic qualities each of which could be long or short, nasalized or non-nasalized. He was able to order the nine qualities along the dimension open-close in reference to the values assigned to the Latin vowel letters *a, e, i, o* and *u*; and by marking length and nasality with diacritics (a superscript accent mark and dot, respec-tively) and leaving their absence unmarked, he kept graphically distinct the thirty-six vowels by the use of just eleven symbols, nine letters and two diacritics. These were required if the orthography was to give an adequate indication of the contrastive pronunciations.

Several consonants occurred as long or geminate in contrast with their short or single counterparts. He suggested writing the long consonants with a capital letter; thus *n* represents [n], and *N* represents [nn]. Conversely, he pointed out that phonetic differences that were depen-dent on their environment need not be marked separately; so the pronunciations [ð] and [θ], at the time both allophones of /θ/, were assigned the single letter *þ*, and the velar nasal [ŋ], an allophone of /n/, could be unambiguously indicated in the letter sequence *ng*.[14]

In addition to his advanced phonological theory, his discovery and demonstration procedures were quite modern. Phonemic distinctions were ascertained by controlled variation of a single segment in a con-stant frame, along such ordered series of words as *sár, sǫr, sér, sęr, sór, sór, súr, sýr,* and they were illustrated by sets of minimally different pairs of words whose difference in meaning depended on the difference of a single letter (one phoneme). The pairs are glossed by being worked into sentences, some of them revealing a racy sense of humour:

Eigi eru *ǫl ǫL* at einu
Not *all ales* are alike;

Mjǫk eru þeir menn *frámer,* er eigi skammask at taka mína konu *frá mér.*
Those men are *brazen,* who are not ashamed to take my wife *from me.*

6—S.H.L.

(The examples are given in the usual Old Norse spellings; only the examples being contrasted are written in the First Grammarian's reformed orthography.)

Whether in his theoretical exposition, his practical applications, or in the style in which he met imagined objections, the First Grammarian is a pleasure to read. Yet the fate of his *Treatise* is a sad one. Shortly after the twelfth century Iceland fared ill, through climatic changes and disease, and became much more sundered from European life and learning. The text remained unpublished until 1818, and after that it was largely unknown outside Scandinavia. Much of the ground it had covered so well was gone over again in the modern era by scholars who were then considered to be pioneers. One must not only have something worthwhile to say, if one is to have an assured place in history; one must also have an adequate cultural situation for it to become known and appreciated.

By far the most interesting and significant development in linguistics during the Middle Ages is the output of 'speculative grammars' or treatises *De modis significandi* ('on the modes of signifying') from a number of writers during the high period of scholastic philosophy (*c.* 1200–1350). Speculative grammar went far beyond the requirements of the teaching of Latin, and the writings in which it was expounded existed side by side with standard teaching manuals such as the *Doctrinale* of Alexander of Villedieu.

Speculative grammar is a definite and distinct stage in linguistic theory, and the different authors, or Modistae, as they are sometimes called, represent substantially the same theoretical point of view, and share the same conception of linguistic science, its objectives, and its place among other intellectual studies. There are, of course, numerous details of presentation in which they differ, as may be expected; a full study and appreciation of this period of linguistics would require proper notice of these differences, but in a historical survey of the subject attention may be concentrated on the broad outlines of the theory that was shared by all those working within it.

Speculative grammar was the product of the integration of the grammatical description of Latin as formulated by Priscian and Donatus into the system of scholastic philosophy. Scholasticism itself was the result of the integration of Aristotelian philosophy, at the hands of such thinkers as St. Thomas Aquinas, into Catholic theology. Scholasticism was a system of thought reinforced by and reinforcing the Christian faith of the day, which could serve to unify within itself all branches and departments of human learning and in which the claims of reason and of revelation could be harmonized. Probably not before and certainly never since has the fabric of knowledge been so undivided at its heart.

The rise and growth of scholastic philosophy came about from a number of historical factors, apart from the emergence of men of first rate intellectual abilities and devotion. The greater tranquillity and settledness of the later Middle Ages have been mentioned. In addition, a knowledge of the Greek language, of Greek writers, and, above all, of Greek philosophy as set out by Aristotle became more readily available to the west from around the twelfth century. This increase of knowledge came from opposite ends of the Mediterranean world. The Crusades, though reflecting little credit on the western participants, resulted in more direct contacts between the Roman Church and the Eastern Empire, and the capture of Constantinople in 1204 stimulated interest in the Greek sources of Aristotelian philosophy (known earlier from Latin translations), and released a number of Greek manuscripts to the west. By the fourteenth century Greek was being regularly taught in a number of European universities. From Spain a considerable amount of Greek philosophical writing was reintroduced into the rest of western Europe through Arabic and Jewish translations and commentaries. During the Arab occupation of Spain, Toledo in particular was a centre of the translation of Arabic versions of Aristotle into Latin. Several of the scholastics knew and studied Aristotelian philosophy through Latin translations rather than in the original Greek, and the commentaries by Arabic scholars, of whom Averroes and Avicenna are the best known, contributed to their interpretation.

Earlier Christian philosophers had laid more weight on Plato and Platonic thought than on Aristotle, partly because Platonic theory was more readily available through the writings of the Neo-Platonists of the third century and after. The works of Aristotle were not accepted without a struggle in all seats of learning, but the teaching of St. Thomas was decisive in making him the dominant philosopher in mediaeval Christian thought.

In the context of scholasticism, the mere description of Latin, as laid down by Priscian and Donatus, was considered inadequate, however useful it might be paedagogically. Commentators had already begun to go further than straightforward elucidation and exegesis, and the view was now expressed that Priscian had not delved deeply enough into his subject in merely describing the language, but that he should have investigated the underlying theory and the justification for the elements and categories that he employed. William of Conches (twelfth century) complained that he had neglected to deal with the causal basis of the various parts of speech and their accidents.[15] Some of the charges against Priscian and the other Latin grammarians show an interesting resemblance to the charges of neglecting explanatory adequacy of theory in favour of mere observational adequacy of data recording, that are made today by generative grammarians against their more purely descriptive predecessors associated with Bloomfield and the dominant trends in linguistic work during the second quarter of the present century. From the twelfth century on, they provided the impetus that led to speculative grammar and to a theory of language set within the philosophy of the times. There was, too, a marked increase in the volume of grammatical research and study that was carried on.[16]

In the middle of the twelfth century Peter Helias wrote a commentary on Priscian in which he sought philosophical explanations for the rules of grammar laid down by him. The examination of Peter Helias's work in relation to a number of commentators preceding him suggests that he was not so much a pioneer in the application of logic to linguistic questions, but rather one of the first grammarians to bring some systematization into earlier rather unordered statements.[17] Thereafter the role of the philosopher in grammar was considered a major one; the theoretical basis of grammar, as distinct from its mere exposition to schoolboys, was the philosopher's province: 'It is not the grammarian but the philosopher who, carefully considering the specific nature of things, discovers grammar'; 'As is the fool to the wise man, so is a grammarian ignorant of logic to one skilled in logic'.[18]

From this attitude consistently arose the conception of an underlying universal grammar, a recurrent quest of theoretical linguists thereafter. Earlier grammarians had not made universalistic claims. They had no need to; their interest was confined first to Greek and then to Greek and Latin, two languages not ill served by the same set of classes and categories. In the Middle Ages Latin remained the only really necessary scholar's language, despite the later increase in men's knowledge of Greek and some study of Arabic and Hebrew. Roger Bacon, who himself wrote a grammar of Greek as well as one of the earliest speculative grammars, and who insisted on the importance of studying Arabic and Hebrew, could declare that grammar was one and the same in all languages in its substance, and that surface differences between them are merely accidental variations.[19] The unity of grammar, realized with superficial differences in different languages, was also compared to the unity of geometry irrespective of the different shapes and sizes of any actual diagrams.[20]

During the scholastic period certain linguistic topics were discussed by writers whose main concern was not linguistic science in the narrower sense. An important distinction was made explicit in semantics, subsequently to be treated under a number of different terms but always maintained as essential in some form. In the thirteenth century, Petrus Hispanus, later to be Pope John XXI, in the course of his *Summulae logicales* referred to the difference between *significātiō* and *suppositiō* as separate but related semantic properties of words.[21] *Significātiō* may be translated as the meaning of a word, and was defined as the relation between the sign or word and what it signified. By virtue of this meaning relation, a given sign may act as a substitute for, or be accepted in place of, a given thing, person, event, etc., or a set of such things; with nouns this is the relation of *suppositiō*. Thus because *homō*, man, means 'man', *homō* or *man* may stand for (*suppōnere*) Socrates, Guy Fawkes, or Harold Wilson. *Significātiō* is prior to *suppositiō*, and when the *significātiōnēs* or meanings of more than one word are brought together in constructions their *suppositiō* may be restricted by this. Thus *homō albus*, white man, can only be accepted for men who are white, not for dark-skinned men nor for white existents other than men. This basic distinction comes up repeatedly, in somewhat different forms and with different interpretations, in such binary oppositions as meaning and reference, connotation and denotation, and intension and extension.

Some logicians and grammarians made a further distinction, involving the opposition of form and matter, that of formal supposition and material supposition. In its formal supposition a word stands for or is accepted for a thing, person, etc., in what later logicians call object language or first order language; in material supposition the word stands for itself, in a metalanguage or second order language. These two types of supposition are exemplified in *Peter is the Pope* and '*Peter*' *is a name*.

This same distinction between form and matter recurs at various points in modistic speculative grammar. The difference between *vox*, sound, and *dictiō*, word, treated by Priscian and, in fact, going back to the Stoics, is expressed thus by Michel de Marbais (thirteenth century): 'A word includes in itself its sound as it were its matter and its meaning as its form'.[22]

Mediaeval modistic linguistics concentrated on grammar; the fact that Latin was everywhere learned as a second language, and pronounced with 'an accent' depending on the first language of the individual and his community, may have been partly responsible for the lack of interest in phonetic detail. The modistae excluded pronunciation from their field, but some writers of the period mention certain features of mediaeval Latin wherein it had changed from the standards of the classical grammarians. In etymology the Middle Ages produced similar absurdities to those all too well known from antiquity. In these two fields no theoretical or practical developments can be reported.

The theory of the speculative grammarians involves a good deal of new technical terminology, and in detail its exposition is a formidable task. In essence, the grammar of Priscian and Donatus was presented as an accurate reflection of the constitution of reality and the powers of the human mind, on which it depended. Considering their universalistic pretensions, it is remarkable how the modistae preserved intact almost all the details of Priscian's Latin morphology, down to subdivisions of word classes quite obviously having reference only to Latin (for example the subclassification of proper nouns into *praenōmina*, forenames, *cognōmina*, surnames, and *agnōmina*, personal titles, all categories strictly limited to Latin onomastics).[23] In dealing with verbal tenses no attempt was made to go descriptively beyond Priscian's rather inadequate formulation or to take Varronian or Stoic theory into account. In these respects a certain naivety appears in the unquestioned descriptive basis of what is otherwise a logically thought-out and internally coherent system of philosophical grammar. It is also a testimony to the place and influence of Priscian in mediaeval linguistic thought.

In the modistic system, things possess as existents various properties or modes of being (*modī essendī*). The mind apprehends these by the active modes of understanding (*modī intelligendī actīvī*), to which there correspond the passive modes of understanding (*modī intelligendī passīvī*), the qualities of things as apprehended by the mind. In language the mind confers on vocal sounds (*vōcēs*) the active modes of signification (*modī significandī actīvī*), in virtue of which they become words (*dictiōnēs*) and parts of speech (*partēs orātiōnis*), and signify the qualities of things; these qualities are now represented by the passive modes of signification (*modī significandī passīvī*), the qualities of things as signified by words.

Two *modī essendī* that were found in all things and underlay our entire apperception of the world and the constitution of our language were the *modus entis*, the property of permanence or persistence in time whereby things may be recognized as things, and the *modus esse*, the property of change and succession (also called the *modus fluxūs*, the *modus fierī*, and the *modus mōtūs*), whereby persistent things may be recognized as undergoing changes or other processes that involve temporal succession.[24]

One may represent the system diagrammatically:

modī essendī

modī intelligendī actīvī	*modī intelligendī passīvī*
modī significandī actīvī	*modī significandī passīvī.*

Again with reference to the distinction between form and matter, the *modī essendī*, the *modī intelligendī passīvī*, and the *modī significandī passīvī* differ formally, since they are on different levels, but they are the same materially, in that they all relate to the properties of things, as they are, as they are understood in the mind, and as they are expressed in language.[25]

The *modī significandī* are the key terms in the system. Every part of speech, or class of words, is distinguished by its representing reality through a particular mode or from some particular point of view; and every category applicable to any word class is itself a mode contributing its own semantic component. This system of description and the theory lying behind it may be illustrated and compared with the Dionysian and Priscianic systems by setting out the modistic definitions of the eight Priscianic word classes of Latin, as they were given by Thomas of Erfurt, the author of a *De modis significandi sive grammatica speculativa* (*c.* 1350), once attributed to Duns Scotus:[26]

nōmen: a part of speech signifying by means of the mode of an existent or of something with distinctive characteristics (this is said to be the equivalent of Priscian's definition involving substance and quality). The mode of an existent is the mode of stability and permanence.[27]

verbum: a part of speech signifying through the mode of temporal process, detached from the substance (of which it is predicated).[28]

participium: a part of speech signifying through the mode of temporal process, not separated from the substance (of which it is predicated).[29]

prōnōmen: a part of speech signifying through the mode of an existent, without distinctive characteristics. The mode of existing without distinctive characteristics comes from the property or mode of being of primal matter (cp. pp. 37 and 58 above).[30]

The remaining, indeclinable, parts of speech were said to have fewer *modī significandī* involved with them and to be derived from fewer properties in things. An earlier modista, Michel de Marbais, had rather loosely compared them with the syncategorematic terms of the logicians.[31]

> *adverbium:* a part of speech signifying by the mode of being constructed with another part of speech that signifies through the mode of temporal process,[32] and further qualifying that mode but without other syntactic relationships.[33]
>
> *coniunctiō:* a part of speech signifying through the mode of joining two other terms.[34]
>
> *praepositiō:* a part of speech signifying through the mode of syntactic construction with a case inflected word, linking and relating it to an action.[35]
>
> *interiectiō:* a part of speech signifying through the mode of qualifying a verb or a participle, and indicating a feeling or an emotion.[36] The specific association of the interjection with verbs and participles seems to spring from its earlier inclusion in the adverb class by the Greek grammarians. Other modistae, such as Siger de Courtrai, did not restrict it in this way, and this accords more with Priscian's definition (p. 58, above) and with Latin usage.[37]

It is apparent that the formal aspects of earlier definitions have been replaced by the ascription of specific meaning categories, some of them shared by more than one word class; but each class is defined by a particular mode of signifying that distinguishes it from all the others. The declinable (inflected) word classes are defined by reference to the categories of scholastic philosophy, ultimately referable to Aristotle's categories of being; but in applying this terminology to the indeclinable word classes, the modistae treated *modus significandī* almost as the equivalent of syntactic function. While class meanings are more readily (if often roughly) ascribable to nouns and verbs, it is much less easy to do this for those classes of words normally found in subordinate positions within syntactic complexes (as were the Latin uninflected words), unless meaning is very much widened to include formal syntactic relations, as the Firthians do explicitly and the modistae did by implication.[38]

The scholastic interpretation of Aristotelian doctrine is apparent throughout modistic grammar. Priscian's grammatical description of Latin was readily adaptable to this, since Aristotelian influence was strongly felt in its source, the system set out in Thrax's *Téchnē*. Defining categories were designated *modī significandī essentiālēs*, and Priscian's *accidentia* became *modī significandī accidentālēs*, covering such categories as case and tense. The definition of the pronoun shows how the descriptive observations of Apollonius and Priscian were made to link this class of words with the representation of the philosophers' *mātēria prīma*.

Although modistic theory was primarily focused on what one might call the morphosemantics of Priscian's Latin grammar, the ascription of a distinct and definite category of meaning to each formal difference exhibited by classes of words, it was in syntax that the speculative grammarians made the greatest innovations and the most significant developments. Perhaps because Priscian had manifestly left this part of his grammar inadequately worked out, in contrast to the completeness of his morphology, they found themselves compelled to pursue research themselves in arriving at a satisfactory syntactic analysis to relate to their basic theory. A number of the fundamental concepts of later syntactic theory can be assigned to this period of linguistic science. A thirteenth-century writer corrected the previous concentration on morphology by declaring that grammar is above all concerned with syntax.[39] Indeed, not only the theoretical modistae but also the writers of the later mediaeval practical manuals and teaching grammars, such as the *Doctrinale* of Alexander of Villedieu, made use of terms and concepts beyond those found in Donatus and Priscian, in particular that of government (*regimen*), in dealing with the syntax of nominal case forms.

Thomas of Erfurt's treatment of syntax may be briefly summarized as an example of modistic theory.[40]

An acceptable sentence (*sermō congruus et perfectus*) arises from four principles, comparable to the four Aristotelian causes:

material, the words as members of grammatical classes (*constructibilia*),

formal, their union in various constructions,

efficient, the grammatical relations between different parts of speech expressed in the inflexional forms (*modī significandī*), that are required by the construction and imposed by the speaker's mind,

final, the expression of a complete thought.[41]

Acceptability required three conditions to be satisfied: the word classes involved must be such as to constitute a syntactic construction (e.g. noun and verb), the words must exhibit appropriate inflexional categories (*modī significandī accidentālēs*), and the words as individual lexical items must be collocable (in the Firthian sense). *Cappa nigra*, black cap, is collocationally appropriate (*propria*), but *cappa categorica*, *categorical cap, though grammatically congruent (*congrua*), is inappropriate (*impropria*) since it involves an unacceptable collocation. A century earlier, and seven centuries before pseudo-sentences like *sincerity admires John* were made famous in discussion, a grammarian had pointed out the unacceptability of *lapis amat fīlium*, *the stone loves the boy, despite its formal correctness[42]; several centuries before that, and quite independently, Indian linguists had formulated the same distinction (p. 145, below).

The construction of noun and verb was taken as fundamental, as in earlier syntactic descriptions, and the terms *suppositum* and *appositum* (subject and predicate) were used to denote the syntactic functions of the two parts of the basic sentence; the *modī significandī essentiālēs* of the noun and the verb (*modus entis* and *modus esse*, respectively) are involved in the interrelations of subject and predicate. The terms *suppositum* and *appositum* were, of course, related to the *subiectum* and *praedicātum* of the logicians, but they were, very properly, kept distinct.

Other constructions were related either to the *suppositum* or to the *appositum*, and the analysis of *Sōcratēs albus currit bene*, white Socrates runs well, comprises a major structure of *suppositum* (*Sōcratēs*) and *appositum* (*currit*), with one subordinate element related directly to each head, but only mediately to the rest of the sentence, introducing an analytical model anticipatory of the more formal immediate constituent type.

Earlier theory had distinguished the subject-verb construction and the verb-object (oblique case) constructions, but the terms *suppositum* and *appositum*, or any comparable syntactic terms, had not been used. The modistae went further, and analysed syntactic relations in terms of dependence and the termination (satisfaction) of a dependence: 'One part of a construction stands to another either as depending on it or as satisfying its dependence'[43]. With various subdivisions, the relation of dependent to terminant was used to characterize constructions such as the following:

Dependent	Terminant	
verb (*appositum*)	noun in nominative case (*suppositum*)	*Sōcratēs currit*
verb	noun in oblique case (object)	*legit librum*
adjective (*nōmen adiectīvum*)	noun	*Sōcratēs albus*
adverb	verb	*currit bene*
noun	noun in genitive case	*fīlius Sōcratis.*[44]

It will be seen that this relation does not coincide with the relation of dependent to head in modern syntax (cp. especially the last example), nor with any single syntactic relation. Its main importance lies in the recognition of syntactic relations in sentence structures other than the surface relations of inflexional concord.

The relation of government (rection) between one word and another had already been identified by the time of Peter Helias,[45] who used *regere*, to govern, in denoting the relation of prepositions to oblique case nouns as well as the types of relation exemplified above in so far as case forms were involved. He is said to have defined this relation as 'causing a word to be put in the particular case in which it is put'.[46] Thomas of Erfurt did not use *regere* or morphologically associated words as technical terms; but in the sense in which *government* is mostly used today in the description of languages like Latin, in reference to the relation of prepositions to certain oblique case forms, he used the verb *dēservīre*, to be subject to, an interesting example of two metaphors drawn from words of opposite literal meanings to bear precisely the same technical sense.[47] *Regere* and *regimen* were used by some modistae as well as by Alexander of Villedieu.

Dependency and its termination are also used to distinguish subordinate clauses and constructions from independent or main constructions. *Sī Sōcratēs currit*, if Socrates runs, is dependent, because the reader or hearer expects more before he accepts the sentence as complete, or the dependency terminated.[48]

Transitive and intransitive as categories of syntactic constructions make their appearance in modistic syntax. The terms were not used in the same sense in which they had been used of verbs by Priscian (following the terminology of Apollonius, p. 37, above), and in which they are used today, but rather a general connection can be traced between them. The modistae apply the terms *constructiō transitīva* and *constructiō intransitīva* to certain syntactic relations between sentence components, or elements of sentence structure, that involve several different classes of words. In a noun-verb-noun sentence like *Sōcratēs legit librum*, Socrates reads a book, the relation between the first noun (*suppositum*) and the verb (*appositum*) is a *constructiō intransitīva*, as is the relation between the noun and the verb in a sentence like *Sōcratēs currit*, Socrates runs; and the relation between *legit* and *librum* is a *constructiō transitīva*, the verb *legit*, reads, acting as the pivot of the whole structure, with dependence on each noun (p. 83, above). The same distinction is made between adjective and noun in concord, *Sōcratēs albus*, white Socrates, a *constructiō intransitīva*, and noun (including adjective) and an oblique case, *fīlius Sōcratis*, son of Socrates, *similis Sōcratī*, like Socrates, *constructiōnēs transitīvae*. The basis of the distinction is that intransitive constructions need involve only one term in the category of person, whereas transitive constructions necessarily involve more than one.[49] It is noteworthy that the later mediaeval grammarians made explicit use of word order in the identification of sentence components, and that the word order assumed as normal was that common to the Romance languages of today, noun verb noun, or subject verb object, rather than the order noun noun verb (subject object verb) characteristic of classical literary Latin.[50] In mediaeval times, Latin of the type exemplified in scholastic writing was a living mode of communication, even though it was everywhere acquired as a second language.

The modistae followed Priscian's morphological description of Latin very closely, but in relating the morphological categories (*modī significandī* in their terminology) to the syntax of sentence construction, they came to make an important distinction between categories (modes) of one word that were directly involved with the categories of other words and those that were not. These were designated *modī respectīvī*, modes involved in further syntactic relations, and *modī absolūtī*, modes not so involved.[51] Some writers further defined the *modī respectīvī* as *principia constructiōnis* (the bases of sentence structure). Thus the essential modes of the noun and verb, the *modus entis* and the *modus esse* (p. 79, above), make possible their relationship as *suppositum* and *appositum* in the sentence, and are therefore both *modī respectīvī*. Likewise among the accidental modes (Priscian's *accidentia*), case, gender, and mood are syntactically relevant categories (*modī respectīvī*), but form (*figūra*,

Thrax's *schêma*), simple or compound (e.g. *dīves*, rich, *praedīves*, very rich), and type (*species*, Thrax's *eîdos*), primary or derived (e.g. *calleō*, I am hot, *callescō*, I become hot), are not, i.e. they are *modī absolūtī*.

The modistae differ in detail on the distribution of particular categories (modes) in these two classes, but broadly a distinction was drawn on syntactic lines between what have been termed in later formal grammar inflexional and derivational formations.[52] The modistic distinction bears some relation also to the distinction made by Varro between *dēclīnātiō nātūrālis* and *dēclīnātiō voluntāria* (p. 50, above), though there is no evidence of an actual use of Varro's work by the modistae. Varro was concerned with morphological regularity and irregularity; the modistae were concerned with syntactic function. The partial correspondence between Varro's *dēclīnātiō voluntāria* and their *modī absolūtī*, and between his *dēclīnātiō nātūrālis* and their *modī respectīvī* arises from the fact that in Latin (as in many other languages) inflexional formations tend to be much more regular and systematic than derivational formations.

The syntactic system worked out by the modistae enabled them to arrive at a clearer picture of the essential function of certain classes of word and in consequence to refine their definitions. The distinction between noun and adjective assumed a position of greater importance. In antiquity adjectives had been assigned to a variety of subclasses of the *ónoma/nōmen* class (pp. 34 and 57, above). Peter Helias referred to a primary division of the *nōmen* into *nōmen substantīvum* and *nōmen adiectīvum*, and Thomas of Erfurt, in describing the *nōmen*, distinguished *nōmen substantīvum* from *nōmen adiectīvum* by their *modī essentiālēs* of syntactic independence (*per sē stantis*) and of construction with a noun (*adiacentis*).[53]

The verb and the participle share the *modus esse*, the category of process in time; but the verb is grammatically distinct from the noun, and in the minimal noun-verb, or *suppositum-appositum* sentence it is one of the two polar terms. The participle, while sharing in much of the syntax and semantics of the verb, including time reference and construction with oblique case forms, can also, with or without other words attached to it, itself act as a nominal element in sentence structure. This distinction was marked by referring to the verb as detached from the substance denoted by the noun (*significans per modum esse distantis ā substantiā*), and to the participle as not separated from this substance (*significans per modum esse indistantis ā substantiā*).[54]

Similarly, the rather unsatisfactory definitions of the preposition by ancient grammarians were replaced by a succinct statement of its function (in Latin), syntactically tied to a case inflected word and relating this to a verb or participle (*ad actum redūcens*). Thomas of Erfurt explicitly rejects the identification of bound morphemes in certain words as prepositions along with the free prepositions, a confusion which had led Priscian into inaccuracy.[55]

The system of relations and categories outlined above is by no means the same as the system used today in traditional Latin grammar or in more strictly formal grammar. But it shows a remarkable growth of syntactic insight and the development of terminology and theory, from which present-day linguists have found a great deal that is applicable and revealing in the formal analysis of the classical languages and of others. It can, in fact, be claimed that a definite and coherent theory of sentence structure and of syntactic analysis was achieved by the modistae, one that dealt with levels of structure deeper than those immediately involved with the morphological categories of the inflected words of Priscian's Latin grammar.

Writers of the speculative grammars did not have to concern themselves directly with the topic that received the greatest attention from mediaeval philosophers. This was the so-called 'question of universals'. While scarcely a linguistic problem except on the most liberal interpretation of the field and scope of linguistics, it was centred on one aspect of the relation between the use of language to talk about the world and the nature of the world in itself. The question primarily refers to the semantic status of the terms or words used to make general propositions, broadly speaking the sort of words that can occur as single predicates or right-hand members of subject-predicate propositions in Aristotelian logic, such as *Socrates is a man* and *man is rational*, and so on. Do such terms stand for real universals existing in their own right apart from and independent of the particular things or persons of which the terms are predicated? Or, do they exist as a common property or character within the particulars? Or, finally, are they no more than general or universal terms used by the speakers of a language, with no status apart from the language and the speaker? These questions, first promoted by Plato's theory of 'ideas' or ideal forms, were brought into particular prominence at the beginning of the mediaeval period by Boethius in his commentary on the writings of the Neo-Platonist Porphyry; and various refinements and modifications of the three fundamental viewpoints on the problem were the subject of continuous debate during the whole of the Middle

Ages (the question is still a living one, and likely to remain so, but it no longer holds the same central position in philosophical enquiry and controversy). The nominalist point of view, that universals are words or names only, with no real existence outside language, has been made famous by one of its exponents, William of Ockham (first half of the fourteenth century), to whom the saying 'entia nōn sunt multiplicanda praeter necessitātem' (Entities are not to be increased in number beyond what is necessary) has been attributed, wrongly in the actual words used, but rightly in the doctrine.

The theory of language set out by the modistae, in terms of the *modī essendī*, *intelligendī*, and *significandī*, however, rests on a 'moderate realism', basically an Aristotelian view as interpreted by St. Thomas Aquinas, and one of the tenets of Thomist philosophy. In this view, as far as human knowledge is concerned, universals are abstracted from real properties of particulars and then considered apart from them by the mind.[56] In modistic terms the mind abstracts the *modī essendī* from things, considers them as *modī intelligendī*, and language permits such abstractions to be communicated by means of the *modī significandī*.

The assumption was that all men carry out this process alike, and that despite superficial differences all languages communicate in the same way, or as the modistae put it, the *modī essendī*, the passive *modī intelligendī* and *significandī* are all the same materially.

This sort of view became harder to maintain when in later years wider linguistic experience and interests showed how very different languages are in their grammatical constitutions and in the semantic categories associated with their most important formal features. More recently linguists have maintained that peoples whose languages and culture are widely separated from those of others must be allowed to live in partly different worlds, or in worlds differently conceived and structured from the 'standard average European' world of the classical European inheritance, and that these differences are in some respects correlated with the grammatical and semantic structure of their languages. Such a viewpoint, in its extreme and scarcely tenable form, that one's language is wholly and irresistibly responsible for one's conception of the world and attitude towards it, has been ascribed, perhaps unjustly, to B. L. Whorf.[57] But in recognizing the far too limited approach to linguistic diversity seen in the modistic speculative grammars, there is no need to go to the opposite extreme. Indeed one may retain modistic terminology, with the sensible provision that the *modī intelligendī* probably differ from language community to language community, and that the traffic is not all in one direction; the *modī intelligendī* give rise to *modī significandī*, but are themselves influenced in the course of years by the *modī significandī* and the actual forms in which they are expressed.

It is worth while studying the work of the speculative grammarians, both to see how their linguistic thought arose from the intellectual context of their time, and to consider its relevance to current problems in the theory and the analysis of language. Apart from their contribution to the theory and the terminology of syntactic description, mentioned above, the modistae raised questions on the most important topics that concern our attempt to understand language and its place in human life and society. Moreover they not unfairly represent some aspects of the mediaeval achievement. They wrote in, and illustrated from, Latin, the international language of European culture during the Middle Ages; but they sought to give a universal validity to the rules exhibited in Latin grammar. Mediaeval scholars wished for a system of knowledge in which all branches and all disciplines would accept the same philosophical and religious principles; and after the confusion of the Dark Ages they endeavoured to establish firmly all sciences on true and stable foundations.

The demand that grammatical description should be integrated into philosophical theory brought about a great change in people's attitudes towards linguistic studies. Philosophy in its widest sense had been the cradle of linguistics and of the first speculation on language in ancient Greece; but since the emergence of the Alexandrian school represented in Thrax's *Téchnē*, whose standpoint remained dominant in Apollonius and his Greek and Latin successors, the study of classical literature and the language and style of reputed poets and prose writers had been the accepted purpose and context of linguistic work. So much had this been an accepted and continuing tradition that after the explicit statement of the tasks and purposes of linguistics at the beginning of the *Téchnē* (p. 31, above), later writers either repeated it summarily, confined themselves to such brief phrases as 'the knowledge of correct speaking and correct writing' (*scientia rectē loquendī rectē scrībendī*), or, as Priscian, felt it unnecessary to give any statement or definition to introduce their subject.[58] But the changed outlook of the later Middle Ages demanded explicit recognition in changed definitions of linguistic science. Siger de Courtrai wrote: 'Grammar is the science of language, and its field of study is the sentence and its modifications, its purpose being the expression of the concepts of the mind in well formed sentences'.[59]

Contemporaries were aware of this change in the definition and conception of the subject. Formerly grammar had been directed towards the *auctōrēs*, the writers of classical literature; now it was exclusively concerned with its place among the *artēs*, the seven liberal arts (p. 69, above), wherein pagan literature had no place unless, like the philosophical writings of Aristotle, it had been officially incorporated into accepted doctrine. The Latin of the speculative grammarians was by classical standards clumsy and inelegant; the forms employed were often unacceptable when considered in relation to the usage of classical Latin authors, and the philosophical theory adduced to justify the theory of modistic grammar was held by later critics of the period to be at best irrelevant and at worst pettifogging and obscurantist. In modern terms the modistae were theory orientated, and the adherents of classical literature and Priscian's grammar as it stood were data orientated. The difference between the two attitudes is illustrated by the choice of examples; the linguists of antiquity and the late Latin grammarians used quotations from classical texts, Priscian being very free with his citations, but the modistae made up their examples almost formulaically, without regard to actual utterance or to situational plausibility; being only concerned with exemplifying a particular structure, they frequently produced sentences that could scarcely have occurred in any other context of situation (the example quoted above, *Sōcratēs albus currit bene*, white Socrates runs well, is quite typical).

This sort of opposition between the *artēs* and the *auctōrēs* was not new in Christian Europe; something similar could be seen in the heart-searching of St. Jerome and others on whether they were guilty of preferring Cicero to Holy Writ; but the rise of the modistic approach to grammar sharpened it and brought it into direct contact with linguistic studies. We find this the subject of a well-known allegory, the *Battle of the seven arts*, in which the *auctōrēs*, classical authors from Homer onwards, are based on Orleans, where classical scholarship and literature had remained entrenched, and go out to do battle with the philosophers and the personifications of the seven arts at Paris, one of the main centres of logic and speculative grammar.[60] It is ironical that Priscian, who in method owed much to Aristotelian models and whose Latin grammar was the foundation of mediaeval grammatical theory, is now, as champion of the *auctōrēs* from Orleans, matched in allegorical combat with Aristotle, who had been made responsible for the assumed

7—S.H.L.

logical basis of grammatical rules and concepts and, as the inspiration of scholastic philosophy, had become a leader of the *artēs*.

In the allegory the *artēs* win, but at the end of the story it is prophesied that in time the true grammar of the classical texts will return in triumph. This indeed happened, but as part of the many and profound movements of thought that characterized the intellectual and cultural side of the Renaissance, which was simultaneously the full-scale revival of classical learning and the birth of the modern world.

FOR FURTHER CONSULTATION

ALEXANDER VILLADEI, *Doctrinale* (ed. D. REICHLING), Berlin, 1893 (*Monumenta Germaniae paedagogica* 12).

H. ARENS, *Sprachwissenschaft: der Gang ihrer Entwicklung von der Antike bis zur Gegenwart*, Freiburg/Munich, 1955, 30–46.

G. L. BURSILL-HALL, 'Mediaeval grammatical theories', *Canadian journal of linguistics* 9 (1963), 40–54.

M. GRABMANN, *Mittelalterliches Geistesleben*, Munich, 1926, volume 1, chapter 4.

E. HAUGEN (ed.), 'First grammatical treatise', *Language* 26.4 (1950), supplement.

R. HUNT, 'Studies on Priscian in the eleventh and twelfth centuries', *Mediaeval and renaissance studies* 1 (1941–3), 194–231, and 2 (1950), 1–56.

J. KOCH (ed.), *Artes liberales*, Leiden and Cologne, 1959.

L. J. PAETOW, *The arts course at mediaeval universities with special reference to grammar and rhetoric*, Urbana, 1910 (*University of Illinois studies* 3.7).

——, *The battle of the seven arts*, Berkeley, 1914 (*Memoirs of the University of California* 4.1).

R. H. ROBINS, *Ancient and mediaeval grammatical theory in Europe*, London, 1951, chapter 3.

H. ROOS, 'Die modi significandi des Martinus de Dacia', *Beiträge zur Geschichte der Philosophie und Theologie des Mittelalters* 37.2 (1952).

J. E. SANDYS, *History of classical scholarship* (third edition), Cambridge, 1921, volume 1.

SIGER DE COURTRAI, *Oeuvres* (ed. G. WALLERAND), Louvain, 1913 (*Les philosophes belges* 8).

THOMAS OF ERFURT (Duns Scotus), *Grammatica speculativa* (ed. M. F. GARCIA), Quaracchi, 1902.

C. THUROT, *Extraits de divers manuscrits latins pour servir à l'histoire des doctrines grammaticales au moyen âge*, Paris, 1869 (reprinted Frankfurt am Main, 1964).

M. DE WULF, *History of medieval philosophy* (tr. P. COFFEY), London, 1909.

J. ZUPITZA (ed.), *Aelfrics Grammatik und Glossar*, Berlin, 1880 (*Sammlung englischer Denkmäler* 1).

NOTES

1. W. P. KER, *The Dark Ages*, London, 1904, chapter 1.
2. ibid., 1.
3. JEROME, *Epistulae* 22 c 30; GREGORY, *Epistulae* 5.53 (*Gregorii I Papae registrum epistularum*, Berlin, 1891, volume 1, 357); *Histoire littéraire de la France*, Paris, 1738, volume 4, 445–6.
4. SANDYS, 1921, 670 (Gram(mar) speaks; dia(lectic) teaches the truth; rhet(oric) adorns the words we use; mus(ic) sings; ar(ithmetic) counts; ge(ometry) measures; ast(ronomy) studies the stars).
5. AUGUSTINE, *Retractatio* 1.6.
6. JEROME, *Epistulae* 57.
7. ZUPITZA, 1880, preface, lines 1–7.
8. ibid., 18–19, 22–4.
9. *Auraicept na n-Éces, The scholars' primer* (ed. G. CALDER), Edinburgh, 1917; B. Ó CUÍV, 'Linguistic terminology in the mediaeval Irish bardic tracts', *TPS* 1965, 141–64.
10. ALEXANDER VILLADEI, 1880.
11. ibid., lxxxix.
12. J. WILLIAMS AB ITHEL, *Dosparth edeyrn davod aur, or The ancient Welsh grammar*, London, 1856, xi.
13. HAUGEN, 1950. On subsequent linguistic studies in Iceland, R. J. MCCLEAN, 'The grammatical terminology of modern Icelandic', *Studia Germanica Gandensia* 4 (1962), 291–300.
14. HAUGEN, 1950, 24, 37–8.
15. 'Causas vero inventionis diversarum partium et diversorum accidentium . . . praetermittit' (ROOS, 1952, 93); SIGER, 1913, (37).
16. SIGER, 1913, (36).
17. HUNT, 1941–3, 1950.
18. 'Non ergo grammaticus sed philosophus, proprias naturas rerum diligenter considerans . . . grammaticam invenit', THUROT, 1869, 124; ALBERTUS MAGNUS: 'Sicut se habet stultus ad sapientem, sic se habet grammaticus ignorans logicam ad peritum in logica', ALEXANDER 1893, xi–xii.
19. GRABMANN, 1926, 118; ROGER BACON: 'Grammatica una et eadem est secundum substantiam in omnibus linguis, licet accidentaliter varietur', SIGER, 1913, (43).
20. By Robert Kilwardby, THUROT, 1869, 127.
21. J. P. MULLALLY, *The Summulae locales of Peter of Spain*, Notre Dame, 1945.

22. PRISCIAN 1.1.1. 2.3.14; p. 24, above; THUROT, 1869, 156: Dictio includit in se vocem tanquam sibi materiam et rationem significandi tanquam sibi formam.
23. THOMAS, 1902, chapter 13.
24. ibid., § 24; SIGER, 1913, 108.
25. THOMAS, 1902, § 12.
26. GRABMANN, 1926, 118–25.
27. THOMAS, 1902, § 25: Nomen est pars orationis significans per modum entis vel determinatae apprehensionis; § 24: modus entis est modus habitus et permanentis.
28. ibid., § 117; Verbum est pars orationis significans per modum esse distantis a substantia.
29. ibid., § 163: Participium est pars orationis significans per modum esse indistantis a substantia.
30. ibid., § 98: Pronomen est pars orationis significans per modum entis et indeterminatae apprehensionis; § 96: modus indeterminatae apprehensionis oritur a proprietate, seu modo essendi materiae primae.
31. THUROT, 1869, 188; THOMAS, 1902, § 183.
32. i.e. a verb or a participle.
33. THOMAS, 1902, § 150: Adverbium est pars orationis significans per modum adiacentis alteri quod per modum esse significat ipsum esse absolute determinans. For the use of *absolute*, see p. 84, above.
34. ibid., § 170: Coniunctio est pars orationis per modum coniungentis duo extrema significans.
35. ibid., § 176: Est praepositio pars orationis significans per modum adiacentis alteri casuali ipsum contrahens et ad actum reducens.
36. ibid., § 181: Interiectio est pars orationis significans per modum determinantis alterum quod est verbum vel participium, affectus vel motus animae repraesentans.
37. SIGER, 1913, 152.
38. cp. J. R. FIRTH, 'The technique of semantics', *TPS* 1935, 36–72.
39. THUROT, 1869, 213.
40. THOMAS, 1902, chapters 45–54.
41. ibid., §§ 185–8.
42. ibid., § 218; THUROT, 1869, 21.
43. THOMAS, 1902, § 187: Unum constructibile est ad alterum dependens vel alterius dependentiam determinans.
44. Socrates runs; he reads a book; white Socrates; he runs well; son of Socrates.
45. THUROT, 1869, 239–43.
46. ibid., 21: Conferre dictionem poni in tali casu, in quo ponitur. Thurot rejects its attribution to Peter Helias.

47. THOMAS, 1902, § 178.
48. ibid., § 227.
49. ibid., §§ 190–216. This may be an extension of Priscian's use of *transitio ab alia ad aliam personam* in reference to transitive verbs (13.5.26, 18.1.4).
50. THOMAS, 1902, § 192.
51. ibid., § 22.
52. B. BLOCH and G. L. TRAGER, *Outline of linguistic analysis*, Baltimore, 1942, 54–5; ROBINS, *General linguistics: an introductory survey*, London, 1964, 256–61.
53. THUROT, 1869, 166; THOMAS, 1902, § 31–2.
54. THOMAS, 1902, §§ 117, 163; cp. p. 79, above.
55. ibid., § 180; cp. pp. 56–8, above.
56. THOMAS AQUINAS, *Summa theologiae* 1, q. 85, a. 1.
57. B. L. WHORF, *Four articles on metalinguistics*, Washington, 1950; J. B. CARROLL (ed.), *Language, thought and reality: selected writings of Benjamin Lee Whorf*, New York, 1956. The expression 'standard average European' is Whorf's; Whorf may not have been such an extreme Whorfian as is sometimes made out.
58. ROOS, 1952, 84–6.
59. SIGER, 1913, 93; Grammatica est sermocinalis scientia, sermonem et passiones eius in communi ad experimendum principaliter mentis conceptus per sermonem coniugatum considerans.
60. PAETOW, 1914; SANDYS, 1921, 676–8.

Five

The Renaissance and after

The Renaissance is traditionally regarded as the birth of the modern world and of modern history, in so far as such inevitably arbitrary divisions of historical time can be meaningful. Most of the features that characterize contemporary history can be seen emerging at this time and continuing without a break up to the present day. Several of them had a direct effect on the directions taken by linguistic studies, and these must be noticed in this chapter; but the Renaissance was also a backward-looking movement, the full rediscovery and reappreciation of the Greco-Roman classical world. Two quite independent events, relatively contemporaneous in occurrence, may symbolize the Janus-like faces of the Renaissance, looking forward to an exciting future and backward to a glorious past. In 1492 Columbus discovered the New World, setting in motion the expansion of Europe over the whole globe, and in 1453 Constantinople, the capital of the Eastern Empire, finally fell to the Turks; thus was brought to an end the last survivor in the uninterrupted succession of the classical Roman Empire, and numbers of Greek scholars were impelled westward to Italy. Manuscripts of classical texts were brought from Constantinople by emigrants and were also actively sought out and carried home by Italian scholars visiting that city and some others. Already in the preceding years Greek scholars had come to the west and begun the revival of Greek learning. At the end of the fourteenth century Manuel Chrysoloras, invited from Constantinople as a teacher of Greek, produced the first modern grammar of that language in the west.[1]

A heightened consciousness of the classical past and an enhanced vigour in the present engendered a tremendous vitality among leading men in all spheres of activity. Few scruples stood in the way of ambition whether good or bad; of the period it has been said that the only crime of which Renaissance man was not guilty was the destruction of ancient manuscripts.[2] From this era of history dates the conception of the 'Middle Ages', a dark and inglorious period lying between antiquity and the new age. The achievements of mediaeval Europe, which have been noticed in the preceding chapter as far as they concerned linguistic scholarship, were gravely underestimated by the men of the Renaissance. Even as late as the nineteenth century Froude could write in his mellifluous prose as he contemplated the end of the Middle Ages: 'A change was coming upon the world, the meaning and direction of which even still is hidden from us, a change from era to era. The paths trodden by the footsteps of ages were broken up; old things were passing away, and the faith and the life of ten centuries were dissolving like a dream. Chivalry was dying; the abbey and the castle were soon together to crumble into ruins; and all the forms, desires, beliefs, convictions of the old world were passing away, never to return. A new continent had risen up beyond the western sea. The floor of heaven, inlaid with stars, had sunk back into an infinite abyss of immeasurable space; and the firm earth itself, unfixed from its foundations, was seen to be but a small atom in the awful vastness of the universe. In the fabric of habit in which they had so laboriously built for themselves, mankind were to remain no longer.'[3] Modern scholarship has done much to raise our estimation of the mediaeval period, and to soften the break between epochs that was formerly imposed. But changes there were, irreversible changes, and their effects were far-reaching.

One direct consequence of these changes as far as linguistics is concerned is that the strands of history become more numerous and more complicated. Hitherto it has been not unreasonable to follow the course of linguistic studies by attending to the study of the Greek language by Greek scholars and the later study of Latin by Latin scholars, together with the theoretical developments built on the foundations of Latin grammar by the speculative grammarians. European work outside these confines was relatively small in extent and, with a few notable exceptions like the work of the 'First grammarian', largely derivative in character. This is no longer true after the end of the Middle Ages. Not only were linguistic horizons widened and the work of non-European linguists beginning to make its impact on the European tradition, but the living languages of Europe were from now on systematically studied, and new lines of linguistic thought, taken for granted today as part of general linguistics, made their appearance. The study of Greek and Latin grammar continued, and the further refinements and developments that carried it from the mediaeval period to modern teaching practice in the classical languages are a proper object of specialist study; but they can no more represent the course of the history of linguistics as a whole.

During the later Middle Ages Arabic and Hebrew had been studied in Europe, and in the University of Paris in the fourteenth century both languages were officially recognized. Roger Bacon wrote a grammar of Hebrew and knew Arabic. Indeed, the necessity of some knowledge of Hebrew, as the language of the Old Testament, had been realized sporadically since the time of Jerome (345–420); but such studies had often been undertaken in a clandestine, half shamefaced manner, Christians fearing charges of associating with the enemies of the Church and Jews fearing the accusation of proselytizing.

Its biblical status had given Hebrew a place alongside Latin and Greek as a language worthy of attention. Isidore (seventh century) along with many others regarded it as the language of God and therefore the first language to be spoken on earth.[4] But with the loosening of clerical bonds during the Renaissance Hebrew was studied more widely and with greater penetration. Greek, Latin, and Hebrew were the three languages in the knowledge of which the *homo trilinguis* of the Renaissance prided himself.[5] A number of Hebrew grammars were written in Europe, in particular Reuchlin's *De rudimentis Hebraicis*.[6] Reuchlin, also a great classical scholar and one of the leaders of the Renaissance in Germany, drew the attention of western scholars to the radically different word class system in use by native Hebrew grammarians; noun, verb, and particle.[7] The former two are declinable and the particles indeclinable. Reuchlin matches the Hebrew grammatical tradition to the Latin tradition by subdividing the noun into noun, pronoun, and participle, and the particles into adverb, conjunction, preposition, and interjection; but he goes on at once to warn his readers that a great part of the categories ('accidents') and their associated theory that apply to the Latin word classes are inapplicable to Hebrew and so require no mention.[8] In 1529 N. Clénard's grammar of Hebrew became definitive for that language in western Europe.

In their increasing knowledge and understanding of Hebrew and their acquaintance with the work of native Hebrew linguists, western scholarship for the first time came into intellectual contact with a non-

Indo-european language and a tradition of grammatical analysis not directly, if at all, derived from the Greco-Roman tradition.

Hebrew linguistic scholarship was developed under the influence of Arabic linguistic work.[9] This was due both to the structural similarities of these two Semitic languages and to the political power of the Arabs after the Islamic expansion over the Near East and north Africa. Technical terms and categories were borrowed from Arabic linguists for the descriptive analysis of Hebrew. A good deal of this work centred on the Hebrew scriptures of the Old Testament. By the end of the twelfth century grammars of Hebrew were being written by Jews living in Spain and in other parts of Europe for their European co-religionists. Among these grammarians the Qimḥi family are well known as the authors of linguistic treatises. Earlier, another Spanish Jew, Ibn Barun, had written a comparative study of the Arabic and Hebrew languages.[10]

Arabic linguistic studies, the inspiration and model of Hebrew scholars, sprang from the Koran. As the sacred book of the Islamic faith, the word of God revealed to the prophet Muhammad, the Koran was the bond of unity over the entire extension of the Arab dominions and the wider Islamic faith, from the seventh century onward. The Koran must not be translated, and therefore non-Arab converts had to learn Arabic to read and understand it (as non-Arab members of the faith still do in Muslim schools in Malaya and elsewhere). Like other sacred texts the book gave rise to a tradition of linguistic exegesis and commentary; there were, too, the needs of the bureaucracy in the training of administrators and officials in the recognized language of the Islamic empire. The teaching of Arabic thus took up a position analogous to that of Latin in the Western Empire.

Some rivalry developed between different philological schools in the Arab world, and, particularly in the school of Basra, Aristotelian influence was felt as part of the wider impact made on Arabic learning by Greek philosophy and Greek science. Basra laid stress on the strict regularity and the systematic nature of language as a means of logical discourse about the world of phenomena; here it is possible that Aristotelian ideas on analogy made an impact (p. 22, above). A rival group of linguistic scholars in Kūfa gave more importance to the diversity of language as it was actually found, including dialectal variations and textual occurrences as they were accepted; in some ways this school maintained 'anomalist' views. The extent, if any, of the influence of Dionysius Thrax's *Téchnē* on Arab grammatical theory is disputed. The work had been translated into Armenian and Syriac early in the Christian era,[11] and may have been studied by the Arabs. But it is certain that Arabic linguists developed their own insights in the systematization of their language, and in no way imposed Greek models on it as the Latin grammarians had been led to do.[12]

Arabic grammatical scholarship reached its culmination at the end of the eighth century in the grammar of Sībawaih of Basra, significantly not an Arab himself but a Persian, thus witnessing to the perennial stimulus to linguistic research lying in culturally imposed language contacts. He was a pupil of Al-khalīl, who had himself worked in metrical theory and lexicography. Sībawaih's work, known just as 'the book', *Al kitab*, fixed in the main the grammatical description and teaching of the Arabic language from then on. Sībawaih, like Thrax, rested on the foundations laid by his predecessors. He set out the grammar of classical Arabic substantially as it is known today, recognizing three word classes, inflected noun and verb and uninflected particle. The description of the verbal inflexions was mostly based on the 'triliteral' roots, familiar in such examples as *k - t - b*, write, whence come *katab*, he wrote, *kitab*, book, etc. Arab lexicographers made these abstract consonantal roots the basis of their dictionary entries.

Additionally Sībawaih achieved an independent phonetic description of the Arabic script. While not up to Indian standards (pp. 141–3, below) it was ahead of preceding and contemporary western phonetic science. He and other Arab grammarians were able to set out systematically the organs of speech and the mechanism of utterance, interpreting articulation as the interference with egressive air in various ways by different configurations of the vocal tract. The modes of interference were designated *maxraj*, literally 'outlet' by which the air made its exit; and working from back to front, from the throat to the lips and the nose, they were able to expound in explicit technical terminology the segmental sounds of the Arabic language. Features such as the velarized articulation of the 'emphatic' consonants and the velarization and palatalization of vowels in certain phonetic contexts were correctly identified. Their only serious observational failure lay in not diagnosing the mechanics of the voice-voiceless distinction in the consonants, though the division of them into two classes was treated as important and the consonants were correctly assigned to them. In view of this omission, Indian influence on the Arabs' phonetic work may be doubted, though it has been suggested. Certainly the articulatory basis of sound classification and the order of description, from the back to the front, agree with Indian practice, and the Arabs' achievement in this branch of linguistics was far more successful in terms of descriptive accuracy than that of the Greeks and the Romans.[13]

Interest in the Arabic and Hebrew languages and the separate scholarly tradition in which they had been treated contributed to the loosening of the bonds that too exclusive an attention to Latin and Greek had imposed on linguistics hitherto. This was reinforced by a powerful drive in the study of the vernacular languages of Europe as themselves worthy objects of intense scholarly effort. In this field too no sharp dividing line can be drawn. During the mediaeval period vernacular grammars of Provençal and Catalan had been written,[14] and Dante, whom some regard as the prophet of the later Renaissance, had done much to foster the study of the spoken Romance dialects as against written Latin, and through his writings in the vernacular had done much to establish a variety of spoken Italian as the literary and later the official language of the peninsula. But the Renaissance itself saw the publication of many of the first grammars of European languages, thus inaugurating an application of linguistic science that has developed without interruption from then on.

The first known native grammars of Italian and Spanish appeared in the fifteenth century, and the first native French grammar at the beginning of the sixteenth (one of the earliest Italian grammars has been attributed to Lorenzo the Magnificent).[15] During the same period grammars were published of Polish and of Old Church Slavonic.

The conditions in which these grammars were written and studied were very different from those prevailing in earlier times. The rise of national states, patriotic feeling, and the strengthening of central governments made for the recognition of a single variety of a territorial language as official; men felt it a duty to foster the use and the cultivation of their own national language. From the end of the fifteenth century Castilian Spanish was so treated in Spain, and Charles V broke with the universalist Latin tradition in addressing the Pope in Spanish.[16] The invention of printing diffused knowledge at a vastly increased rate, and the rise of a commercial middle class spread literate education through wider circles of society and encouraged the study of modern foreign languages. The publication of dictionaries, both unilingual and bilingual, accompanied the publication of grammars, and has gone on ever since. In England, because of the introduction of French as the language of the conquerors after the Norman invasion and its continued use by the upper classes for some centuries thereafter, a number of grammars and practical manuals of the French language were produced during the Middle Ages. But the systematic study and teaching of French in England can really be said to begin with the publication in 1530 of J. Palsgrave's *L'esclarcissement de la langue françoyse*, a work of more than a thousand pages, dealing with French orthography, pronunciation, and grammar, the last in very great detail.[17]

Secular and humanist needs were reinforced by the rise in status of the vernacular languages of Europe after the translation of the Bible into them, one aspect of the religious Reformation. Luther's German Bible was printed in 1534, and by this time the Scriptures had been translated into a number of western European languages. A widespread interest in the theory and the technique of translation is indicated by the Frenchman E. Dolet's brief essay on the subject.[18]

On the whole the written languages of the educated classes were made the centre of grammatical study, and as with Renaissance Latin studies (p. 108, below), literature rather than logic became the prime authority for grammatical rules and correctness. But written languages were also spoken, and written to be pronounced. The pronunciation of mediaeval Latin had been relatively unimportant and varied with the first language of the speaker, while the grammars mechanically reproduced the not very scientific phonetic descriptions of Priscian and the classical grammarians. The new grammars of modern languages paid great attention to the relations between spelling, now being standardized in printing, and pronunciation. Problems of orthography and of spelling reform took on a fresh significance, and, while the confusing equation of letter and spoken sound continued, phonemic inadequacies of existing spellings were noted and resented. Thus early Italian grammars show new letter signs to distinguish open and close *e* and *o* ($/\varepsilon/$ and $/e/$; $/ɔ/$ and $/o/$).[19]

The serious study of the neo-Latin (Romance) languages can be said to have been instituted by Dante's *De vulgari eloquentia* in the early fourteenth century, wherein he extolled the merits of spoken languages learned unconsciously in early childhood and contrasted them with written Latin consciously acquired as a second language at school through grammatical rules.[20] In a celebrated passage Dante made a plea for the cultivation of a common Italian vernacular which should serve to unify the peninsula of Italy in the way that centralized royal courts did for other peoples.[21]

The relationship between the Romance languages and Latin provided what the ancient world had always lacked, a proper theoretical framework for dealing with diachronic linguistics. The rediscovery of classical antiquity in all its glory as part of the revival of learning gave Renaissance man a historical perspective such as the Middle Ages had not had. The sound changes (expressed as changes of letters) by which Spanish, French, and Italian words could be historically related to the corresponding 'parent' Latin forms were systematically recorded and seriously studied; and, perhaps more significantly, the questions that arise from changes in grammatical systems were faced and answered. The Romance vernaculars were not just corrupted Latin, but languages of merit and standing, in their own right, sprung from Latin and related to it in interesting ways.

The causes of this linguistic change were discussed, and writers referred to the factors of linguistic contacts and mixtures, and of the gradual independent changes that take place in the transmission of a spoken language from one generation to the next. Scholars recorded the origin of the Romance futures from Latin infinitives followed by forms of the verb *habēre*, to have, and the fact that the caseless nouns of the modern Romance languages had replaced the paradigms of separate case forms found in Latin. This latter change provoked an important reappraisal of the role of prepositional constructions. While most of the Romance prepositions can be formally matched with their corresponding Latin originals, there is a marked difference between those whose syntactic and semantic uses broadly continue those of the Latin forms, as with Italian *in*, in, and *con*, with, and those like French *de* and Italian *di*, which on the whole correspond semantically to Latin oblique case inflexions, usually the genitive, without any preposition. In 1525 Pietro Bembo raised the question whether these latter were prepositions properly speaking or rather just case-signs, *segni di caso*;[22] and the matter was discussed by his contemporaries, one writer arguing that *di* in *padrone di casa*, master of the house, is a *segno di caso*, but that it is a preposition in *sono partito di casa*, I have left the house.[23] It is easy to say that historical and descriptive linguistics are not adequately distinguished here; but what is important is the beginning of the process of setting free the grammatical description and teaching of modern languages from categories imposed for no other reason than their relevance to Latin, a process to be seen at work also in the succession of grammars of English after the Renaissance, despite the lack in this case of a direct genetic relationship (p. 119, below). In like manner the Priscianic system of eight word classes was not left unquestioned. Systems of fewer and of more classes were proposed. Nebrija in his *Gramatica de la lengua castellana* (1492) set up ten.[24] However the definite separation of nouns and adjectives into distinct classes had to wait until the eighteenth century.

Among the Renaissance grammarians Pierre Ramée (Petrus Ramus, born *c.* 1515) is well known, and has been hailed as a precursor of modern structuralism.[25] More generally he is regarded as one of the thinkers who marked the transition from the mediaeval to the modern world. His educational reforms were widely influential in northern Europe, and with his celebrated rejection of Aristotle in his master's degree disputation ('*quaecumque ab Aristotele dicta essent commentitia esse*', 'everything Aristotle said is wrong') he went on to revivify the study of the liberal arts in Paris, formerly the stronghold of Aristotelianism and modistic grammar. He vigorously championed the humanistic teaching of the classical languages, through their literature rather than through scholastic Aristotelianism. After becoming involved in the religious strife of the times, he was murdered in the massacre of St. Bartholemew in 1572.[26]

Ramus wrote grammars of Greek, Latin, and French, and set down his theory of grammar in his *Scholae grammaticae*.[27] While in his grammar of French he made didactic use of references to Latin grammar, he showed a proper appreciation of each individual language. Rather than follow philosophical arguments on grammar, which, he said, did not save the scholastics from barbarisms,[28] he stressed the need in the ancient languages to follow the observed usage of the classical authors, and in the modern languages the observed usage of native speakers. His grammatical descriptions and classifications are formal in today's sense, relying neither on semantics nor on the categories of logic but on the relations between actual word forms.

Ramus's grammar of French contains one of the earliest treatments of the pronunciation of the language; and he took care also to point to the differences between Latin as formerly spoken by Latin-speakers and Latin as variously pronounced by those who subjected it to their own phonological patterns after learning it at school.[29] In Latin grammar he preserved the Priscianic eight word classes, but in demanding purely formal criteria for their identification he made inflexion for number and its absence the basic division between them, contrasting nouns, pronouns, verbs, and participles (which he regarded as nouns) with all the rest.[30] This reliance on number as the principal category for grammatical classification was influential; whereas case inflexion on which the ancient grammarians had relied so much had largely disappeared in the modern languages, number still remained as an inflexional category. Ramus made use of the same distinction in his French grammar,[31] and it was taken up after him by some writers of English grammars (p. 120, below).

In his account of Latin morphology he reorganized the traditional system of declensions by making his basic criterion for classification the parisyllabicity or imparisyllabicity of the case forms of a noun or adjective (whether the different cases did or did not substantially agree in the number of their syllables).[32] Latin verbs are distinguished primarily by whether their future tense is formed with -b- (amābō, etc.) or not, thus largely corresponding to the traditional first and second conjugations on the one hand and the third and fourth on the other.[33] Interestingly Ramus remarked that though Priscian and the other grammarians of Latin did not make use of this classification themselves, they none the less provided the material on which such a formal classification could be made.[34]

Ramus's syntax was also based on the distinction between words with number inflexion and words without it, and was systematized by reference to the two categories of syntactic relation, concord and government (in this he was indebted to mediaeval grammatical theory).[35]

Contacts between European linguistic scholarship and the work of Jewish and Arabic grammarians during the later Middle Ages have been mentioned already. These were by no means the only non-European languages with which Europeans became acquainted in the Renaissance. Colonization of the New World and voyages of discovery round the globe, the establishment of trading stations and expatriate settlements, and the despatch of missionaries all played their part in awakening scholars to the hitherto undreamed wealth of linguistic diversity in the world. This process continued unchecked, and indeed is still in progress, with missions playing a leading part. Appropriately Firth referred to the linguistic aspect of the expansion of Europe as the 'discovery of Babel'.[36]

From the New World, grammars of Quechua (Peru) and of Guarani (Brazil) were published in 1560 and 1639 respectively; in Europe a Basque grammar appeared in 1587 and the seventeenth century saw grammars of Japanese and Persian published. Among the linguistic work done under the control of missionary activities, mention should be made of the achievements of the *Propaganda Fide* department of the Roman Church and of Jesuit missionaries during the sixteenth, seventeenth, and eighteenth centuries. India, south-east Asia, and the Far

East were all visited, and several of the languages there encountered were first subjected to a roman transcription by Catholic missionaries for the translation of the Scriptures. The alphabets devised by these missionaries for some of the languages of India and Burma, and the phonetic observations accompanying them have been praised by linguists of the present century,[37] and the transcription made by Alexander de Rhodes for Vietnamese in 1651 is still, with minor alterations, the official writing system of Vietnam.

Some study of Sanskrit was undertaken, and isolated observations were made on certain apparent resemblances between that language and Italian, Greek, and Latin (p. 135, below).

Trade routes had linked China and the Roman Empire overland through central Asia, and the western world was dimly aware in antiquity of the Seres (far away to the east). Early in the fourteenth century Marco Polo had travelled through Asia as far as China and had studied a number of Asian languages during his residence. But prolonged direct contacts between European scholars and the Chinese really started with the arrival of traders and missionaries in the Far East. Francis Xavier had established Jesuit missions in China and Japan by the time of his death in 1552, and several members of these missions became masters of different varieties of Chinese. Of them Ricci is one of the best known.

Trigault, who translated Ricci's famous diary into Latin, recorded the salient differences between the Chinese languages and those of western Europe that strike the first year student of Chinese today: the almost complete lack of morphological paradigms such as had received so much attention in Latin and Greek and were seemingly essential to grammatical structure, the distinction of what would otherwise be lexical homophones by differences in pitch (tones), and the existence of a common written language (Chinese characters) readily intelligible to literate persons irrespective of the differences, amounting often to complete barriers to intercommunication, that existed between several of the varieties of spoken Chinese.[38]

China had developed an indigenous tradition of linguistic studies by the time western scholars made contact with the country and its languages. A character writing system, properly defined as the graphic representation of individual morphemes by separate symbols, had been in use since 2000 B.C. and was of native origin, despite certain superficial similarities to character systems in other parts of the world. This mode of representing the language in writing, together with the isolating, analytic structure of Chinese grammar, determined the course taken by linguistic studies in Chinese civilization.

From the end of the sixteenth century the nature of the Chinese writing system was known in Europe and it played an important part in some directions of linguistic research (pp. 113-4, below), besides making European scholars aware of the existence of a group of languages whose phonological, grammatical, and lexical organization differed markedly from those of languages with which earlier generations had been familiar. The first actual grammar of Chinese published in Europe did not appear until 1727 with J. H. de Prémare's *Notitia linguae Sinicae*.[39]

The virtual absence of morphological paradigms in Chinese did not encourage early grammatical study, apart from some attention to the class of particles. A distinction was made between 'full words', those capable of standing alone and bearing an individual lexical gloss, and 'empty words' or particles, serving grammatical purposes within sentences containing full words but scarcely having a statable meaning in isolation. This passed through Prémare into general linguistic usage.[40] Full words were further divided into 'living words', verbs, and 'dead words', nouns. But the main linguistic efforts of the Chinese were turned on to lexicography and phonology.

Dictionaries were produced in China from the second century A.D. onward. As elsewhere the stimuli were the linguistic changes in the lexicon of the literary language. These made some characters obsolete and altered the meanings of others, thus increasing the difficulties of studying the ancient classics of Chinese literature. One of the earliest known Chinese dictionaries, the *Shuo wên* (c. A.D. 100), making use of the revised writing system that had been standardized three centuries earlier, arranged the characters in the manner employed ever since, by 'radicals', though the number of the 'radicals' has since been reduced. Each character is analysed into two components in lexicography, a 'radical', which in part correlates with the general meaning of some of the characters containing it, and the 'phonetic', which sometimes gives an indication of the pronunciation of the character, though semantic and phonetic changes have made these indications very patchy and at best only approximate. The 'radicals' are ordered serially starting with those containing one stroke, in ascending order of numbers of strokes; and the characters containing each 'radical' and so listed under it are likewise arranged in ascending order of numbers of strokes in the 'phonetic' (certain characters consist of 'radical' only; these come first in the lists).

Later dictionaries attempted to deal with the problem of indicating the pronunciation of characters, in view of phonetic changes that had taken place in the language since the classical literary era. This provided the matrix for the development of the phonological study of literary Chinese. The character represented the morpheme rather than the word, though in classical Chinese especially many words were mono-morphemic; and, broadly speaking, the morpheme was phonologically represented by a single syllable, falling within a limited number of possible syllable structures. There was no segmental representation of the components of the syllable in Chinese character writing, and the focus of Chinese phonological thinking was on the isolated mono-syllable and on the means of indicating the pronunciation of characters that had become obsolete or had formerly had different phonetic values.

At first the only method available was the citation of a homonym of the character concerned, but from the third century A.D. onward the syllable was analysed into initial and final components, the final being taken as everything coming after the initial consonant, and including the tone. The pronunciation of a character could now be indicated by the citation of two other characters whose pronunciation was assumed to be known, the initial of the first and the final of the second giving the syllabic composition and so the pronunciation of the character in question. Thus the character read /ko/ with a rising tone followed by the character read /hwɛ/ with a level tone would indicate the pronun-ciation of a character read /kwɛ/ with a level tone.

By the time this technique was in use Buddhist missionaries were already active in China, and it is possible that even this limited phono-logical analysis of the syllable was inspired by acquaintance with an alien alphabetic script. Certainly it was with the aid of Buddhist monks that in A.D. 489 the Chinese tones were for the first time systematically defined as integral components of spoken syllables, although Chinese had been a tone language from time immemorial.[41]

The next advance in phonological analysis was directly influenced by Sanskrit linguistic studies (pp. 141-3, below). In the eleventh century the well-known rhyme tables set out the total of the occurrent syllables of literary Chinese, represented by characters, on a chart in which the vertical columns held the initials and the horizontal rows listed the finals, now further analysed so as to distinguish medial (post-initial) semivowels such as /-w-/, final vowel or vowel plus consonant, and the tone. This two-dimensional classification enabled Chinese scholars to distinguish, as the Stoics had already done in the west (p. 24, above), between non-occurrent but phonologically possible forms and forms excluded by the rules of Chinese syllable structure. Indian influence is marked in the ordering of the initials by their articulation; the plosives and nasals were arranged in groups of four by place and manner of articulation, /k/, /kh/, /g/, /ŋ/, /t/, /th/, /d/, /n/, etc., and articulatory terminology was used to differentiate them. These rhyme tables are of the greatest importance in the reconstruction of the spoken forms of Chinese syllables in this period of the language, but their historical significance lies in their evidence of the development under Sanskritic influence of a segmental analysis in the face of the tradition engendered by a morphemic-syllabic script, which had first suggested an analysis into initials and finals much more like Firthian prosodic phonology than segmental phonemics.[42]

Various modifications and elaborations were made in this system of phonological analysis during the mediaeval and modern periods of Chinese linguistic scholarship. The emphasis changed from the study of the language of classical literature to the contemporary colloquial northern Chinese of Peking, along with other varieties of spoken Chinese. In the seventeenth century Pan-lei, an excellent phonetician and dialectologist, travelled all over China studying the dialect variations of the different regions. But little of further general importance took place before European scholarship began seriously to interest itself in the linguistic problems presented by the Chinese language (or languages), including the transcription of Chinese syllables in roman letters, an interest very much to the fore at the present time.

It has been seen how important a part was played by linguistic contacts from outside in the development of Chinese phonological analysis. But China herself was the source of a linguistic problem and of its solution, the adaptation of the Chinese character writing system to an unrelated language of very different structure.

The Japanese language is genetically unrelated to Chinese, but from the fifth century A.D. onward there was considerable contact between Japan and China, and the Japanese borrowed freely from Chinese literature and other aspects of Chinese culture, with large numbers of Chinese words being taken into the language. Writing was introduced from China, and the problem at once arose of adapting the characters that in Chinese represented unchanging monosyllables to the requirements of a language rich in agglutinative derivations and inflexions. At first the problem was solved by ignoring it; the agglutinated elements of words were left unrepresented and the characters were used as they would have been in Chinese sentences. Ultimately the situation still in use today was evolved, wherein the characters are used to represent invariable words and the constant root element of variable words, while the derivational and inflexional parts of word structures are written in the *kana* syllabary, a set of syllabic signs derived from bits of particular characters used for their phonetic value alone.

An intermediate stage, however, is worthy of notice. In this the character represented the root of the word, but other grammatical elements, as well as certain particles in close syntactic relationship with it, were indicated graphically by means of diacritical marks written at different positions round the character itself. Thus the verb *kasikom-*, to fear, would be represented by a particular character bearing a similar meaning in Chinese, and a small circle at its lower left hand corner would further indicate the word *kasikomite*, fearing, and a diagonal stroke at the top right-hand corner would indicate the word *kasikomitari*, (he, etc.) feared.[43] This orthographic system did not remain in use, but it is of interest in its similarity to certain linguistic speculations and experiments in Europe during the sixteenth and seventeenth centuries (p. 117, below).

To many thinking people in the first phase of the Renaissance in Europe, the revival of ancient learning and the new awareness of the glories of the Greco-Roman classical world were probably the most significant characteristics of the age. Indeed, the words 'Renaissance' and 'revival of learning' testify to this conception. It is noticeable how numbers of early Renaissance writers quote freely from classical sources to justify and illustrate their arguments, looking directly to antiquity, no longer under any taint of paganism, but rather seen as a period of exalted humanism with which Renaissance thinkers, in stressing the worth and dignity of man in his own right, felt an intellectual and moral kinship. Such men of the Renaissance considered themselves to be continuing the work of ancient civilization. The classical texts available in Europe were now approximately those available today, and the study of ancient literature took on the forms recognizable in the present age in the classical curricula of schools and universities.

The Greek and Latin classics were read for their own merits and in the original languages, not by means of translations or through the official interpretations of scholastic theologians. In the Renaissance the conception may be said to have been formed of the study of classical literature as the basis of a liberal education.

This changed attitude towards Latin and Greek had its effect on the linguistic study of these languages, especially of Latin. The emphasis was set on Latin as the language of Cicero and Vergil, the language of the ancient world, not on mediaeval Latin as a *lingua franca* of education and intellectual intercourse. Latin as an elegant language enshrining a great literature was the proper object of study. Some scholarly works continued for a time to be written in Latin, but the rise in status of European vernaculars and the spread of secular learning in secular states fostered national languages as proper media for scholarly and scientific publication. Indeed, the very standards of correctness and elegance now insisted on militated against the use of Latin as an international language. As we find with English today, the acceptance of the role of an international or a world language entails an acceptance of regional variations of all kinds and the relaxation of standards of correctness from those enjoined in metropolitan literature.

Many of the technical advances in descriptive efficiency realized during the Middle Ages were retained, and in places mediaeval didactic grammars like that of Alexander of Villedieu continued in use; but the general conceptions of the speculative grammarians were severely attacked by Renaissance grammarians as being philosophically pretentious, educationally undesirable, and couched in a barbarous degeneration of the Latin language.[44] The return to preeminence of the *auctōrēs* foretold in the *Battle of the seven arts* had indeed come to pass.

Scholastic grammarians had done little more than copy Priscian's account of Latin pronunciation, and the actual speaking of Latin largely depended on the phonetics of the first language of the persons concerned. This feature of Latin speaking continued as it still does today; but concern for what was considered to be the correct pronunciation, that is to say the pronunciation of the time of Cicero and the other golden age authors, was expressed in writings on the Latin language even if their practical effect on most pupils was, as it still is, relatively small.

Erasmus (1466–1536) wrote on the correct pronunciation of Latin and Greek, and his system of Greek pronunciation was accepted in northern Europe.[45] Among other observations on Latin, he established along with others that the Latin letters *c* and *g* represented velar articulations in all positions in classical Latin, although the currently spoken Romance languages with only a few exceptions (Illyrian and Sardinian) had sibilant or affricate pronunciations of these letters before front vowels. The orthographers, whose work on the phonetic interpretation of current spelling systems has already been noticed (p. 100, above), also turned their attention to this hitherto neglected aspect of classical scholarship in Europe.[46] In the writing of Latin, Ramus introduced the letters *j* and *v* to represent the semivowel pronunciations (in words such as *jam* (*iam*), now, and *virtūs*, virtue), as distinct from the vowel pronunciations [i] and [u]; *u* had previously been the cursive form of *V*. The two letters *j* and *v* were known for a time as the 'Ramist consonants'; one notices that *v* still survives but not *j* in the usual way of writing Latin.[47]

The teaching of Latin and Greek grammar gradually took on the form in which it is known today in the standard school textbooks. Essentially this process involved the incorporation of mediaeval syntactic notions into the morphological systematization of the late Latin grammarians, ultimately with further developments such as the final separation of the adjective from the noun class (though as late as Madvig's Latin grammar the terms 'noun substantive' and 'noun adjective' remained in use[48]), and the merging of the participle into the inflexions of the verb.

Among the Renaissance grammars of Latin one may note the works of two near contemporaries. J. C. Scaliger's *De causis linguae Latinae* was a theoretical and closely argued, contentious book, whose style fits what we know of the author's character from his bitter attacks on Erasmus who as a cultivated teacher and writer of Latin had suggested that Cicero was not the only model of good Latin prose.[49] Sanctius (Sanchez) wrote a less theoretical textbook, *Minerva seu de causis linguae Latinae* that was highly esteemed.[50]

In England W. Lily's Latin grammar enjoyed the distinction of being officially prescribed for school use by King Henry VIII in 1540 (the official version, in fact, contained contributions from other contemporary grammarians as well).[51] Lily's grammar in the main follows the Priscianic system, with eight word classes or parts of speech. It is severely practical and didactic, and does not engage in linguistic or philosophical theory or speculation. A century later Bassett Jones published his *Essay on the rationality of the art of speaking*,[52] expressly as a supplement to Lily's grammar. He laid claim to the support both of Aristotle and of Francis Bacon, but his allegedly rational explanations of some grammatical facts are mostly either unoriginal or absurdly fanciful.

The effects on linguistic studies brought about by the rise of humanism, nationalism, and secular government, along with the overseas expansion of Europe, have been noticed. The Renaissance period was also the first age of printing in Europe (independently China had invented paper in the first century A.D. and block printing in the tenth). From then on literacy and the demand for education grew steadily, even though universal education was not achieved in Europe before the nineteenth century. Knowledge travelled faster and spread more widely. The study of foreign languages as well as that of the classical languages was immeasurably enlivened by the multiplicity and availability of printed texts, grammars, and dictionaries. These same factors made the exchange of knowledge and theoretical discussion between scholars in different lands much easier and more speedy, and as time went on some of the features of the present-day world of learning began to take shape. Learned societies, sometimes fostered by national governments, came into being as centres for scholarly debate and scientific research. In Britain the Royal Society was founded in 1662 and its early years were much concerned with linguistic research; and in France Cardinal Richelieu established the *Académie française* in 1635 to keep permanent watch and ward on the literary and linguistic standards of the French language. Learned and specialized journals, such as now play so great a part in the development of linguistics, and the other branches of knowledge, grew up around the societies and institutions, though this process was not fully achieved before the nineteenth and twentieth centuries.

It was seen in earlier chapters how the course of linguistic science in antiquity and the Middle Ages was in part determined by its involvement in controversies between opposing points of view on questions wider in extent than the study of language itself. In the sixteenth, seventeenth, and eighteenth centuries the philosophical world was preoccupied with the debate between empiricists and rationalists, and the views held by each group of thinkers produced their effects on the treatment of linguistic questions.

Empiricism had arisen as part of the challenge to the accepted ideas of mediaeval scholasticism. The rise of a modern scientific outlook ready to confound authority with observed fact and to remodel theory to incorporate newly discovered data was famously exemplified in the work of Galileo, Copernicus, and Kepler. Empiricism as a philosophical standpoint was a particularly British contribution; Francis Bacon had stressed the observational origin of all knowledge and the importance of induction as opposed to deduction, and Locke, Berkeley, and Hume wrote what are now the accepted expositions of this phase of philosophy.

The centrepiece of empiricism was the thesis that all human knowledge is derived externally from sense impressions and the operations of the mind upon them in abstraction and generalization. Its extreme form appears in Hume's total rejection of an *a priori* component of knowledge. Opposed to this in many ways was the rationalist position, expounded by Descartes and his followers. The rationalists sought for the certainty of knowledge not in the impressions of the senses but in the irrefutable truths of human reason. In some respects the Cartesian position was the more traditional, but both schools of thought agreed in their reliance on mathematics and Newtonian science in place of scholastic Aristotelianism as the foundation of philosophical reasoning.

A celebrated aspect of the empiricist-rationalist controversy turned on the question of 'innate ideas'. Locke, Berkeley, and Hume denied the existence of any ideas implanted in the human mind prior to experience; the Cartesian rationalists regarded certain innate ideas as the basis of any certainty in our knowledge; these included the ideas of number and figure, and logical and mathematical conceptions. To some extent the two sides were nearer in fact than in terminology. Experience of the world and knowledge are not merely sense impressions, and the part played by the rationalist innate ideas corresponds somewhat to that of Locke's admitted 'operations of our minds within'.[53] But the two schools considered that they differed on a matter of philosophical importance, and that is what is relevant historically.

During the sixteenth and seventeenth centuries a number of separate but related movements made their appearance in linguistic research, springing from the intellectual condition of the times. In them both rationalist and empiricist influences may be seen at work.

The breakdown of Latin as the international language of learning and authority, the emergence of the European vernaculars into full recognition, and the new discoveries in the field of languages overseas all helped to create the feeling that it was in men's power to improve and even to create languages to suit the needs of the age.

Francis Bacon had deplored the unnecessary controversies caused by the inadequacies of existing languages, part of the 'idols of the market place', and envisaged a vast improvement based on the analogy of words with things, not just with one another. In distinguishing the descriptive grammar of a particular language from a philosophical or general grammar he seems to have had the idea of constructing an ideal language for the communication of knowledge from the best parts and features of a number of existing languages.[54] The invention of printing made standardized spellings more important, and, in turning attention to the relations between writing and pronunciation, aroused interest, since then perennial, in the problem of spelling reform. One gets the impression of numbers of scholars in England and on the continent working, partly in collaboration and partly in rivalry, on various aspects of language improvement and language planning.

The most radical proposal of the age was the invention of a new language for the advancement of learning and commerce throughout the civilized world. Latin as the erstwhile *lingua franca* was dead or dying, and the extent of the world's linguistic Babel had been revealed; these projects of new universal languages were attempts at 'debabelization' or a restoration of the situation.[55] At this time people did not so much envisage a universal language like modern Esperanto created from the material of existing languages; rather, they had the bolder scheme of devising a system in which knowledge, thought, and ideas could be directly and universally expressed in symbols created for this purpose and for which pronunciations could be given. Leibniz (1646–1716) looked forward to the day when controversies would be resolved by the mere invitation to sit down and calculate by means of a newly devised universal symbolization of thought, free from vagueness and uncertainties of natural language. His *Specimen calculi universalis* anticipates some features of modern symbolic logic, though it is based on the Aristotelian syllogism.[56]

If such symbol systems were not to be hopelessly clumsy, human knowledge must be classified and reduced to an ordered conspectus. The inspiration that a universal language of this kind was practicable sprang from a number of sources: great faith in the power of human rationality, the classifications of the now rapidly expanding empirical sciences, the appreciation of the power of mathematical symbolism (Arabic numerals as written symbols with a pronunciation appeared in some projected languages[57]), and a misunderstanding of the nature of Chinese character writing, which had been known in Europe since the end of the sixteenth century.

Mathematics is a genuinely language-free mode of symbolization, though it has not got the semantic range or expressive power of a natural language (to speak of the 'language of mathematics' or 'mathematical language' is to use a metaphor, and the analogy should not be pressed too far). Chinese characters were at the time thought to be the direct representation of 'ideas' (*ideograph* is still a popular term for a Chinese character). This is not so; the written language of Chinese literature can be read and understood by educated speakers of mutually unintelligible varieties of spoken Chinese, but for all that it is a language like other languages, belonging to and evolved by a particular speech community or set of speech communities, and its characters represent morphemes, which can be given pronunciations, though different ones in different dialect areas. This written language has grammatical classes and grammatical rules as any other written language does, and cannot be understood or translated, except for very short and transparently obvious sentences, without a knowledge of the grammar. This was not grasped by sixteenth- and seventeenth-century Europe; the real study of the Chinese type of language began only later in the eighteenth and nineteenth centuries.

In the seventeenth century various people devised universal languages or 'real characters' as they were sometimes called. In France M. Mersenne, probably influenced by Descartes, suggested the creation of the best of all possible languages by which all men's thoughts could be put into the same words with brevity and clarity; anticipating Jespersen he recognized the rather general phonaesthetic associations of [i]-like vowels with thinnesss and littleness.[58] In England similar projects were advanced by such men as George Dalgarno, and Bishop John Wilkins, to whom Mersenne's work was known, and of these Wilkins's *Essay towards a real character and a philosophical language* is the most famous.[59] It was published with the support of the recently founded Royal Society, and is mentioned by Roget as one of the main inspirations of his *Thesaurus* nearly two hundred years later.[60]

Wilkins's project was nothing less than the creation of systematically worked out and universally applicable principles of a language, written and spoken, for communication between members of all nations of the world. The *Essay*, which runs to 454 pages, after criticizing the shortcomings of existing natural languages sets out what purports to be a complete schematization of human knowledge, including abstract relations, actions, processes, and logical concepts, natural genera and species of things animate and inanimate, and the physical and institutionalized relations between human beings in the family and in society.

All these classes and their subdivisions, and the various semantic relations and modifications involved with them are represented by written shapes, built into semantically self-sufficient and perspicuous 'real characters', each standing for an ideal word, translatable into or from the words of a natural language. A simple example may be given:

'father' is represented by the character ⌐, which consists of the

basic sign ⌐, for the genus 'economical' (interpersonal) relation, to which are added a right oblique line on the left, indicating the first subdivision, in the case of economical relations that of consanguinity, an upright line on the right indicating the second subdivision, in the case of consanguinity marking the relation of direct ascending, and a semi-circle above the middle of the character, indicating male. Should the character be used metaphorically, this can be specified by the addition of a short vertical line over the left end of

the character: ⌐.

In order to provide a spoken form corresponding to each such character, Wilkins set out a system of universal phonetics, or of 'letters' standing for the major categories of articulation such as were said to be found in the known languages of the world. Each component of a character had its own syllable or single letter assigned to it, from which an equally perspicuous spoken word form could be built up. Thus in the spoken word for the character 'father', *Co* stands for economical relation, *b* and *a* for the two subdivisions, consanguinity and direct ascendant, respectively, giving *Coba*, parent, and the further addition of *ra* for male gives *Cobara* (probably [kobara]), father.

A universal grammar was proposed, consisting of word classes valid for all communicative needs. Syntactic rules were to be kept to a minimum, and the class membership and grammatical relations of words were to be indicated graphically by special signs affixed to or interposed between the characters, and phonetically by additions and modifications to the pronounced words.

In a final chapter Wilkins compared his 'philosophical language' with Latin as the nearest existing approach to a universal language, and the 'real character' aspect of it with Chinese character writing. He condemned the unnecessary lexical redundancy, grammatical complexity, and the irregularities of Latin, as contrasted with his own proposed language, and the formal complications of Chinese characters and their lack of semantic analysability and perspicuity, though he approved of the tendency to group characters for semantically related concepts under the same radical (p. 105, above).[61]

The efforts of men like Wilkins show how far linguistic theory and linguistic thought had moved since the Middle Ages. They also show a deep and subtle penetration into the way languages must in fact be naturally organized in order to fulfil the tasks successfully imposed on them. Nothing practical came of these suggestions for artificially constructed universal languages, and it is easy to perceive the naivety of Wilkins's attempts at the componential analysis and classification of all human knowledge and experience. But the current work of some generative grammarians in attempting to formalize the intuitive knowledge that native speakers have of the correct use of their language and the semantic interpretation of the words in it seems to proceed on somewhat similar lines, and has been described as an effort directed towards the 'atomization' of meaning.[62] The successful employment and understanding of the lexical resources of our native language is something that is performatively given to us while we are yet children, but the full explication of it seems still to be hidden from the wisest.

The notion of a universal thought structure possessed by mankind, or at least by all civilized mankind, basically independent of any particular language and therefore expressible in a universal language, was a conception perhaps natural to the rationalists. Similar attitudes towards the grammar of actual languages are found in the work of the rationalist Port Royal grammarians (p. 123, below), and repeat in a different form the older universalism of the scholastic speculative grammarians. The interdependence of thought and language and the significance of linguistic as well as of cultural relativity were more readily appreciated in the climate of the later Romantic era.

Apart from the advancement of knowledge, the avoidance of sterile controversies, and the ease of communication between men of education in all lands, other considerations were in men's minds when they pondered the creation of universal languages: the facilitation of trade, the unity of the Protestant churches, and the science of cryptography. The possession of a new 'real character' serving Protestantism as Latin had once served the formerly universal Roman Church may have been only a minor factor; its extent is a matter for debate. During the English Civil War the codes and cyphers of each side attracted attention to certain structural features and frequencies of occurrence in the English language, and in 1641 Wilkins had written a work on secret communication.[63]

The cryptography of the time was intimately associated with another application of linguistics that flourished in England from the reign of Elizabeth I, the devising of systems of shorthand or 'characterie' as they were then called. Stenographic methods had been in use in ancient

Rome, but like much else they appear to have been lost during the mediaeval period.

Modern shorthand, depending both on the use of phonetic symbols and on representations of particular words or word roots by specific outlines, may be traced back to British work in the sixteenth century. The name most associated with this is Timothy Bright, who worked out systems of shorthand employing both individual letter signs and character-like signs for words standing for classes of objects. Interest in shorthand and universal languages went together, and the same motives were adduced. Bright referred to the alleged ideographic nature of Chinese characters, independent of any particular language, and commended his system of 'characterie' as both a universal means of written communication and a device for preserving secrecy.[64]

In one respect Bright exploited a process very like that applied at one stage by the Japanese in their adaptation of the Chinese character script (p. 108, above). Grammatical additions or alterations to basic word forms, such as plurality in nouns, past tense in verbs, and comparison in adjectives, were indicated by marks, or 'pricks', on the right or left of the word sign itself. Some other grammatical forms were indicated by the use of a word sign to represent a homographic and homophonic morpheme, and by extension other semantically and grammatically related morphemes as well. Thus *friendship* was to be written with the *ship* sign below the *friend* sign, but below the *neighbour* sign this same *ship* sign stood for the *-hood* of *neighbourhood*.

One aspect of English empiricism in linguistic studies during the sixteenth and seventeenth centuries was the beginning of systematic phonetic description of the sounds of the English language, and of the formal analysis of English grammar, now that men felt free to challenge and modify the grammatical model enshrined in Priscian and Donatus.

Phonetic studies began seriously in England in the attention turned on spelling and its relation to pronunciation through the invention of printing and the diffusion of literacy, as on the continent. From the sixteenth to the eighteenth century work was carried on around phonetic questions under the titles of orthography and orthoepy (the term *phonetics* is first recorded in the nineteenth century); but the research was on what today would be called phonetics and phonology, and the empirical attitude in British philosophy from Francis Bacon to David Hume, as well as the nature of English spelling, fostered a tradition that has been given the title of 'the English school of phonetics'.[65] J. Hart, W. Bullokar, A. Hume, R. Robinson, C. Butler, J. Wallis, and

W. Holder[66] are among those who wrote on English pronunciation in the sixteenth and seventeenth centuries, in some cases as part of a full-scale grammar of English. The formative influences of the times are shown by the fact that Wallis, besides his work on English, held the chair of geometry at Oxford University and was also a natural scientist. It is interesting to see, in addition to questions of spelling, modern objectives already in close association with phonetic studies, such as English language teaching for foreigners, teaching speech to the deaf, and the cultivation of standard English or 'the King's language'.[67]

The work of these orthographers and orthoepists has been much used in the reconstruction of the English pronunciation characteristics of their times[68]; in the history of linguistics their importance lies rather in the stage they had reached in phonetic theory and practice, and in the work they bequeathed to their better known nineteenth-century successors.

Among them W. Holder was perhaps the most successful. After some delay due to jealousy on the part of rivals such as Wallis, Holder's *Elements of speech* was published in 1669 by the Royal Society, of which he was a member. Holder was an observational phonetician and he achieved remarkable succinctness and accuracy in describing the articulation of speech sounds. He set down a general theory of pronunciation, referring consonantal differences to differences of 'appulse' between one organ and another, total in the case of stops and partial in fricatives and continuants; he referred vocalic differences to different degrees of aperture, with the further distinctions of front and back tongue raising and of lip rounding.[69] His conception of speech as 'determined by the alternation of appulse and aperture' has a very modern ring.

Holder came nearer than any other western scholar, before contact was made with Indian phonetic work, to a correct articulatory diagnosis of the voice-voiceless distinction in consonants. His correct insight escaped the attention of his contemporaries and was left unremarked for over a century. He wrote, using 'voice' in its modern technical sense: 'The larynx both gives passage to the breath, and also, as often as we please, by the force of muscles, to bear the sides of the larynx stiff and near together, as the breath passeth through the rimula, makes a vibration of those cartilaginous bodies which forms that breath into a vocal sound or voice.' The excellence of his phonetic theory and the conciseness of his expression are shown in his summary statement on the nature of English vowels: 'The vowels are made by a free passage

of breath vocalized through the cavity of the mouth, without any
appulse of the organs; the said cavity's being differently shaped by the
postures of the throat, tongue and lips. . . . Vowels . . . being differ-
enced by the shape of the cavity of the mouth'.[70]

In the next century A. Tucker noted the prevalence of [ə] in English
as a hesitation form and in the 'weak forms' of words unstressed in
connected speech, forms almost wholly unmarked in orthographic
writing.[71]

Problems of spelling in relation to pronunciation were the occasion
for the invention of new typographical symbols for particular sorts of
sound, and several of the phonetic symbols used today in the International Phonetic Alphabet were first suggested or invented during this
period. Some writers went beyond English to suggest international
alphabets, such work being often linked with systems of shorthand.
F. Lodwick published an *Essay towards a universal alphabet* in the
Philosophical transactions of the Royal Society in 1686, consisting of
invented symbols systematically corresponding to articulatory differences; and Wilkins included in his *Essay* a sound chart which can be
compared with early editions of the International Phonetic Alphabet,
and an 'organic alphabet' with pictures of the articulation of eight
vowels and twenty-six consonants, representing general phonetic categories, in which were shown the positions of the lips and, by a cut-away
section, the positions of the tongue as well.[72]

The sixteenth and seventeenth centuries also saw the reworking of
English grammar. Men started with the framework handed down from
the late Latin grammarians and suggested by Aelfric as suitable for
Old English as well as for Latin (pp. 70–1, above); but the intellectual
climate of the post-Renaissance world, a love of their own language,
and English empiricist attitudes all encouraged them to test the categories against observation, and we can observe the different degrees to
which this testing and reappraisal took place in the allocation of words
to word classes or parts of speech.

English grammarians of the sixteenth, seventeenth, and early eighteenth centuries usually started from the Latin system of the eight Priscianic classes enshrined in Lily's grammar, in that they either followed
it or felt the need to express and justify their disagreements with it.
Some, for example Bullokar,[73] set up the Latin system and assigned
English words to each class. The English articles, *a(n)* and *the*, having
no Latin counterpart were not given the status of a part of speech, but
merely referred to as notes or signs set before nouns to identify them

as nouns. Others treated the articles as a subclass of nouns adjective,[74] and Ben Jonson assigned them to a class of their own.[75]

A rearrangement of the Latin system in which the influence of Ramus may be seen is found in those grammarians such as A. Gill, who made number inflexion versus its absence a major binary distinction, setting off nouns and verbs from the rest, which he designated *dictiones consignificativae* in reference to their principal functions in subordinate relations with nouns and verbs, a distinction also made by the ancient grammarians (pp. 26, 37, above).[76] Butler linked nouns and verbs more closely in his system by regarding them both as having number and case inflexion; nominal case is illustrated by such forms as *man* and *man's*, and past tense and past participle inflexions (*loved, fallen*) are designated as oblique cases of the verb, the present tense form being the 'rect'.[77] This usage harks back to that of Aristotle.

Some other grammarians were influenced by Port Royal theories (p. 124, below) to divide the eight Latin classes according as they were held to denote objects of thought (noun, pronoun, participle, preposition, adverb (and article)), or manners of thought (verb, conjunction, interjection). This was applied to English by the writer (or writers) of a grammar attributed to J. Brightland,[78] though the systematization is not very clearly worked out.

More radically, Wilkins and C. Cooper distinguished two main classes, on semantic grounds, integrals and particles; Wilkins intended his system to be of universal applicability. Integrals were said to have a definite meaning of their own, while particles only consignify, relating or modifying the meanings of the integrals. Nouns and verbs are integrals; in Wilkins's systematization, which is more explicit and worked out as part of his philosophical grammar,[79] verbs are not given a separate class, but are regarded as nouns adjective (active, passive or neutral (intransitive)) always in association with or containing in their own form a copula (e.g. *lives*=*is living*; *hits*=*is hitting*). This analysis is similar to that of the Port Royal grammarians. Derived adverbs (from nouns adjective, like *badly*) are also integrals. The particle class is divided into essential (the copula verb, *to be*) and occasional; this latter group includes pronouns, articles, prepositions, non-derived adverbs, and conjunctions, and also modes and tenses (*can, may, will,* etc.). This treatment of the verbal auxiliaries, which Cooper follows for English, though inexplicitly,[80] bears some analogy with some analyses of English verbs current today.

The Latin tradition is seen in the retention of the adjective within the noun class, though formally this has less to commend it in English than in Latin, and in the preoccupation of most of the grammarians with the participle, treated either (purely traditionally) as a class in its own right, or as a noun adjective having particular derivational associations with the verb.

Perhaps because Wilkins was framing a system of universal or philosophical grammar, applicable to English but not based simply on English, he was the most radical in revising the Priscianic-Lilyan tradition. Certainly he went further than his closest follower among grammarians of the English language, Cooper. The great interest in the work of the quite considerable number of writers on English grammar during this period is to be found in the attempts they were making to test the traditionally accepted framework of grammatical description and teaching against their actual observations of the forms and structures of the language, even though by later standards they do not appear to have moved so very far.[81]

Grammars of English have continued to be written from this period up to the present day, gradually remodelling tradition in the interests of formal correspondence with the actual patterns and paradigms of English. Two early nineteenth-century grammars are well known, by Lindley Murray and by William Cobbett. Though they are similar in theory and presentation, their social settings are interestingly dissimilar and reflect the different contexts in which English grammar has been and is taught and studied.

Murray was an American citizen who settled in England after the War of Independence. Established near York, he wrote his celebrated *English grammar*, primarily with the needs of young students in mind. First published in 1795, it achieved very wide acceptance and ran into numerous reprintings during the first half of the nineteenth century. Somewhat conservative in theory, it may be taken as an example of a successful teaching grammar of English during this period. It is divided into four parts: Orthography, with an account of the various pronunciation values of the letters of the English alphabet, 'Etymology' (i.e, morphology, the parts of speech, their forms and inflexions), Syntax, and Prosody and punctuation. Prosody is divided into the rules of versification and the description of those features such as length, stress, pause, and intonation ('tone'), to which the term 'prosody' had been applied in antiquity (p. 38, above) in a manner in several ways anticipatory of its use by Firthians (p. 218, below).

In his grammar Murray considered that three cases should be

recognized in English nouns: nominative, genitive, and objective or accusative.[82] He argued this on the analogy of Latin, wherein despite the sameness of form between nominative and accusative in many nouns the cases were separately recognized. His argument is hardly valid formally, because the distinction of the cases is primarily set up on the basis of those nouns wherein different constructions do require distinct inflexional forms. One does see in Murray the 'modern traditional' set of word classes for English: article, noun, adjective, pronoun, verb, adverb, preposition, conjunction, and interjection, with no suggestion of merging the adjective with the noun or of treating the participle as a separate word class.

Murray's style is clear and systematic, if rather unexciting and unoriginal. His concern for the general well-being of his young readers appears throughout his book. In the preface and in a final 'address to young students' he declares his wish to 'promote the cause of virtue as well as of learning', and the examples chosen display a gentle piety: *I will respect him, though he chide me*; *Duty and interest forbid vicious indulgences*; *Idleness produces want, vice, and misery.*[83] Quite apart from differences of theory, his choice of examples puts him and his work in a very different context from that of some modern writers who have favoured examples like *I'm going to get one for Bert*, and *All the people in the lab consider John a fool.*[84] Neither the one nor the other style is necessarily the better field for the exemplification of a grammatical description or a linguistic theory.

The repute of Murray's grammar may be seen in the prudence of Mrs. Jarley, the waxworks proprietor in Dickens's *Old Curiosity Shop*, when her audience was to comprise young ladies from select boarding schools, in 'altering the face and costume of Mr. Grimaldi as clown to represent Mr. Lindley Murray as he appeared when engaged in the composition of his English grammar'.

Though the theoretical framework and the categories employed are very similar, the contemporary, less well-known, *Grammar of the English language* by Cobbett, the radical politician (London, 1819), was conceived in quite a different setting. Written in the form of a series of letters to his son James, it was 'intended . . . more especially for the use of soldiers, sailors, apprentices, and ploughboys'. A later edition includes 'six lessons intended to prevent statesmen from using false grammar, and from writing in an awkward manner', and contains a dedication to Queen Caroline in which with radical eloquence Cobbett presses the case for the literary education of the 'labouring classes':

'The nobles and the hierarchy have long had the arrogance to style themselves the pillars that support the throne. But, as your Majesty has now clearly ascertained, Royalty has, in the hour of need, no efficient supporters but the people'.

In doctrine so alike, in style so different, these two English grammars embody two themes that had been prominent in the teaching of English ever since the Renaissance had ushered in an epoch of social mobility in English society: the careful maintenance of the linguistic standards appropriate to superior social status, and the acquisition of such standards as a vital step in any social advancement.

Just as empirical attitudes fostered descriptive phonetics and the grammatical independence of different languages, so did the rationalist movement make itself felt in the production of philosophical grammars, especially those associated with the French Port Royal schools. These religious and educational foundations were set up in 1637, and disbanded in 1661 owing to political and religious strife;[85] but their influence was longer lasting in educational ideas, and their work in grammar can be seen continuing in the *grammaires raisonnées* and 'general grammars' of the eighteenth century. The Port Royal grammar was reprinted as late as 1830.[86]

The rationalist grammars were in several ways the successors of the mediaeval scholastic grammars. Though the educational system of Port Royal included sound classical instruction, one or two of its members declared a prejudice against the pagan literature of classical antiquity. Port Royal numbered among its company writers on logic, and in their grammar the influence of logic on linguistics was strongest. They were writers of universal grammars, not in the same sense as either the universal language planners or the mediaeval grammarians. Unlike the language planners they were not inventing new systems of communication but expounding a general theory of grammar through the medium of such languages as Latin and French. Unlike the scholastics they asserted the claims of human reason above authority and they made Descartes rather than Aristotle the basis of their teaching. They did not seek a philosophical universalist explanation of all the details of Priscian's Latin grammar, ignoring other languages, but they did attempt to reveal the unity of grammar underlying the separate grammars of different languages in their role of communicating thought, itself comprising perception, judgment, and reasoning.

On the basis of this general grammar Port Royal scholars took the nine classical word classes, noun, article, pronoun, participle, preposition, adverb, verb, conjunction, and interjection, but redivided them semantically, the first six relating to 'the objects' of our thought and the last three to the 'form or manner' of our thought. The basic noun-verb dichotomy survived, but the repartition of the other classes around it was a different one. There was no attempt to follow the grammar of Donatus and Priscian as they had set it out, but a good deal of the tradition of Latin grammar was thought to underlie all languages and to find expression in various ways. Thus the six cases of Latin are, at least operationally, assumed in other languages,[87] though some of them were expressed by prepositions and word order in the 'vulgar languages' (i.e. modern European languages; the term is not pejorative); and Greek was said to have an ablative case always alike in form to the dative. This last statement is misleading; the translation equivalence of the Latin ablative is divided between the Greek dative and the Greek genitive. Collectively cases and prepositions were intended to express relations,[88] but the two categories were kept theoretically distinct despite their common exponence in the 'vulgar languages', and the purely case-like usage of French *de* and *à* was contrasted with their genuinely prepositional functions, as had been done in earlier comparative studies of the classical and modern Romance languages (p. 101, above).

Despite some similarities with the modistae and a like stress on the universal necessary features of all languages being variously manifested, there are striking differences in attitude. The universalist foundation envisaged by Port Royal was human reason and thought. The elaborate interrelations of the *modi essendi* of the external world and the *modi intelligendi* by which they were perceived and interpreted in the mind have no place in the Port Royal system, and the somewhat modistic explanation of the essential difference between noun and verb given by J. C. Scaliger, based on the categories of permanence and transience, was expressly criticized as both irrelevant and inadequate.[89]

Structural interpretations of the functions of certain classes of word may be noticed. Adverbs are no more than an abbreviation of a prepositional phrase (*sapienter*, wisely, = *cum sapientia*, with wisdom). Verbs are properly words that 'signify affirmation' and, in other moods, desire, command, etc.[90] This returns the Port Royal grammarians to an analysis suggested by Aristotle[91] of all verbs other than the copula, to be, as logically and grammatically equivalent to this verb plus a participle, making *Peter lives* (*Peter is living*) structurally analogous with *Peter is a man*; the categories of intransitive and transitive (and

active and passive) are said properly to belong not to the words commonly called verbs but just to the 'adjectival' element in them.[92].

This analysis, it should be noted, is not an alleged historical explanation, nor is it a surface description of verbal morphology, as Bopp was
later to try to make it; it was the positing, in modern terms, at a deeper
structural level, of elements that in actual sentences were represented
conjointly with other elements.[93] The Port Royal grammarians might
have claimed support from our wider knowledge today of languages in
which virtually any root can be nominalized or verbalized by an appropriate affix, so that the distinction maintained in the surface grammar
of European languages, at least, between *Peter is a man* and *Peter lives*
disappears.[94]

The downgrading or subordinating function of relative pronouns
(Latin and French *qui*, etc., English *who*, *which*, etc.) is described in
terms on which transformationalists lay stress as an anticipation of their
own theories. A single proposition *the invisible God has created the
visible world* is related to the more explicit form *God, who is invisible,
has created the world, which is visible*, and, in a still more elementary
representation, is said to unite the three propositions or judgments
(underlying sentences), *God is invisible*, *God created the world*, and *the
world is visible*, by including ('embedding' in modern usage) the first
and the third in the 'principal and essential' second proposition as the
matrix.[95] However, the Port Royal grammarians seem to have worked
in other than purely formal terms, because the proposition *the valour of
Achilles has been the cause of the taking of Troy* is said, unlike the other
proposition, to be a simple one, no more than one judgment or affirmation. It is hard to follow this reasoning, as in transformational terms
this latter sentence would be treated very similarly to the other.

The Port Royal grammarians made a genuine attempt to write a
general grammar. Drawing examples from Latin, Greek, Hebrew, and
modern European languages, they sought to refer them to alleged universal characteristics of language, underlying them. A wider knowledge
of non-European languages does not appear to have interested them, or
they might have revised their classical framework more radically. They
envisaged general grammar as underlying the actual make-up of all
languages, rather than as particularly exemplified in any one; but as
scholarly patriots they took pride in the perspicuity, elegance, and
beauty that they saw in the French language,[96] a testimony to the
change in men's attitude to the European vernaculars wrought by the
Renaissance.

Once the diversity of languages was properly accepted, and vernaculars were recognized as equally worthy of study and cultivation with the classical languages, linguistic scholars had to face the question of language universals. The ancient world had almost ignored the problem, being only interested in Greek and Latin; the scholastics had in practice assumed that Latin as described and analysed by Priscian in fact represented the universal infrastructure of all languages; after the Renaissance, the empiricists stressed the individual variations of particular languages and the need to adjust categories and classes in the light of observation, while the rationalists still looked for what was common to all languages below surface differences. The whole question is still very much alive. Hjelmslev in his early *Principes de grammaire générale* demanded a universal *état abstrait* comprising the possibilities available to languages and differently realized in the *états concrets* of each particular one; failing this, linguistic theory would lapse into 'nihilism'.[97] The descriptivists of what is now called the 'Bloomfieldian' epoch reduced the assumption of universals to a minimum and made the description of the observed forms paramount, by means of *ad hoc* categories and classes devised for each language independently and having little in common between different languages; Bloomfield declared that 'the only useful generalizations about language are inductive generalizations'.[98] Likewise, Firthians spoke of general theory, but remained very cautious of general categories or universal grammar.[99] More recently Chomsky and the transformationalists have reasserted, in terms strikingly similar to those both of the rationalist philosophical grammarians and of Hjelmslev in 1928, the importance of language universals, suggesting that in the deeper levels of linguistic structure languages will be found to share aspects of form that are a common human possession realized differently at the surface in different languages; indeed they claim that without this conception linguistics is doomed to confinement within a narrow empiricism and relative lack of significance.[100] In linguistics as in other realms of thought the old problems continue to present themselves, though in different ways to different generations.

The author of a later general grammar, Beauzée, expresses an attitude similar to that of the Port Royal scholars; grammar has two sorts of principles, those of universal validity arising from the nature of human thought, and those resulting from the arbitrary and mutable conventions that constitute the grammars of particular languages. The former, which are the objects of general grammar, are logically anterior to any given language and concern the very possibility and necessary conditions of the existence of any language.[101]

Though Beauzée's doctrine is in agreement with Port Royal, his grammatical system is somewhat different in its organization, and despite tributes to Descartes and Arnauld (a major Port Royal grammarian) in his preface, there are some explicit criticisms of certain Port Royal statements in the text. Beauzée's word classes are more modern in that the adjective is taken as a quite separate class, and the specific Port Royal bipartition of the classes is not mentioned. As in any general grammar, the classes must be defined in terms applicable to any language, and appeal is made to general semantic notions. Typical is the distinction between noun and pronoun on the one hand and verb and adjective on the other: nouns and pronouns express individual things, persons, and abstractions; adjectives and verbs express the qualities, states, and relations with which they are associated.[102] In some respects Beauzée, though a universalist, is less rigid. No attempt is made by him to impose a single system of cases on all languages, and the Port Royal scholars are reproved for insisting on their six cases in Greek in defiance of the forms actually observable in Greek nominal inflexions.[103]

Even a brief survey shows how much more varied were the lines taken by linguistic science after the Renaissance. All the main intellectual, social, and political developments that were to bring into being the modern age of history and mark it off from the preceding Middle Ages, as well as those that linked it more securely to the world of classical antiquity, made their impact on the study of language and of languages. From the sixteenth century the philosophical debate between empiricist and rationalist tended to polarize attitudes to language, although certain developments are seen to have drawn inspiration from both currents.

During the period, and to some extent even in the later years of the Middle Ages, ways of thought about language began to emerge on topics which had either not been considered before or, if they had been, had fallen into terms that could not lead to any very useful conclusions. This has already been noticed in the beginnings of the historical linguistics of the Romance languages (pp. 100–1, above). Towards the end of the eighteenth century the historical approach to languages deepened and was enriched by new insights. Historical study was linked with typological comparison, and both found new and significant material in the languages then known to scholarship and in specially collected vocabularies and texts from previously unstudied fields.

From the end of the century the linguistic situation was quite transformed by one of the most important events in the history of linguistics, the full discovery of the language and scholarship of ancient Sanskritic India. But as the effects of this belong to the nineteenth and the twentieth centuries, it will be well to deal with them in subsequent chapters.

FOR FURTHER CONSULTATION

D. ABERCROMBIE, 'Forgotten phoneticians', *TPS* 1948, 1–34.

R. W. ALBRIGHT, 'The International Phonetic Alphabet: its backgrounds and development', *IJAL* 24.1 (1958), part 3.

H. ARENS, *Sprachwissenschaft: der Gang ihrer Entwicklung von der Antike bis zur Gegenwart*, Freiburg/Munich, 1955, 47–88.

R. R. BOLGAR, *The classical heritage and its benefactors*, Cambridge, 1954.

F. CADET, *Port Royal education* (tr. A. D. JONES), London, 1898.

N. CHOMSKY, *Cartesian linguistics*, New York, 1966.

G. B. DOWNER, 'Traditional Chinese phonology', *TPS* 1963, 127–42.

J. R. FIRTH, *The tongues of men*, London, 1937, chapters 5 and 6.

——, 'The English school of phonetics', *TPS* 1946, 92–132.

O. FUNKE, *Die Frühzeit der englischen Grammatik*, Berne, 1941.

F. P. GRAVES, *Peter Ramus and the educational reformation of the sixteenth century*, New York, 1912.

L. KUKENHEIM, *Contributions à l'histoire de la grammaire italienne, espagnole, et française à l'époque de la Renaissance*, Amsterdam, 1932.

——, *Contributions à l'histoire de la grammaire grecque, latine, et hébraïque à l'epoque de la Renaissance*, Leiden, 1951.

——, *Esquisse historique de la linguistique française*, Leiden, 1962.

V. G. SALMON, 'Language planning in seventeenth-century England; its context and aims', C. A. BAZELL, J. C. CATFORD, M. A. K. HALLIDAY, and R. H. ROBINS (ed.), *In memory of J. R. Firth*, London, 1966, 370–97.

J. E. SANDYS, *History of classical scholarship* (third edition), Cambridge, 1921, volume 2.

E. VORLAT, *Progress in English grammar 1585–1735*, Louvain, 1963.

NOTES

1. SANDYS, 1921, 17–21.

2. B. RUSSELL, *History of western philosophy*, London, 1946, 523.

3. J. A. FROUDE, *History of England from the fall of Wolsey to the defeat of the Spanish Armada*, London, 1875, volume 1, 61–2.

4. *Origines*, 1.3.4.
5. KUKENHEIM, 1951, 88.
6. J. REUCHLIN, *De rudimentis Hebraicis*, Pforzheim, 1506; L. GEIGER, *J. Reuchlin*, Leipzig, 1871.
7. REUCHLIN, op. cit., 551.
8. ibid., 552, 585.
9. H. HIRSCHFELD, *Literary history of Hebrew grammarians and lexicographers*, London, 1926, 7.
10. P. WECHTER, *Ibn Barun's Arabic works on Hebrew grammar and lexicography*, Philadelphia, 1964.
11. E. O. A. MERX, 'Historia artis grammaticae apud Syros', *Abhandlung für die Kunde des Morgenlandes* 9.2 (1889, Leipzig).
12. cp. H. FLEISCH, *Traité de philologie arabe*, Beirut, 1961, volume 1, 1–49.
13. A. SCHAADE, *Sibawaihi's Lautlehre*, Leiden, 1911 (several corrections are suggested by M. H. A. EL SARAAN, *A Critical study of the phonetic observations of the Arab grammarians* (Ph.D. thesis, University of London, 1951)).
14. KUKENHEIM, 1932, 95.
15. ibid., 6.
16. ibid., 205.
17. K. LAMBLEY, *The teaching and cultivation of the French language during Tudor and Stuart times*, Manchester, 1920.
18. *La manière de bien traduire d'une langue en aultre*, Paris, 1545.
19. KUKENHEIM, 1932, 37–8.
20. Book 1, chapter 1.
21. Book 1, chapters 18–19.
22. KUKENHEIM, 1932, 140.
23. G. RUSCELLI, *Commentarii della lingua italiana*, Venice, 1581, 100.
24. KUKENHEIM, 1932, 98–9.
25. KUKENHEIM, 1962, 18; this is disputed by P. A. VERBURG, *Taal en functionaliteit*, Wageningen, 1952, 172–84.
26. GRAVES, 1912.
27. *Scholae grammaticae*, Frankfurt, 1595; *Gramere*, Paris, 1562.
28. *Scholae* 7–14, 95.
29. *Gramere* 10–11.
30. *Scholae* 95–6, 205–6.
31. *Gramere* 41.
32. *Scholae* 118.
33. ibid. 223.
34. ibid. 118.
35. GRAVES, 1912, 130 (where see chart).
36. FIRTH, 1937, chapter 5.

37. e.g. FIRTH, 'Alphabets and phonology in India and Burma', *BSOS* 8 (1935–7), 517–46.

38. L. S. GALLAGHER, *The China that was*, Milwaukee, 1952, 42–8.

39. Hongkong, 1893.

40. PRÉMARE, op. cit., 36; J. VENDRYES, *Le langage*, Paris, 1921, 98–9.

41. LAI MING, *A history of Chinese literature*, London, 1964, 4.

42. B. KARLGREN, *Philology and ancient China*, Oslo, 1926; R. A. D. FORREST, *The Chinese language*, London, 1948; DOWNER, 1963.

43. G. B. SANSOM, *An historical grammar of Japanese*, Oxford, 1928, chapter 1.

44. M. GRABMANN, *Mittelalterliches Geistesleben*, Munich, 1926, volume 1, 141–3.

45. SANDYS, 1921, 127–32; ERASMUS, *De recta Latini Graecique sermonis pronuntiatione*, Basle, 1528.

46. S. HAVERKAMP, *Sylloge altera scriptorum qui de linguae Graecae vera pronuntiatione commentarios reliquerunt*, Leiden, 1740, 124–5; KUKENHEIM, 1932, 182.

47. GRAVES, 1912, 124–5.

48. I. N. MADVIG, *Latin grammar* (tr. G. WOODS), Oxford, 1856, § 24.

49. Lyons, 1540; SANDYS, 1921, 129–30.

50. Amsterdam, 1587.

51 KUKENHEIM, 1951, 47; FUNKE, 1941, 49.
    In England, Sir Thomas Smith (1514–77) and Sir John Cheke (1514–57) strove to reform the pronunciation of classical Greek on the basis of Erasmus's teaching. This was ultimately successful, and in itself it stimulated orthographic and phonetic studies in this country (SANDYS, 1921, 230–3; FIRTH, 1946, 100–1).

52. London, 1659.

53. J. LOCKE, *An essay concerning human understanding*, London, 1690, 2.1.4.

54. J. M. ROBERTSON, *The philosophical works of Francis Bacon*, London, 1905, 119–20, 264, 523–4.

55. FIRTH, 1937, chapter 6; C. K. OGDEN, *Debabelization*, London, 1931.

56. C. J. GERHARDT (ed.), *Die philosophischen Schriften von Gottfried Wilhelm Leibniz*, Berlin, 1890, volume 7, 200, 218–27.

57. FIRTH, 1937, 72.

58. SALMON, 1966, 373, 388–9.

59. London, 1668.

60. R. A. DUTCH (ed.), *Roget's Thesaurus*, London, 1962, xxxv.

61. WILKINS, *Essay*, 452.

62. J. J. KATZ and J. FODOR, 'The structure of a semantic theory', *Language* 39 (1963), 170–210; KATZ and P. M. POSTAL, *An integrated theory of linguistic descriptions*, Cambridge, Mass., 1964; D. W.

BOLINGER, 'The atomization of meaning', *Language* 41 (1965), 555-573.

63. SALMON, 1966; WILKINS, *Mercury: or the swift and secret messenger*, London, 1641.
64. T. BRIGHT, *Characterie*, London, 1958 (first published 1558); W. J. CARLTON, *Timothy Bright*, London, 1911.
65. FIRTH, 1946.
66. B. DANIELSSON, *John Hart's works on English orthography and pronunciation*, Stockholm, 1955; FIRTH, 1946; E. J. DOBSON (ed.), *The phonetic writings of Robert Robinson* (Early English Text Society, original series 238, 1957).
67. FIRTH, 1946.
68. cp. E. J. DOBSON, *English pronunciation 1500–1700*, Oxford, 1957.
69. W. HOLDER, *Elements of speech*, London, 1669, 35–6, 80–90.
70. ibid., 23, 80.
71. ABERCROMBIE, 1948, 18–26.
72. WILKINS, *Essay*, 358, 378. See further FIRTH, 1937, chapter 6; id., 1946; ABERCROMBIE, 1948, ALBRIGHT, 1958.
73. W. BULLOKAR, *Bref grammar for English*, London, 1586.
74. e.g. J. WALLIS, *Grammatica linguae Anglicanae*, Oxford, 1653, a work reprinted several times and much praised.
75. B. JONSON, *The English grammar*, London, 1640.
76. *Logonomia Anglicana*, London, 1621.
77. *The English grammar*, Oxford, 1634, chapter 3, § 3.
78. J. BRIGHTLAND, *A grammar of the English tongue*, London, 1711; VORLAT, 1963, 73.
79. WILKINS, *Essay*, 298.
80. COOPER, *Grammatica linguae Anglicanae*, London, 1685.
81. Further details in VORLAT, 1963, and FUNKE, 1941.
    The close connection seen in this period between English scientific empiricism and the formal study of language is evident in the eighteenth century in the linguistic interest shown by the natural scientist J. Priestley (1733–1804): *A course of lectures on the theory of language and universal grammar*, Warrington, 1762; *The rudiments of English grammar*, London, 1761 (page vi: 'Grammar may be compared to a treatise of natural philosophy').
82. L. MURRAY, *English grammar* (thirty-fourth edition), York, 1821, 54–6.
83. ibid. 75, 127, 137.
84. FIRTH, 'Personality and language in society', *Sociological review* 42 (1950), 44; N. CHOMSKY, *Syntactic structures*, The Hague, 1957, 79.
85. CADET, 1898.
86. KUKENHEIM, 1962, 49. Cartesian influence on linguistic studies is seen

in G. CORDEMOY's *Philosophicall discourse concerning speech, conformable to the Cartesian principles*, London, 1668 (translated from the French original of 1667).

87. *A general and rational grammar, translated from the French of Messieurs de Port Royal*, London, 1753 (first published in French in Paris, 1660), chapter 6. See further CHOMSKY, 1966.

88. *A general and rational grammar*, chapter 11.

89. ibid., 94–5; SCALIGER, *De causis linguae Latinae*, 137, 220.

90. *A general and rational grammar*, chapters 12 and 13.

91. *De interpretatione* 12; *Metaphysica* 1017 a 29.

92. *A general and rational grammar*, chapter 18.

93. cp. CHOMSKY, *Current issues in liguistic theory*, The Hague, 1964; id., *Aspects of the theory of syntax*, Cambridge, Mass., 1965. cp. pp. 173–4, below.

94. E. SAPIR and M. SWADESH, *Nootka texts*, Philadelphia, 1939, 235–43.

95. *A general and rational grammar*, chapter 9; CHOMSKY, *Current issues*, 15–16.

96. *A general and rational grammar*, 154.

97. L. HJELMSLEV, *Principes de grammaire générale*, Copenhagen, 1928, 15, 268.

98. L. BLOOMFIELD, *Language*, London, 1935, 20.

99. FIRTH, 'A synopsis of linguistic theory', *Studies in linguistic analysis* (Special volume of the Philological Society), Oxford, 1957, 21–2.

100. CHOMSKY, *Current issues*, chapters 1 and 5; id., *Aspects*, 117–18.

101. M. BEAUZÉE, *Grammaire générale ou exposition raisonnée des éléments nécessaires du langage pour servir de fondement à l'étude de toutes les langues*, Paris, 1767, ix–xi.

102. ibid., volume 1, 403: 'Les noms et les pronoms expriment des êtres déterminés, au lieu que les adjectifs et les verbes expriment des êtres indéterminés'.

103. ibid., volume 2, 160.

Six

The eve of modern times

Both in general history and in the history of particular subjects the Renaissance is justifiably regarded as the beginning of the modern age. But the early nineteenth century saw a yet sharper turn towards the world to which we are now accustomed. Even in spite of the rapid changes during the present century, it requires less effort of the historical imagination to study the life and work of nineteenth-century people through their own lives and in their own context. Among the modern nation states of Europe, Germany and Italy achieved their independent existence during this century, and the patterns of industrial civilization spread over and transformed the predominantly agricultural life that had characterized Europe since antiquity.

Intellectually, too, the nineteenth century saw the emergence of modern conditions. New universities were founded in Europe and America, and the interplay of European and American scholarship, now so vital a force in education, only began seriously in this century. Popular education spread ever wider and the goal of universal literacy was for the first time made a practical proposition for governments. Learned societies and periodicals associated with them had already made their appearance, but many of those best known today in university libraries began publication in the nineteenth century, and improved communications made the exchange of articles and the systematic reviewing of books the dominant feature of academic life to which we are now accustomed.

In linguistics many of the scholars whose work was done in the nineteenth century are known to students well before they consciously delve into the history of the subject. Grimm, Whitney, Meyer-Lübke,

Max Müller, Brugmann, and Sweet are just a few examples of nine-teenth-century scholars who were partly responsible for shaping their branches of linguistics in the broad patterns still taught in present-day textbooks.

If any single year can, albeit artificially, be taken to mark the start of the contemporary world of linguistic science, it is the year 1786, just over a decade before the turn of the century. 1786 has been declared by a contemporary scholar to have initiated the first of the four really significant 'breakthroughs' in the modern development of linguistics up to the present day. In this year, as is now well known, Sir William Jones of the East India Company read his famous paper to the Royal Asiatic Society in Calcutta, wherein he established beyond doubt the historical kinship of Sanskrit, the classical language of India, with Latin, Greek, and the Germanic languages.

Jones's statement, though quoted in so many books already, should be set out here, because its effects in the circumstances of the time were so profound and far-reaching: 'The Sanskrit language, whatever may be its antiquity, is of a wonderful structure; more perfect than the Greek, more copious than the Latin, and more exquisitely refined than either; yet bearing to both of them a stronger affinity, both in the roots of verbs and in the forms of grammar, than could have been produced by accident; so strong that no philologer could examine the Sanskrit, Greek, and Latin, without believing them to have sprung from some common source, which, perhaps, no longer exists. There is a similar reason, though not quite so forcible, for supposing that both the Gothic and the Celtic had the same origin with the Sanskrit.' [1]

What is vital about this event is not that it marked an absolute beginning to historical linguistics. Historical questions had been tackled before, and with some individual successes and insights; indeed, a special relationship between Sanskrit and some European languages, ancient and modern, had been surmised before Sir William Jones. But hitherto observations in these areas of linguistics had been in the main isolated and fragmentary. Historical significance characterizes events that can be seen to be linked in an enduring causal chain, where-by later participants start from the positions taken up by their pre-decessors. Such a state of affairs is observed in the development of grammatical theory and grammatical analysis in ancient Greece, and the same features dominate the course of historical linguistics during the century following Jones's statement, during which it constituted the major branch of linguistic studies.

The progress of comparative and historical linguistics must be traced in its most significant theoretical aspects during the nineteenth century; but the results of the introduction of serious Sanskrit study into Europe, which followed the demonstration of its historical relationships, were not confined to historical linguistics. Modern descriptive linguistics shows no less the effects of contact with ancient India, even though in this case the full realization took place much less immediately.

Roman Catholic missionaries had opened up the field of Indian languages in earlier centuries (p. 104, above). The first known reference to Sanskrit came at the end of the sixteenth century, when the Italian Filippo Sassetti wrote home from India reporting admiringly of the *lingua Sanscruta*, and pointing out a number of resemblances between Sanskrit and Italian words. Subsequently likenesses were noticed between Sanskrit and some European languages by the German B. Schulze and the Frenchman Père Cœurdoux[2]; but little came of these observations.

Jones's discovery was not only of a more profound nature than previous pronouncements on Sanskrit by Europeans, but it came propitiously on the eve of an awakening interest in Near Eastern and Indian studies on the part of European scholars. The Napoleonic wars were partly responsible, and during his supremacy Napoleon deliberately encouraged French archaeological work in Egypt and the Near East, inaugurating a long association of French scholarship with the non-European languages of the Mediterranean.

The German scholar F. von Schlegel was initiated into Sanskrit studies while he was in Paris in 1803; his brother A. W. von Schlegel, who in 1819 became Professor of Sanskrit in the University of Bonn (founded in 1818), wrote: 'I would count myself fortunate if I could do something towards establishing Sanskrit studies in Germany.'[3] With governmental support he achieved his object. In the expansion of university education in Prussia after the wars chairs of Sanskrit and of historical linguistics were set up and appointments made to them under the influence of Wilhelm von Humboldt, who served for a time as minister for public instruction in the Kingdom of Prussia.

The first Sanskrit grammar in English was published early in the nineteenth century, and from 1800 translations were made into European languages of the classical Sanskrit literature of India.

The linguistic study of Sanskrit by Europeans had a twofold effect; the comparison of Sanskrit with languages of Europe formed the first stage in the systematic growth of comparative and historical linguistics, and, additionally, in Sanskrit writings Europeans now came into contact with the independently developed tradition of linguistic scholarship in India, whose merits were acknowledged at once and whose influence on several branches of European linguistics was deep and lasting.

Linguistics in India goes back further than in western Europe, and has been maintained by a continuity of native scholarship ever since. It attained its classical period early in its history, and by the time Europeans became aware of it, Indian scholars had recognized definite schools and distinct doctrines, together with acknowledged texts and sources followed by successions of commentaries and exegesis.

Indian linguistics was not itself historical in orientation, though its roots lay in the changes languages undergo in the course of time. But the topics covered by modern descriptive linguistics: semantics, grammar, phonology, and phonetics, were all treated at length in the Indian tradition; and in phonetics and in certain aspects of grammar, Indian theory and practice was definitely in advance of anything achieved in Europe or elsewhere before contact had been made with Indian work. The stimulation afforded by Sanskritic linguistic scholarship carried by Buddhist monks into China has already been noticed (pp. 106–7, above). European scholars realized immediately that they had encountered a mass of linguistic literature in India of the greatest importance and stemming from an independent source, even though their interpretation and full appreciation of it was in part halting and delayed.

So far as we can tell, the original inspiration for linguistics in India was the need that was felt to preserve certain ritual and religious orally transmitted texts coming from the Vedic period (c. 1200–1000 B.C.), the oldest known stage of Sanskrit literature, from the effects of time. The preservation without alteration of linguistic material handed down through the generations by oral transmission is an artificial process, an attempt to halt what is everywhere the natural outcome of linguistic continuity. Changes in pronunciation, grammar, and word meanings were observed in the rest of the language, and the dialectal divergences in the speech of different areas may have made even more apparent the special position of the Vedic texts, and, in a manner similar to the contrasts between Hellenistic Greek and classical literary Greek, made necessary an apparatus of phonetic, grammatical, and semantic interpretation.

Such was the stimulus, but the response went far beyond these immediate needs; and, as a modern writer observes, 'a scientific curiosity, coupled with keen audition and an effective methodology, led to descriptions which must surely have transcended their original terms of reference'.[4]

In Greece we have preserved for us the stages through which linguistic scholarship passed virtually from its beginnings. In ancient India most of the linguistic literature that we have, and especially the best known piece of linguistic composition, Pāṇini's Sanskrit grammar, manifestly came at the end and as the culmination of a long line of previous work of which we have no direct knowledge. Pāṇini's grammar is known as the *Aṣṭādhyāyī*, or 'Eight books'; it is divided into eight main sections. It is not known whether its author wrote it down or put it together orally; its date, too, is uncertain, and it has variously been assigned to around 600 B.C. and around 300 B.C. Clearly, however, linguistics in India must have been seriously under way well before the middle of the first millennium B.C.

Sanskrit Indian scholarship served as the model for the rest of India. It was the inspiration for the *Tolkāppiyam*, one of the earliest grammars of Tamil, a Dravidian language of central and south India (? second century B.C.).

Indian scholars covered virtually the whole field of synchronic linguistic studies, though their best known representative, Pāṇini, restricted his work to the intensive treatment of a limited range. In reviewing the Indian achievement as it was when it made its impact on European linguistics, it is legitimate to span several centuries together and to consider the work of Indian scholarship, divergent in time though united by the continuity of scholarly tradition, under three principal headings: general linguistic theory and semantics, phonetics and phonology, and descriptive grammar.

General linguistic theory was debated by Indian scholars as it was by scholars in the west, though before the end of the eighteenth century there was no contact between them. Language was considered against the background both of literary studies and of philosophical enquiry; and a number of the topics familiar to western scholarship and almost inevitable in a serious examination of language were also familiar to Indian linguists from early times.

Various questions involved in understanding the nature of word and sentence meaning were discussed from different points of view. Indian linguists considered the extent to which meanings could be regarded as a natural property of words, or the extent to which onomatopoeia could be taken as the model for describing the relationship between word and thing. As in the western nature-convention argument (p. 18, above), men soon realized the very limited part that such a factor can play in language, and how much more typical of language is the arbitrary conventional relation between a form and its meaning.

Much thought was given to the variability and extensibility of word meanings, one of the major characteristics of language, enabling it to fulfil the unlimited requirements placed on it with its necessarily limited resources. Meanings were seen to be learned both from observation of the contexts of situation in which words were actually used in sentences and from direct statements by elders and teachers on particular words and their uses. While limits could hardly be set to actual usage, collocation often restricted the meaning range of a word by the exclusion of certain otherwise acceptable meanings of the word in isolation. Thus *dhenuḥ* which by itself could mean both 'mare' and 'cow', could only be taken as meaning 'cow' in such a collocation as *savatsā dhenuḥ*, cow with calf.[5] The almost unanswerable question was faced in India, as elsewhere, on the extent to which single word forms with multiple meanings should be regarded as polysemous words or as a number of different but homophonous words. Within this context much attention was paid to the relations between what was considered the primary meaning of a word, which was said to be understood first, and the various meanings arising from its metaphorical use (lakṣaṇā), both on everyday discourse and for particular literary effects.

While these were questions of great literary importance, the Indian logicians debated, again as did western logicians, whether words primarily denoted particulars, classes, or abstract universals, and how far word meanings were positive in identifying an object for what it was or negative in distinguishing it from the rest of reality. It was also realized that a word, e.g. *fire*, can stand for itself as well as for its primary denotation.

A question that is far from being solved today is that of the semantic relation between a sentence and its component words. Sentences are clearly more than the sum of their juxtaposed words, whether considered from the semantic or the grammatical point of view. The western tradition tended to concentrate on words as individual minimal meaning bearers and to regard the sentence as the product of word combinations in specific types of logical proposition. Plato and Aristotle mostly discussed meaning in relation to words as isolates, and Aristotle stressed the semantic minimality (in his view) and independence of the word as such (p. 26, above). The Stoics appear to have pointed to the further limitation of a word's field of reference or its disambiguation as the result of specific collocations (pp. 21–2, above), and this doctrine was developed in the course of the distinction between *significatio* and *suppositio* in the Middle Ages (p. 77, above). Indian linguists debated the whole question of the primacy of the word as against that of the sentence. One set of thinkers maintained a view very like the general western attitude that the sentence is built up of words each contributing its meaning to the total meaning of the sentence. But an opposite view, particularly associated with Bhartṛhari, author of *Vākyapadīya* (*c.* seventh century A.D.), regarded the sentence as a single undivided utterance conveying its meaning 'in a flash', just as a picture is first perceived as a unity notwithstanding subsequent analysis into its component coloured shapes. Given the conception of the word unit, sentences can be identified as one-word sentences or as many-word sentences, but for the speaker and hearer they are primarily single sentence unities, words and word meanings being largely the creation of linguists and self-conscious speakers trying to analyse and classify sentence meanings in terms of smaller components. As an example of Bhartṛhari's attitude, the sentence *fetch a cuckoo from the woods* is not understood first as a sequence of words put together, because the full meaning of *fetch* in the sentence (i.e. the mode of fetching) is only grasped together with the meaning of *cuckoo*, and someone ignorant of the meaning of the word *cuckoo* is therefore to some extent ignorant of the meaning of the rest of the sentence.[6]

Such a view may be criticized, and it was, as extreme. It is echoed in Malinowski's dictum that 'isolated words are in fact only linguistic figments, the products of an advanced linguistic analysis',[7] and perhaps underestimates the psychological reality of the word as a viable unit for the native speaker as well as part of the linguist's analytical apparatus (the bound morpheme is probably a better example of an analytical creation, and it is noteworthy that *morpheme* is generally a technical term, or translated by a technical term, whereas words for *word* are found in a very large number of languages, both written and unwritten). It is, however, a necessary corrective against the typical western tendency to concentrate semantic enquiries on the word as a wholly independent unit only subsequently put into sentences.

This Indian appreciation of the semantic unity of the sentence is parallel to and may have been connected with their early appreciation of the phonological and phonetic differences between words as pronounced isolates and words pronounced in connected spoken sentences (*sandhi*, pp. 142–3, below).

An inevitable problem in any serious linguistic thought is the relation between the perceived utterances, spoken and written, of a language and the language itself, whether regarded from the point of view of what the speaker possesses as his linguistic competence or from that of what the linguist sets up as the system or systems of elements, categories, and rules underlying and accounting for the infinitely varied output of a living language. *Langue* and *parole*, *abstraction* and *exponent*, *emic* and *etic unit*, *form* and *substance*, are all examples of recent attempts to compass and express this relation. Indian linguists sought to express it in the theory of *sphoṭa*. This theory was formulated somewhat differently by different Indian scholars and has been much discussed. Essentially, in any linguistic element or constituent two aspects are distinguished, the actual event or individual realization (*dhvani*) and the unexpressed and permanent entity (*sphoṭa*) actualized by each occurrent *dhvani*. Sentence *sphoṭa*, word *sphoṭa*, and sound unit (*varṇa*) *sphoṭa* were all envisaged.

The *sphoṭa* of a sentence as a single meaningful symbol is realized or actualized by a succession of articulated sounds. At a lower level the word, in so far as it is a meaningful symbol in its own right, may be regarded as a unitary *sphoṭa* also actualized by a succession of sounds. But sounds do not function simply as audible disturbances of the air; a particular abstract and permanent unit of distinctive sound signalling capable of semantic differentiation is actualized by the multitude of slightly different pronunciations each varying with the individual's voice, his style, and the physical situation in which he speaks. This last conception of the *varṇa sphoṭa* was especially associated with Patañjali (*c.* 150 B.C.). Bhartṛhari, on the other hand, in consonance with his theory of the primacy of the sentence, seems to have held the sentence *sphoṭa* to be the real *sphoṭa*. He, in fact, envisaged three levels in the realization of the sentence *sphoṭa* as a unitary meaningful symbol: the integral symbol itself, graphically and phonically ineffable, the sequential phonological pattern that expresses it, as normalized by the elimination of all individual variations (*prākṛta dhvani*), and the realization of this in the individual utterances of the sentence (*vaikṛta dhvani*). It would appear that the mediate stage would correspond to some interpretations of *varṇa sphoṭa*, and the entire scheme may be compared with the interlevel status accorded to phonology in relation to grammar and lexis on one side and to phonic utterance on the other by some linguists today.

A further development of the *dhvani-sphoṭa* relationship is seen in

Ānandavardhana's theory of poetic language (*Dhvanyāloka*, ninth century A.D.). Just as the sounds reveal the meaningful entities themselves, so in poetry the chosen words and their literal meanings reveal further suggested senses and the beauty of the poem as a whole. Here one remarks a striking parallel with Hjelmslev's conception of stylistic analysis as the treatment of the content plane and the expression plane of a natural language in some specific usage as themselves together forming the expression plane of a higher order 'connotative semiotic'.[8]

Much of what has been briefly noticed in ancient Indian speculation on semantics and the theory of language strikes chords already familiar in the western tradition, though their approach is often rather different. What is most remarkable about Indian phonetic work is its manifest superiority in conception and execution as compared with anything produced in the west or elsewhere before the Indian contribution had become known there. In general one may say that Henry Sweet takes over where the Indian phonetic treatises leave off.[9] We have seen how Greek and Roman linguists made the major classifications of letters, as the representatives of speech sounds, in terms of their acoustic impressions. But at this stage in linguistics, prior to the technology and equipment needed for the scientific analysis of sound waves, articulatory description was the only possible frame for an accurate and systematic classification. And in view of the primacy and the observational accessibility of the speech organs in the act of phonation, articulation still remains fundamental in phonetic description, even though modern acoustic categories may supplement and even supersede articulatory ones in phonological analysis.[10]

The Greeks and the Romans made articulatory features secondary in their phonetic descriptions; Arabic grammarians went further and achieved more in articulatory phonetics; but above all their contemporaries and successors before the nineteenth century were the ancient Indian phoneticians, whose work is preserved in a number of phonetic treatises which have been tentatively ascribed to the period 800–150 B.C.[11]

Once their terminology is mastered or translated, the Indian phonetic writings on Sanskrit are, apart from relatively few points, easy to follow for the modern reader acquainted with phonetic theory and phonetic descriptions. As a result, more is known certainly about the pronunciation of the Sanskrit that they described (the ritual and sacred texts) than about any other ancient language. In certain matters their detailed statements can be readily interpreted today, whereas the

nineteenth-century scholar W. D. Whitney, though he realized their
worth and importance, was led to a too hasty dismissal of some of
their reported observations.[12]

The place of phonetics was seen as the linking of grammar to utterance, and phonetic description was organized under three main headings, the processes of articulation, the segments (consonants and
vowels), and the synthesis of the segments in phonological structures.

The articulatory organs were divided into intrabuccal and extrabuccal, extrabuccal being the glottis, the lungs, and the nasal cavity.
These three are responsible for the distinctions of voice and voicelessness, aspiration and non-aspiration, and nasality and non-nasality,
giving in the phonological system of Sanskrit a five term system at
different articulatory positions, which may be exemplified by the bilabial series /b/, /p/, /bh/, /ph/, and /m/. Within the buccal cavity the
articulatory organs are described from the back to the front, ending
with the lips, and four degrees of stricture are distinguished: total
buccal obstruction (stops and nasal consonants), fricative constriction,
semivowel constriction, and absence of constriction, this last constituting
vocalic articulation. The mechanism of articulation is described in
terms of a stationary point of articulation (*sthāna*), for example the hard
palate, and a moving articulator (*karaṇa*), e.g. the tongue. This conception was extended to cover bilabial and glottal articulation, where it is
scarcely plausible to regard one of the parts involved as stationary and
the other as moving.

The correct diagnosis of the glottal activity in voicing is rightly
regarded as one of the phonetic triumphs of the ancient Indians. The
nearest approach to an accurate description in the west had been that
of Holder in the seventeenth century (p. 118, above), which went un-
heeded at the time. The Indian linguists distinguished voice from
voicelessness according as the glottis was closed or open in articulation,
noticed the tendency for otherwise voiceless consonants to be voiced in
intervocalic position (a common phonetic occurrence in a number of
languages), and, against the nineteenth-century incredulity of Max
Müller and Whitney, properly accounted for the production of voiced
h ([ɦ]).[13]

Junction features and certain prosodic features of stretches of speech
in connected utterance received careful attention. This is witnessed by
the now universal technical use of the Sanskrit term *sandhi*, joining
together, to denote the differences between disconnected words, morphemes, and the like, and the same elements combined into concaten-

ated sequences. Indeed, as some Indian linguists asserted the priority of the sentence over the word as a meaningful unit, some of the phonetic treatises denied the word an independent phonetic existence outside or apart from the text; the breath group was the basic unit of phonetic description and word isolates were primarily paedagogical devices. Sanskrit orthography represented connected discourse, rather than successions of isolated words, such as was the practice of Greek and Latin orthography and is largely European orthographic practice today; but with some texts parallel versions were in use, a normal *sandhi*-marking text and a text written in word isolate forms, a *pada* (word) text.

The phonetics of word and morpheme juncture features associated with initiality and finality in the breath group, vowel length and syllable quantity, tone, and tempo were all described in precise detail. Vedic Sanskrit had three distinctive pitches, high, low, and falling (*udātta, anudātta, svarita*); these had disappeared by the Christian era.[14] Thanks to the Indian phonetic treatises we can compare Sanskrit with Ancient Greek, joint preservers of what was probably the tonal system of unitary Indo-european.

In their descriptive work it is clear that the Indian phoneticians operated within an intuitive conception of phonemic principles. The treatises do not discuss a concept like the phoneme as a theoretical abstraction, though some aspects of the *sphoṭa* theory may be seen to approach certain modern interpretations of the phoneme. They show themselves, however, well aware of certain phonetic differences which, being environmentally determined should be noted in a description but not assigned to separate distinctive sound units, for example the [φ] and [x] allophones of /h/ before labials and velars respectively; and in describing the high and low tones Patañjali pointed out that their distinctiveness rested on their relative not their absolute pitch levels.[15]

The Sanskrit alphabet or syllabary has been shown to have been devised on segmental phonemic lines, the only redundant symbol being the one standing for the palatal nasal consonant [ɲ(a)], since [ɲ] only occurs as an allophone of /n/ in juxtaposition with a palatal consonant.[16] And here this very redundancy of symbols arose from an equally sound phonological analysis which governed the usual arrangement of the alphabet, since [ɲ] stood to the palatal plosives in precisely the same phonetic relation as did the other nasal consonants, /ŋ/, /ɳ/, /n/, and /m/, to their corresponding plosive series.[17]

Worthy as the phonetic works of the ancient Indians are now seen to have been, it is for their grammatical theory and the grammatical analysis of their own language, Sanskrit, that Indian linguistic scholarship is best known today, and among Indian grammarians the name of Pāṇini stands out above all. Though his date is uncertain, quite definitely his is the earliest grammatical treatise extant on any Indoeuropean language, and the earliest scientific work in any Indo-european language, and in Bloomfield's words 'one of the greatest monuments of human intelligence'.[18] However, while it brings almost to perfection its avowed intentions in the field of Sanskrit grammar with which it deals, it is not what would ordinarily be called a complete grammar of the Sanskrit language.

Pāṇini's grammar includes as its main component an exhaustive statement of the rules of word formation of the Sanskrit language. These rules are expressed in short statements, or aphorisms as they are often called, giving either definitions, or processes of word formation. They are referred to as *sūtras*, threads, a term also used of the ritual instructions in some of the earlier Vedic literature. There are also appendices giving a list of verbal roots, a list of similarly inflected words, and a list of the sounds of Sanskrit. The rules, like the rules of today's generative grammarians, have to be applied in a set order; and apart from the completeness with which Pāṇini covers every aspect of Sanskrit word formation, those who have studied his work, whether in India or later in Europe, have been most struck by the ingenuity with which he achieved the extreme economy of his statements. This quest for economy was evidently part of the context of early Indian grammatical composition; a commentator remarked that the saving of half the length of a short vowel in framing a grammatical rule meant as much to a grammarian as the birth of a son.[19] This demand for economy may have been inspired primarily by the needs of oral recitation and commitment to memory, but it clearly became a canon of scholarly merit in its own right. It does, however, make the task of the reader enormously complicated; the *Aṣṭādhyāyī* is a grammarian's grammar, not a learner's or a teacher's manual (in this respect it is quite unlike Dionysius Thrax's *Téchnē*). As Bloomfield observes, it is 'intelligible only with a commentary',[20] and it has been the subject of continuous comment and explication ever since it was composed. Patañjali's *Mahābhāṣya* ('Great commentary') is the major Indian commentary, and most subsequent Indian work has been comment on comment.

Though Pāṇini's composition is about as far removed as could be from one's conception of a teaching grammar, the teaching and presentation of Sanskrit today, as well as several important directions and features of descriptive linguistics can be traced back immediately to his genius.

Pāṇini's grammar is set in a context wherein the rest of the grammatical description of the language and its underlying theory are implicit. The phonetic description of the language is equally taken for granted; the set of sound units represented in the Sanskrit alphabet, and listed in the *Aṣṭādhyāyī* is given without further comment, though the sounds are ordered in sequences that are both phonetically and morphologically relevant to his grammatical rules. Actual phonetic statements in Pāṇini are very few.

Indian linguists made use of four classes of words: nouns and verbs (inflected), and prepositions and particles (uninflected). The basic Indian theory of sentence structure required that for words to constitute a sentence they must fulfil three requirements: they must have mutual expectancy as members of appropriate grammatical classes in proper constructions, or they would be no more than a lexical list devoid of further significance; they must be semantically appropriate to one another, or we would have to accept apparently grammatical non-sentences like *he wets it with fire*, such as have, in fact, troubled linguists in the east and the west throughout the history of linguistic thought and still tease us today; and they must occur in temporal contiguity, or they could not be carried in the memory or understood as a single utterance at all. The Sanskrit terms for these three requirements were *ākāṅkṣā, yogyatā*, and *saṃnidhi*; they may be compared to the somewhat corresponding Firthian relationships of colligability and collocability of the elements and temporal sequence of their actual exponents.[21]

In addition to the phonological term *sandhi*, Indian grammatical names for the different types of word compounding, a subject to which they devoted considerable attention, have passed into general currency. One may instance the terms *tatpurusha* (*tatpuruṣa*), attributive compound (e.g. *doorknob, blackberry*), and *bahuvrihi* (*bahuvrīhi*), exocentric compound (e.g. *turnkey, humpback*).[22]

The verb, inflected for person, number, and tense, was taken as the core of the sentence (in Sanskrit, as in Latin and Greek, the verb could stand alone as a complete sentence). Other words stood in specific relations to the verb, and of these the most important were the nouns in their different case inflexions. Nouns standing in different relations to the verb were designated by the term *kāraka*; the *kārakas* were classified by the different types of relation between the action or process referred to by the verb and the denotata of the nouns. 'Agent' and 'object' were two of them; but the *kārakas* are not to be equated with cases, as normally understood; the Sanskrit genitive in its most general use is not considered to express a *kāraka*, because it relates nouns to nouns as its main grammatical function, not nouns to verbs. The exponents of *kārakas* included the case endings of case inflected words, but the same *kāraka* could be expressed in more than one formal structure.[23]

The rules of Sanskrit grammatical word formation, which form the bulk of Pāṇini's *Aṣṭādhyāyī*, are set in the general grammatical context sketched above. They are difficult to describe and exemplify without reference to the Sanskrit language. Bloomfield in an extended review gives a good summary of Pāṇini's method and of how a Pāṇinian description of the relevant parts of English grammar would appear and what it would accomplish.[24]

The generation of the word form *ábhavat*, he, she, it was, from the root *bhū-*, to be, passes through the following stages (the numbers refer to some of the relevant *sūtras*):[25]

bhū-a	3.1.2,	3.1.68.			
bhū-a-t	1.4.99,	3.1.2,	3.2.111,	3.4.78,	3.4.100.
á-bhū-a-t	6.4.71,	6.1.158.			
á-bho-a-t	7.3.84.				
á-bhav-a-t	6.1.78.				
ábhavat.					

Only the final representation is the form of a real word as pronounced in isolation; those preceding it illustrate the ordered application of rules, covering, of course, the formation of large numbers of words other than this one. The whole descriptive procedure may be compared with the stages by which the transformational-generative grammarians, more than two thousand years later, arrive at an actual form through successive representations of elements combined with each other in accordance with ordered rules. Thus from the stem *dīsayd-*, the following stages are passed through in order:[26]

dīsayd-iv
dīsayz-iv
dīsays-iv
dīsaysiv.

Pāṇini's descriptions involve the isolate identification of roots and affixes, which directly inspired the morpheme concept of present-day grammatical analysis. The study of Hebrew and Arabic had led later mediaeval Europe to recognize the abstract root as a constant that underlies inflexional paradigms, but the typical European model of grammatical description continued to be the one handed down by Dionysius Thrax and Priscian, a thorough-going word-and-paradigm one. Such a model, indeed, with its very obvious paedagogical advantages, continues strongly in use in language teaching, especially the teaching of ancient languages.

Formal variations among functionally equivalent elements, such as are handled under the modern concept of allomorphs of single morphemes, were dealt with by Pāṇini morphophonemically. He set up abstract basic forms, called *sthānin* ('having a place', 'original'), which by the rules of morphophonological change and internal *sandhi* were converted into the actual morphs of the resultant words; the formal replacements were called *ādeśa* ('substitute'). General rules were given together with exceptions; in English the past tense formation of verbs with /-d/ would have been related to the environmentally determined variants such as /-t/ (*walked*) and /-id/ (*plodded*), with separate mention of individual irregularities like *run, ran*.[27] Bloomfield's *Menomini morphophonemics* has been regarded as Pāṇinian in method and inspiration.[28]

In the interests of the extreme economy of statement referred to earlier, Pāṇini's rules are set out in such a way that the repetition of a rule in relation to a subsequent rule in word formation is rendered unnecessary. Economy is further served by a number of special devices; the distinctive sound units listed by Pāṇini are arranged in a special order, bringing together those sounds jointly involved in the statement of certain rules. These sequences are further divided by the interposition of sound units used demarcatively, so that a succession of sounds can be abbreviated to the first sound and the marker following the last. Thus from the sequence *a i u* (*ṇ*), *a i u* can be indicated by *aṇ*, and from *a i u* (*ṇ*) *ṛ ḷ e o* (*ṅ*) *ai au* (*c*), *ac* can be used to mean 'all vowels' (*ṛ* and *ḷ* stand for vocalic *r* and *l*, respectively).[29] This type of abbreviation is extended to grammatical elements; *sup* refers to all nominal case endings and *tiṅ* to all verbal personal endings.

A rather famous example of Pāṇini's economy of verbiage is his final *sūtra* (8.4.68), which takes the form '*a a*', that is to say that *a* (which had been treated (e.g. in 6.1.101) as the qualitative equivalent of *ā*, so that the *sandhi* rule of vowel coalescence could be economically stated as i-i = $\bar{\imath}$, u-u = $\bar{u}$, a-a = $\bar{a}$) is in fact a closer, more central vowel sound.[30]

A descriptive device familiar to linguists today, zero representation of an element or category, is owed directly to Pāṇini. Apparently irregular forms may be made to appear more regular at the more abstract levels of representation and analysis by the assumption of a morpheme represented by a zero morph, i.e. with no overt exponent in the phonic material. Thus since most English noun plurals include an overt morph, usually a suffix, examples like *sheep* as a plural can be analysed as being /ʃiːp/-Ø.

Pāṇini sets up as the minimal grammatical structure of a noun form the sequence root + stem suffix + inflexional suffix. In most noun forms each of these elements can be linked to actual phonetic segments as their exponents, but not in all nouns. Thus in *-bhājam*, sharing (accusative singular), *-bhāj-* represents the root, *bhaj-*, and *-am* the final, inflexional suffix. Pāṇini's rules for such nouns specify a descriptively earlier segment *v* representing the stem-forming suffix (3.2.62), and a later rule deprives this *v* of overt representation, that is to say represents it by zero (6.1.67).

Many different uses have been made of the zero concept in modern linguistics; some have protested against its excessive exploitation; but there are forms in many languages that are most economically analysed by means of a zero element. All of these uses derive from Pāṇini's first known application of this device; the most Pāṇinian example outside Sanskrit is de Saussure's analysis of Greek nominative case forms like *phlóx* (/pʰlóks/), flame, in which /pʰlóg-/ represents the root, /-s/ the nominative singular suffix, and the stem formative (as in *híppos* (/hípp-o-s/), horse) is represented by a zero suffix (/phlóg-Ø-s/).[31]

The impact of the work of Pāṇini and the other Indian linguists on Sanskrit studies in Europe from 1800 was deep and far-reaching. Two of the earliest Sanskrit grammars published in English, W. Carey's *Grammar of the Sungskrit language* (Serampore, 1806) and C. Wilkins's *Grammar of the Sanskrita language* (London, 1808) pay tribute to the work of their Indian predecessors, which they had studied with the aid of living Sanskrit pundits in India.[32]

Concentration on the historical aspects of linguistic studies during the nineteenth century, itself the immediate result of the discovery by Europeans of the Sanskrit language and its relationships with the classical and modern languages of Europe, had the effect of delaying the full appreciation of Indian grammatical concepts and methods in descriptive work, but in phonetics the Indian insights were influential in the stimulation and development of both theory and practice throughout the century.

The study of Sanskrit was the prime incitement to early nineteenth-century comparative and historical work. But it came at a propitious time and to a Europe prepared for it. From Dante onward, through and after the Renaissance, various disconnected attempts had been made at linguistic history and at historically orientated comparisons between languages; but the bulk of linguistic scholarship, as has been seen in earlier chapters, had been directed at the description and analysis of languages, synchronic theory, paedagogy and other applications, and approaches to what can loosely be called the 'philosophy of language', general theories of the place and the working of language in human affairs.

During the eighteenth century, however, speculation was turning towards historical questions, though in a rather general way. The origin of language, while for ever beyond the reach of any conceivable linguistic science, has always fascinated linguistically minded people and in different forms has been a focus of attention throughout recorded history. Psammetichus of Egypt's attempt to discover the 'oldest', i.e. the original, language allegedly by recording an utterance (Phrygian *bekos*, bread) from a child carefully brought up in a speechless environment is a forerunner of other similar tales, told of other personages and other languages.[33] But several linguistic thinkers of the eighteenth century in different European countries asked and tried to answer the question, what lay between the beginnings of human language and its obviously elaborate present form, and how the seeds of language as it was known in historical times could have been sown in man's prehistory. Men further sought historical explanations of the observed forms of words in accordance with supposedly universal principles of linguistic development. While all this was far from the systematic historical study of specific and determined families of languages such as grew up in and dominated the next century, it was nourished by the increasing knowledge, albeit often partial, of newly discovered languages of the expanding world of European colonization, missions, and trade.

Attempts at seriously thought-out explanations of the origin and development of language in mankind, considered as a single species, united philosophers of the empiricist and rationalist persuasions characteristic of the eighteenth century and earlier with those working well within the counter-rationalist Romantic movement of its later years and the turn of the century. This is not surprising, since it is in language that men both communicate the collectively accumulated knowledge, argument, and principles of reasoning, such as were held in so high esteem by men of the rationalist Enlightenment, and, equally, give expression to the emotions and individual sentiments on which the Romantics laid such stress. *Vernunftmensch*, the man of reason, and *Gefühlsmensch*, the man of feeling, realize themselves through the resources of their language.

Half-way through the eighteenth century two French philosophers discussed the origin and early development of human speech. In 1746 E. B. de Condillac devoted the second part of his *Essai sur l'origine des connoissances humaines*[34] to language, and in 1755 Rousseau treated the same topic more briefly in part of his discourse on the origin of inequality among men, making favourable mention of Condillac's views.[35] A later work published posthumously in 1782 was his essay on the origin of languages.[36]

Condillac wrote within the rationalist-empiricist tradition, relying a good deal on Locke's theory of knowledge, whereas Rousseau looked forward to the Romantic movement that was to follow; indeed, in many respects he can be said to have been one of its heralds. Their conceptions of the genesis of language were very similar. Language originated in deictic and imitative gestures and natural cries, but since gestures were less efficient as communicative signals the phonic element in human language became dominant, as specific sound sequences were semantically associated with existents and phenomena and as the power of human thought increased. Condillac envisaged a mixed stage in which spoken verb forms were accompanied by gestures indicating time reference, these latter subsequently replaced by vocal symbols uttered after the verb itself and finally, in the stage reached by Latin, agglutinated to it.[37] Rousseau suggested an almost deliberate agreement to make this substitution from gesture to speech on the lines of the social contract.[38]

Both Condillac and Rousseau considered that abstract vocabulary and grammatical complexity developed from an earlier individual concrete vocabulary with very few grammatical distinctions or constraints; and both regarded reliance on tonal contrasts in the manner of Chinese as a survival of a primitive feature, and likewise the attention paid to the intonation of declamatory speech in classical antiquity,[39] and both considered poetry to have sprung from chanting as the earliest literary form of language. On this, however, their different philosophical attitudes revealed themselves. Condillac dispassionately compared Latin and French oratory, and refused to express a value judgment as between the stylistic merits of Latin with its grammatically free word order and French with its more analytic structure and more fixed word order.[40] Rousseau on the other hand rejoiced in the supposed vivacity and passion of the earlier stages of human language, when poetry had not been chilled into reasoning, and before writing, unable to symbolize the stress and pitch differences and the vocal inflexions of speech, had substituted 'exactitude for expression' and enervated the liveliness of language itself: 'All written languages have to change their character and lose vigour in gaining clarity'.[41] Rousseau, who could dream of the noble savage uncorrupted by property and civil government, could also write of 'languages favourable to freedom; these are sonorous, prosodic, harmonious languages, which can be heard and understood from afar. Our languages are designed for the buzzing of the drawing room'.[42]

The widespread interest during the second half of the century in resolving problems concerning the origin of language is instanced by the prize offered by the Prussian Academy in 1769 for an essay answering the questions whether man could have evolved, unaided, language as it was known then, and if so how he went about it. This enquiry was in part a reaction against hitherto unsatisfactory statements and against the scientifically hopeless assertion of Süssmilch in 1754 that the complexity and perfect ordering of languages could only be explained as the direct gift of God to mankind, a view also expressed by Rousseau on divine guidance in the evolution of language, hinted at by Plato, and found in a number of traditional mythological accounts in the Old Testament and elsewhere.[43]

Herder's solution to the questions put by the Academy won him the prize and was published in 1772 as his *Abhandlung über den Ursprung der Sprache*.[44] It was written in great haste and with great feeling (he had, in fact, set down a few years before some of his opinions on language in a number of essays[45]). Probably few other academic prize compositions contain so many exclamation marks or exhibit so impassioned a rhetoric.

Herder asserted the inseparability of language and thought; language is the tool, the content, and the form of human thinking.[46] The close connection between thought and language had been a commonplace of philosophy since antiquity, but earlier writers from Aristotle to the modistae had taken for granted the hierarchic dependence of language on prior thinking and abstraction. Herder's assumption of the common origin and parallel development of both together through successive stages of growth and maturity was rather new; and he stated that, since language and thinking were interdependent, the thought patterns and the popular literature of different peoples could only properly be understood and studied through their own languages.[47] Such opinions had been expressed before, but at the beginning of the European and especially of the German Romantic era, and with the forces of European nationalism about to become a dominant theme of nineteenth-century politics, the assertion of the individuality of a nation's speech and its intimate bonds with national thought, national literature, and national solidarity was readily appreciated and initiated a continuing trend of linguistic theory. Sapir may be right in attributing much of Humboldt's distinctive thought on language to Herder's inspiration, and if this is so both the adherents of Whorfian theories and the generative grammarians today can each trace links back to this formative philosopher of language.[48]

Herder answered the question on the priority of language or of thought, by saying that since each depended on the other for its existence the two had a common origin and mankind had advanced in each by equal stages, developing a faculty uniquely possessed by man as distinct from all the rest of the animal kingdom. The first step was the abstraction and recognition of a recurrent entity with its own relatively constant and distinctive characteristics from the 'whole ocean of experience',[49] and at the same time its designation by a vocal symbol. He assumed that hearing was the sense whose data were first isolated and named in this way, and the lamb was hailed as 'the bleeter' ('Ha! Du bist das Blöckende!'[50]). From the vocal symbolization of things by their auditory characteristics mankind moved outwards to the data provided by the other senses. Herder's arguments in support of the centrality of the auditory sense may endure little examination today as they stand, but the phonaesthetic component of so many vocabularies wherein visual and other features (littleness, spikiness, nearness, etc.) manifestly correlate with certain types of sound feature, lends some support to his hypothesis.[51] The first word stock was a 'simple vocabulary',[52] one largely confined to observable beings and events, and thereafter lexical diversity and grammatical differentiations grew with the accumulating treasure of men's thought.

This hypothetical reconstruction of the prehistory of speech, despite its obvious naiveties of expression, is as good as many other probings of events that lie beyond the reach of scientific observation. In particular it was a distinct advance on some earlier talk on the origin of language that had put the question in the form, how did language originate in man considered in all other respects as he was known at the time of asking and differing only by the lack of articulate speech.

Herder retained the traditional monogenetic theory of all languages, as of all cultures; and his theory suffered from the restricted time perspective allotted in the eighteenth century to man's existence on the earth, with a consequential attempt to see enduring characteristics of the early stages of language in alleged 'primitive languages' existing in the present. This carried with it such silly suggestions as that the verb enjoyed temporal priority of emergence among the word classes (in fact *word class* can have no meaning unless at least two classes are distinguished in a language); and Herder buttressed his assertion with the equally fallacious analogy with the child's use of language.[53]

It is less of a reproach to Herder, writing when he did, that he resorted to such arguments than to modern writers in whose speculations into the prehistory of speech these same outworn analogies still make their unmerited appearance.

Herder lay between the rationalist and the Romantic movements and came under the influence of both; this gives great significance to his writings on history as well as those on language.[54] His own theory of the origin of language, though passionately expressed, was not out of key with rationalist thinking. Interestingly, by the time the news reached him that he had won the prize for his essay, he had moved further towards the Romantics and was anything but happy with what he had written.[55]

A prominent representative of the universal philosophical theory of grammar in England during the eighteenth century was James Harris, whose *Hermes or a philosophical enquiry concerning language and universal grammar* was published in 1751.[56] Harris's thought can be associated with the so-called Cambridge Platonists; while continental expositions of universal rationalist grammar based themselves in the main on Descartes. Harris, who was an Aristotelian scholar and very well read in ancient philosophy and literature, looked to Aristotle for the philosophical foundations of grammar. Like all universalists Harris had to distinguish between the individual structural differences of particular languages and 'those principles that are essential to them all'.[57] In his theory of word meaning he followed Aristotle closely; words are related to what they designate by convention and language is 'a system of articulate voices significant by compact'.[58] Sentence and word as universals are defined in Aristotelian terms as, respectively, a 'compound quantity of sound significant, of which certain parts are themselves also significant', and a 'sound significant, of which no part is itself significant'.[59]

Harris's system of grammar requires two 'principals', nouns (including pronouns) or 'substantives', 'significant of substances', and verbs or 'attributives', 'significant of attributes'.[60] Verbs include what are formally distinguishable as verbs proper, participles, and adjectives; this is very much in agreement with Plato and Aristotle on the *rhēma* (pp. 26–7, above). Adverbs are a special type of attributives, being attributives of attributives, or second order attributives. Apart from the 'principals', languages distinguish two 'accessories', which lack independent meaning and may be compared to the Aristotelian *sýndesmoi* (except for his inclusion of personal pronouns among them), divided into 'definitives' (articles and some pronominal words), which construct with a single word, and conjunctions (conjunctions and prepositions), which construct with two or more words.[61] Unlike the Greek grammarians, but following the Latin practice, Harris recognized interjections as a separate component of languages, though not a part of speech in the same way as the others.[62]

While basing his theory of universal grammar on Aristotelian doctrine, Harris was, unlike Aristotle, well aware of and interested in the surface differences between various languages; but just because the same function, as he considered it, was served by case inflexions in Latin and by prepositional phrases in English (*Brūtī, of Brutus*), one must look more deeply for the identification of those universal categories of grammar and relations which alone can give significance to the purely formal grammars of particular languages.[63]

In his theory of meaning Harris regarded the 'principal' words, that had independent meaning, as 'primarily, essentially and immediately' the symbols of general ideas, and only secondarily and via these general ideas the symbols of particular ideas.[64] He defended the concept of innate ideas against the prevalent English empiricist attitude, and along with his insistence on universal grammar he considered that the capacity of mankind to frame universal or general ideas, of which words were the signs, was certainly God-given.[65] As a philosopher he paid most attention to language as the means of expressing logical propositions; but while he linked his theory of language with Aristotle and with philosophical universalism, in a number of ways he looked forward to developments characteristic of the thought of the later eighteenth century. Indeed, his use of the Aristotelian distinction between matter and form (*hýlē* (ὕλη) and *eîdos* (εἶδος)) with reference to the phonic substance and the semantic function of speech foreshadows the important doctrine of *innere Sprachform* set out in the work of W. von Humboldt early in the nineteenth century.[66]

In stressing the importance of universals in the use of language, Harris agreed with Condillac as well as with Herder, who praised his work,[67] in linking the faculty of speech with the faculty of abstraction and the recognition of recurrent phenomena and persisting entities resembling one another. Condillac cited Locke in this part of his treatise; Locke attributed generality to ideas, though his more rigidly empiricist successors, Berkeley and Hume, considered that generality could be properly predicted only in terms, i.e. of words, not ideas.[68] With Herder, Harris shared the recognition of the significance to be seen in the individual peculiarities of each language. Though he erected his linguistic theory on underlying universals, as a philosophical grammarian must, he laid more weight on the individuality of languages and their intimate connection with the history and life of the people who speak them than some previous philosophical grammarians had done, and in this he looked forward to the linguistic attitudes most characteristic of the Romantic movement.[69] In an eloquent passage he enlarged and illustrated his theme in his eulogy of the twin excellences of Greek thinkers and writers and of the Greek language uniquely fitted to give them expression.[70]

Harris's *Hermes* is somewhat better known than it might otherwise have been because it was the target for attack by Horne Tooke. Tooke was a man of wide interests and involvements; he wrote a number of political pamphlets, and played a leading part in an appeal for subscriptions in aid of relatives of American colonists killed by British troops at Lexington in 1775, for which in the illiberal manner of authorities engaged in warfare King George's justices fined him £200 and imprisoned him for a year (he attributed his later gout to the poor quality of the claret available in the King's Bench prison). As Tooke was a natural rebel and Harris occupied a position in what today would be called 'the establishment', Harris was an obvious opponent,[71] and it happened that Tooke's thinking about language was violently antagonistic to the tradition of philosophical grammar such as had been expounded by Harris.

It was not difficult to fault Harris for his obscurity of language in several places, and for apparent self-contradictions, as when, struggling with the semantics of some of his 'accessories' (a problem on which linguistic theory is still unsettled), Harris declared that conjunctions shared the attributes both of words having signification and of those having no signification of their own,[72] nor to criticize his erection of an alleged universal system of grammar on the basis of an inadequate factual knowledge of languages, as when he allowed a place for prepositions, but not for postpositions such as are found with comparable syntactic and semantic functions in Hungarian and Turkish (and in several other major languages not cited by Tooke).[73] Harris also opened his defences to Tooke's onslaught when he declared that a 'distant analogy' determined that the sun and moon are naturally assigned nouns of masculine and feminine genders respectively, in defiance or ignorance of the facts of the Germanic languages and of Russian.[74]

Tooke's ideas on language are set out in a number of dialogues in which he gives himself a part, somewhat loosely and inconsequentially put together in *Epea pteroenta or the diversions of Purley*,[75] first published in two volumes in 1786 and 1805. Tooke's style is often pungent and racy; the following passage from a footnote (typically attacking Harris and seeking to explain away his undoubted estimation) may be cited as characteristic of the author and his writing: 'For which [Harris's reputation] however I can easily account; not by supposing that its doctrine gave any more satisfaction to their minds who quoted it than to mine; but because, as judges shelter their knavery by precedents, so do scholars their ignorance by authority: and when they cannot reason, it is safer and less disgraceful to repeat that nonsense at second hand which they would be ashamed to give originally as their own.'[76]

Tooke's approach to grammar is partly in line with modern formal doctrines; gender for him is, as a grammatical category, primarily an exponent of syntactic constructions involving nominals in those languages wherein it appears.[77] His theory, however, in so far as he can be said to have formulated a theory, shows a total mixture of synchrony and diachrony. Language as we know it, he declared, developed from natural cries (a theory put out by others in this period), with which he identified interjections ('the dominion of speech is erected upon the downfall of interjections'[78]). For this reason he chided other grammarians, of whom Harris was one, though with reservations, for admitting them as a part of speech.

Tooke admitted only two essential parts of speech, the noun and the verb[79]; every other class of word is the result of 'abbreviation' or corruption, by which language is made to run more smoothly. He laid great weight on this concept of abbreviation, and gave a good deal of detailed etymology, some correct but much of it wildly incorrect, to try to show that conjunctions, adverbs, and prepositions were the result of abbreviated or mutilated noun and verb words. Adjectives and participles were nouns and verbs used adjectivally ('adjectived') by position and syntax.[80]

Like others in the eighteenth century and afterwards, Tooke regarded inflexional and derivational elements in words as fragments of earlier independent words agglutinated to the root word. Again, some of his identifications were correct, as with the English adjectival suffix *-ful* (*beautiful*, etc.), but others were extravagantly wrong, as when he derived Latin *ībō*, I shall go, from *ī-*, to go, plus *b-* (= Greek *boul-* (βουλ-), to wish) plus (*eg*)*o*, I, and *audiam*, I shall hear, from *audī*(*re*), to hear, plus *am*(*ō*), I love (i.e. I want to hear)![81]

The view, also found in Condillac (p. 150, above) that morphological variation in word forms arises from the agglutination of independent words is borne out by historical evidence in a number of formations in languages. We can trace the coalescence, no doubt after the word order became fixed, of *dōnāre habeō* to *donnerai*, I shall give, in French, and similar forms in other Romance languages; and the suffixed articles of the Scandinavian languages and of Rumanian are derived from earlier demonstrative pronouns occupying a position immediately after the nouns to which they referred (local late Latin *lupus ille* > Rumanian *lupul*, the wolf). A sort of half-way stage can be seen today in the much more tightly bound and positionally fixed pronouns and negative elements in French verbal expressions as compared with their freely mobile antecedents in Latin. This is partly recognized orthographically in the hyphenation of such forms when occurring postverbally (e.g. *montrez-le-nous*, show it to us!, cp. Italian *mandatecelo*, send it to us!). But it is naively simplistic to suppose that all morphology can be ascribed to this process, and still more so to attempt to identify the independent originals of all the bound morphemes of contemporary or attested languages.

Moreover, whatever the adequacy or inadequacy of Tooke's historical explanation of inflexions and derivations, and of the parts of speech other than nouns and verbs as originating in these, his arguments are irrelevant to the question, clearly understood by the sixteenth- and seventeenth-century empirical English grammarians, of their definition and classification in a synchronic description of a language. His failure to grasp the point of descriptive grammar weakens the force of some otherwise merited criticisms of Harris and of other writers on language. In dealing with the semantics of fairly restricted ranges of words such as prepositions, one must analyse their semantic system as an articulated whole. Wilkins saw this in his diagram of the spatial relations expressed by English prepositions; Tooke unjustifiably criticized him over this, on the ground that 'he overlooked the etymology of words ... in which their secret lay'.[82] That etymology is popularly confused with correct semantic analysis is no justification for this confusion in what purports to be scholarly investigation.

Harris's linguistic work was highly valued by another eighteenth century British linguist, James Burnett (Lord Monboddo), a prominent figure in the literary and scientific life of Edinburgh, who wrote a six-volume treatise *Of the origin and progress of language*,[83] which included extensive accounts of the classical languages and some modern European languages and a discourse on literary style. Like Harris, Monboddo did not wish to deny divine intervention in the creation of so wonderful and complex a faculty as language,[84] but he turned his attention more towards its historical development than to the assertion of linguistic universals. He saw the intimate connexion between human society and human speech, but only envisaged a unilateral dependence between them, in that society may have existed for many ages before the invention of language, but this invention depended on the prior existence of society. He was quite prepared to admit the polygenesis of language, and though 'primitive languages' were said to lack facilities for abstract expressions, Monboddo asserted that man must have formed ideas of universals before he invented the words to symbolize them.[85] Herder's conception of the parallel origin and development of speaking and thinking is much more plausible.

Monboddo was among an unfortunately large number of linguists who have thought that the origin of language could be partly brought to light by the study of certain existing languages, seeking evidence of primitivity and the continuance of early characteristics in the languages of culturally primitive and illiterate peoples. These arguments that 'primitive languages' contain little abstract vocabulary and an inadequate grammatical organization are also seen in Herder, who knew and approved of Monboddo's work and saw the first volume translated into German in 1784.[86] They are also found in later writers, with less and less justification as linguistic descriptions of remote languages grew in numbers and in quality.

Monboddo's evidence of linguistic underdevelopment in the existence of one word expressions for a thing and its possessor was singularly
unfortunate,[87] since he needed to look no further than Hungarian and
Finnish among European languages to find precisely the same formation (Hungarian *lábam*, my foot, *virágunk*, our flower; Finnish *käteni*,
my hand); and descriptive study of the languages of preliterates and
culturally primitive people in no way bears out Monboddo's allegation
that such languages are without the differentiation of word classes and
syntactic rules.[88] His linguistic limitations are seen on the one hand in
his dismissal of the language of the Chinese as 'exceedingly defective'
and his assumption that in consequence they could not have made
any progress in philosophy, and on the other in his statement that
Sanskrit was 'formed . . . upon principles of philosophy, like Wilkins's
artificial "real character"'.[89]

It is all too easy to find fault with eighteenth-century attempts at the
historical study of language. What is noteworthy is that thinkers in
different countries and with diverse backgrounds were drawn towards
the history of language on the eve of a century wherein the history of
languages, enlivened by a flash of light from the east, was to make
unprecedented advances.

FOR FURTHER CONSULTATION

W. S. ALLEN, *Phonetics in ancient India*, London, 1953.

H. ARENS, *Sprachwissenschaft: der Gang ihrer Entwicklung von der Antike
bis zur Gegenwart*, Freiburg/Munich, 1955, 88–132.

S. K. BELVALKAR, *Systems of Sanskrit grammar*, Poona, 1915.

T. BENFEY, *Geschichte der Sprachwissenschaft und orientalischen Philologie
in Deutschland*, Munich, 1869.

J. BROUGH, 'Theories of general linguistics in the Sanskrit grammarians',
TPS 1951, 27–46.

——, 'Some Indian theories of meaning', *TPS* 1953, 161–76.

H. E. BUISKOOL, *The Tripādī*, Leiden, 1939.

P. C. CHAKRAVARTI, *The philosophy of Sanskrit grammar*, Calcutta, 1930.

——, *The linguistic speculations of the Hindus*, Calcutta, 1933.

E. B. DE CONDILLAC, *Essai sur l'origine des connoissances humaines* (*Oeuvres
de Condillac*, Paris, 1798, volume I).

B. FADDEGON, *Studies on Pāṇini's grammar*, Amsterdam, 1936.

O. FUNKE, *Zur Sprachphilosophie des achtzehnten Jahrhunderts: James
Harris's 'Hermes'* (*Studien zur Geschichte der Sprachphilosophie*, Berne,
1927, 5–48).

O. FUNKE, *Englische Sprachphilosophie im späteren 18 Jahrhundert*, Berne, 1934.

E. HEINTEL, *Johann Gottfried Herder: sprachphilosophische Schriften*, Hamburg, 1964.

J. G. HERDER, *Abhandlung über den Ursprung der Sprache* (*Herder's sämmtliche Werke* (ed. B. SUPHAN), Berlin, 1891, volume 5, 1–156).

K. K. RAJA, *Indian theories of meaning*, Madras, 1963.

L. RENOU (tr.), *La grammaire de Pāṇini*, Paris, 1948–54.

R. ROCHER, '"Agent" et "objet" chez Pāṇini', *JAOS* 84 (1964), 44–54.

J. J. ROUSSEAU, *Essai sur l'origine des langues* (*Oeuvres de J. J. Rousseau*, Paris, 1822, volume 13, 163–257).

E. SAPIR, 'Herder's "Ursprung der Sprache"', *Modern Philology* 5 (1907–8), 109–42.

J. F. STAAL, 'A method of linguistic description: the order of consonants according to Pāṇini', *Language* 38 (1962), 1–10.

——, 'Context-sensitive rules in Pāṇini', *Foundations of language* 1 (1965), 65–72.

P. THIEME, 'Pāṇini and the pronunciation of Sanskrit', E. PULGRAM (ed.), *Studies presented to Joshua Whatmough*, The Hague, 1957, 263–70.

NOTES

1. Quoted, *inter alia*, in J. E. SANDYS, *History of classical scholarship* (third edition), Cambridge, 1921, volume 2, 438–9; C. F. HOCKETT, 'Sound change', *Language* 41 (1965), 185–204.
2. ARENS, 1955, 58; BENFEY, 1869, 336–8; L. KUKENHEIM, *Esquisse historique de la linguistique française*, Leiden, 1962, 31.
3. BENFEY, 1869, 380.
4. ALLEN, 1953, 6.
5. RAJA, 1963, 51.
6. BROUGH, 1953, 167–8.
7. B. MALINOWSKI, *Coral gardens and their magic*, London, 1935, volume 2, 11.
8. CHAKRAVARTI, 1930, 84–125, 1933, 42–7; BROUGH, 1951; M. A. K. HALLIDAY, 'Categories of the theory of grammar', *Word* 17 (1961), 244; L. HJELMSLEV, *Prolegomena to a theory of language* (tr. F. J. WHITFIELD), Baltimore, 1953, 73–6.
9. ALLEN, 1953, 7.
10. R. JAKOBSON, *Selected writings I: phonological studies*, The Hague, 1962, 438 and *passim*.
11. ALLEN, 1953, 5.
12. ibid., 3–7, 90.
13. ibid., 35.
14. T. BURROW, *The Sanskrit language*, London, 1955, 114.

15. ALLEN, 1953, 50, 89.
16. M. B. EMENEAU, 'The nasal phonemes of Sanskrit', *Language*, 22 (1946), 86–93.
17. Details in ALLEN, 1953. The development of /ɲ/ as a phoneme in some Middle Indian dialects may have been a contributory factor (EMENEAU, op. cit., 90–2).
18. L. BLOOMFIELD, *Language*, London, 1935, 11; P. THIEME, *Pāṇini and the Vedas*, Allahabad, 1935, ix.
19. B. SHEFTS, Grammatical method in *Pāṇini*, New Haven, 1961, ix.
20. *Language* 5 (1929), 270.
21. BROUGH, 1953, 162–3; J. R. FIRTH, 'Synopsis of linguistic theory', *Studies in linguistic analysis* (Special volume of the Philological Society, Oxford, 1957), 17; HALLIDAY, 'Categories', 254–5; see further B. K. MATILAL, 'Indian theorists on the nature of the sentence', *Foundations of language* 2 (1966), 377–93; cp. p. 82, above.
22. CHAKRAVARTI, 1930, chapter 8; BLOOMFIELD, *Language*, 235. The Sanskrit terms themselves exemplify the categories that they refer to: *tatpuruṣa*, his-servant; *bahuvrīhi*, (possessing) much-rice.
23. ROCHER, 1964.
24. *Language* 5 (1929), 267–76.
25. BUISKOOL, 1939, 12–13.
26. N. CHOMSKY, *Current issues in linguistic theory*, The Hague, 1964, 74; cp. STAAL, 1965.
27. cp. BLOOMFIELD, *Language* 5 (1929), 272–4.
28. *TCLP* 8 (1939), 105–15; ALLEN, 'Zero and Pāṇini', *Indian linguistics* 16 (1955), 106–13 (112).
29. The sounds used as demarcative symbols are bracketed.
30. ALLEN, 1953, 58, suggests an appropriate translation: 'a = [ə]'.
31. ALLEN, 'Zero and Pāṇini'; F. DE SAUSSURE, *Cours de linguistique générale* (fourth edition), Paris, 1949, 255–6; H. A. GLEASON, *Introduction to descriptive linguistics*, revised edition, New York, 1961, 76; W. HAAS, 'Zero in linguistic analysis', *Studies in linguistic analysis*, 33–53.
32. BENFEY, 1869, 383, called Wilkins 'the father of European Sanskrit studies'.
33. HERODOTUS 2.2.
34. CONDILLAC, 1798.
35. F. C. GREEN (ed.), *Discours sur l'origine et les fondements de l'inégalité parmis les hommes*, Cambridge, 1941 (reference to Condillac, pages 41–2).
36. ROUSSEAU, 1822.
37. CONDILLAC, 1798, 368–9.
38. *Discours*, 45.

39. CONDILLAC, 1798, 276–7, 278–301.

40. ibid., 299–301, 413–15.

41. ROUSSEAU, 1822, chapters 5 and 7.

42. ibid., 255: 'langues favorables à la liberté; ce sont les langues sonores, prosodiques, harmonieuses, dont on distingue le discours de fort loin. Les nôtres sont faites pour le bourdonnement des divans'.

43. J. P. SÜSSMILCH, *Versuch eines Beweises dass die erste Sprache ihren Ursprung nicht vom Menschen sondern allein vom Schöpfer erhalten habe*, Berlin, 1766; ROUSSEAU, *Discours*, 48–9; PLATO, *Cratylus* 397 C, 425 D; ALLEN, 'Ancient ideas on the origin and development of language', *TPS* 1948, 35–60.

44. HERDER, 1891.

45. *Herder's sämmtliche Werke*, ed. B. SUPHAN, Berlin, 1877, volume 2.

46. *Werke* 2, 24–6.

47. ibid., 26–8.

48. SAPIR, 1907–8, 141; CHOMSKY, *Current issues*, 17–21, *Aspects of the theory of syntax*, Cambridge, Mass., 1965, 4, 8–9, 51; pp. 208, 228, below.

49. HERDER, 1891, 34–5.

50. ibid., 36.

51. ibid., 64–7; O. JESPERSEN, *Language*, London, 1922, chapter 20; FIRTH, *Speech*, London, 1930, chapter 6.

52. HERDER, 1891, 82–9.

53. ibid., 52–4, 134.

54. F. MCEACHRAN, *The life and philosophy of Johann Gottfried Herder*, Oxford, 1939, 32 and *passim*; R. G. COLLINGWOOD, *The idea of history*, Oxford, 1946, 86–93.

55. SAPIR, 1907–8, 137–8.

56. Pagination from the third edition, London, 1771.

57. HARRIS, op. cit., 7, 11.

58. ibid., 314–15, 328–9; ARISTOTLE, *De interpretatione*, 2, 4 (p. 19, above).

59. HARRIS, op. cit., 19–20.

60. ibid., 23–6, 192–3, 291–2.

61. ibid., 30–31.

62. ibid., 289–90.

63. ibid., 25–6.

64. ibid., 347–9.

65. ibid., 350–402.

66. ibid., 315; p. 175, below.

67. *Werke* 15, Berlin, 1888, 181–2.

68. CONDILLAC, 1798, 395–6; J. LOCKE, *An essay concerning human understanding*, London, 1690, 2.11.9, 4.7.9.

222223434444

444

69. HARRIS, op. cit., 409–11; FUNKE, 1934, 8–18.
70. HARRIS, op. cit., 419–24.
71. J. HORNE TOOKE, *Epea pteroenta or the diversions of Purley*, London, 1857, 37.
72. HARRIS, op. cit., 259; TOOKE, op. cit., 61.
73. TOOKE, op. cit., 154–5.
74. HARRIS, op. cit., 45; TOOKE, op. cit., 27.
75. ἔπεα πτερόεντα, 'winged words', a stock phrase in Homer.
76. TOOKE, op. cit., 62.
77. ibid., 28.
78. ibid., 32.
79. ibid., 24.
80. ibid., 657, cp. 626–7.
81. ibid., 629.
82. ibid., 249–50; J. WILKINS, *Essay towards a real character and a philosophical language*, London, 1668, 311.
83. Edinburgh, 1773–92 (reference to HARRIS, volume 1, 8).
84. ibid., volume 1, 191–2.
85. ibid., volume 1, 196–7, 302, 395–400.
86. R. HAYM, *Herder*, Berlin, 1880–5, volume 2, 224.
87. MONBODDO, op. cit., volume 1, 364–5.
88. ibid., volume 1, 370.
89. ibid., volume 2, 432–3, 481.

Seven

Comparative and historical linguistics in the nineteenth century

It is a commonplace in linguistics to say that the nineteenth century was the era of the comparative and historical study of languages, more especially of the Indo-european languages. This is broadly justified, but it does not mean either that no historical research based on the comparison of languages was undertaken before that time or that all other aspects of linguistics were neglected during the nineteenth century. It is, however, the case that this century saw the development of modern conceptions, theoretical and methodological, of comparative and historical linguistics, and the greatest concentration of scholarly effort and scholarly ability in linguistics was devoted to this aspect of the subject rather than to others. As late as 1922, O. Jespersen, who did as much as many to foster synchronic, descriptive, linguistics, could write in the still prevailing nineteenth-century climate of opinion that linguistics was mainly a historical study;[1] and some of the most stimulating ideas on language structure suggested at the start of the century were applied first to a primarily historical view of language.

One can rightly speak of pre-nineteenth-century historical work on languages as sporadic, not because it necessarily lacked insight or an appreciation of what was involved, but because people's suggestions and researches remained largely in isolation, and since they were not taken up and developed by a continuous succession of scholars, each new thinker had little to build on or to react to. This was not so after 1800, when one is brought face to face with a remarkable continuity of scholarship focused on a specialized field of theory and practice, in which generations of men, mostly Germans or scholars from other countries trained in Germany, built up their subject on the basis of what had been done by their predecessors or earlier contemporaries. They might start from where those before them had left off, or they might react against what they had considered errors of fact or misdirections of theory; but the sense of continuity of achievement, leading to a culmination, though not, of course, a stopping point, towards the end of the century, must be regarded both as a tribute to the scholarship of the time and as an inspiration to those looking back today on this remarkable century of successful endeavour.

Work on the historical relations of particular groups of languages by European writers may be said to have begun with Dante (1265–1321), though the relationship of Icelandic and English by virtue of resemblances in word forms had been asserted in the twelfth century by the brilliant 'First Grammarian' (p. 72, above). Dante's *De vulgari eloquentia* has already been mentioned in connection with the post-mediaeval rise in status of the European vernacular languages (pp. 99–100, above); this same work gives an account of the genesis of dialect differences and thence of different languages from a single source language as the result of the passage of time and the geographical dispersion of speakers.[2] Dante recognized three properly European language families: Germanic in the north, Latin in the south, and Greek occupying part of Europe and adjacent Asia.[3] He divided the contemporary Latin area into three distinct vernacular languages all descended from the Latin preserved by the grammarians; this common descent was shown by the considerable numbers of words that each shared with the others and which could be referred to a single Latin word.

As diagnostic marks of his language divisions Dante used a method seen again in J. J. Scaliger (p. 167, below) and enshrined as a labelling device in the much later binary division of Indo-european into the *centum* and *satem* groups. He chose a single word meaning and noted its expression in different languages; thus the Germanic languages reply in the affirmative with 'iò' (*ja*, etc.), and the three Latin-derived languages use 'sì' (Latin *sic*) in Italy, 'oc' (Latin *hoc*) in southern France, and 'oïl' (Latin *hoc ille*) in northern France (*hoc ille*, he (does) this, had become generalized as the affirmative reply to a question in this area[4]). From this division spring the names of the main linguistic regions of France, *Langue d'oc* (Provençal) in the south and *Langue d'oïl* in the north.

Within these language areas Dante was keenly aware of dialectal differences, and in subsequent chapters he gives a most detailed and well exemplified survey of the Italian dialects, together with aesthetic judgments pronounced on them, in which none is rated perfect but the Tuscan of his day is declared one of the worst.[5]

All this detailed classification is set within the conception of linguistic differentiation in the world having arisen in the way described in the story of the Tower of Babel (Genesis 11), Hebrew being the first language spoken on earth before the building of the Tower, the language spoken by Adam as the gift of God.[6]

The monogenesis of all languages and the ascription of the status of the original or oldest language to Hebrew was a generally held idea during the first centuries of the Christian era, when science had to be reconciled with the literally interpreted creation story of Genesis. It may be compared with the early efforts of geologists and zoologists to fit their observations into the apparent chronology and sequence of events given in the Old Testament.[7] The monogenesis of all languages in Hebrew continued to be accepted for several centuries and, perhaps more important theoretically, when it was challenged, it was challenged by the submission of a rival language as the surviving original or 'oldest language'. The fact that Latin, the parent of the Romance languages, also survived as a written language in use during the period before the Renaissance, and as the spoken language of Roman Catholic church services and as a *lingua franca* for educated persons, may have made the conception of a more general surviving linguistic ancestor more plausible. Notorious in this sort of challenge was Goropius Becanus, who in a marvellous series of etymologies argued that the 'first' language, 'Cimmerian', survived in Dutch-Flemish;[8] but he was not the only one.

Alternative models of the historical relations of languages were not lacking during the period from Dante to Sir William Jones (early studies in the history of the Romance languages by Renaissance scholars have been noticed above, pp. 100–1); it was just that they were not taken up and developed by their contemporaries. J. J. Scaliger (1540–1609), son of J. C. Scaliger (p. 110, above), a scholar of wide and varied learning, dispensed with two fallacious dogmas that distorted the historical dimension of language study, the supposed linear historical relation between Greek and Latin, whereby Latin was thought to be directly descended from a dialect of Greek with some alien admixtures (p. 49, above), and the alleged origin of all languages in Hebrew. Scaliger recognized eleven language families, four major and seven minor ones, covering the continent of Europe, within which the member languages were genetically related but between which no relationship could be established. These families agree broadly with modern groupings in so far as their member languages are concerned, but comprise what are now recognized as subfamilies of separate larger families, among them Indo-european and Finno-ugrian.

The families which Scaliger conceived as the products of earlier single languages, on the model of Latin and the Romance languages, he designated *Muttersprachen* or *Matrices linguae* (mother tongues). The four major families in his eleven correspond to the present-day Romance, Greek, Germanic, and Slavic groups within Indo-european. Working on the basis of lexical similarities between members of a family, he named each family by reference to the words for 'God', which showed obvious likenesses in form within each but not with the words in the other three. Thus he wrote of *Deus* languages, *Theós* languages, *Godt* languages, and *Boge* languages, respectively. In view of his insight and its results one must regret that he did not look further into word forms exhibiting rather obvious similarities across the four families, before denying any relationship between them either lexical or grammatical.[9]

It is typical of the period that Scaliger's groupings and his justification of them were not properly examined or made the basis of further work by his contemporaries. But towards the end of the seventeenth century a more developed model of historical relationship between languages was put forward by two Swedish scholars. A. Stiernhielm (who continued to regard Hebrew as the source of all languages), in his edition of the Gothic Bible, set side by side the inflexions of Latin *habēre* and Gothic *haban* (to have), and despite the non-cognation of the roots, of which he was unaware, he could argue from the personal endings that the two languages were closely related descendants of a single ancestor.[10] In a public lecture, A. Jäger spoke of an ancient language spreading, as the result of migrations, over Europe and part of Asia and producing thereby 'daughter' languages which in turn produced the languages known today as Persian, Greek, the Romance languages, the Slavic languages, Celtic, Gothic and the Germanic languages, while no trace of the original mother tongue survived.[11]

Nearly a century after Scaliger, Leibniz (1646–1716) turned his attention to historical linguistics in the course of his better known philosophical speculations and discussions of synchronic linguistic questions (p. 113, above). Leibniz saw no reason to discount a monogenetic theory of the world's languages, but he did not seek their origin in any actually living or attested language, and he firmly placed Hebrew within the Arabic family. Leibniz went to the opposite extreme from Scaliger; like Scaliger's, his smaller groups correspond with those made today, and Leibniz was one of the first to posit historical relations between Finnish and Hungarian, but he went further and on the basis of alleged common word 'roots' he set up two major divisions of the original language, Japhetic or Kelto-Scythian (a term used also by others) and Aramaic, covering respectively the languages of the north, including all Europe, and the languages of the south; thus he could link his system of relations between languages with the Biblical story of the sons of Noah (Genesis 10).[12]

While Leibniz seems to have been guided by inspired and insightful guesses rather than by systematic research, writing rather loosely about speech 'mixtures' to explain relationship between languages, he laid clear a number of the methodological principles by which historical linguistic research is fruitfully undertaken. He pointed to the evidence in place-names and river names of the earlier distribution of languages over areas from which they had later receded either through the expulsion of the speakers or the replacement of the language after the arrival of newcomers; Leibniz refers to the Basque language, now confined to a corner of the Franco-Spanish border country in the western Pyrenees, whose extension over a larger area in the Iberian peninsula is attested in this way.[13]

In view of the importance of etymological study in historical linguistics, Leibniz pressed for the preparation of grammars and dictionaries of the languages of the world, linguistic atlases, and a universal roman-based alphabet into which the non-roman scripts of languages could be transliterated. In particular he tried to encourage the rulers of Russia to begin surveying the many non-European languages of their territory and the collection of word lists and standard texts from them.[14]

The systematic gathering of material that was going to serve in the comparative study of languages had been going on as a notable feature of the centuries after the Renaissance when the European world was expanding so rapidly. Word lists and language surveys, interlingual dictionaries, and texts, usually those forming part of Christian worship and in particular the Lord's Prayer, were laboriously prepared and published, more especially in the eighteenth century. Two such surveys went under the title *Mithridates*, in deference to the polyglot monarch of ancient Pontus (p. 47, above), the first by the Swiss C. Gesner in 1555, the second on the eve of the new era of historical studies in 1806 and 1817 by J. C. Adelung.[15]

Adelung's exposition stands typically on the borders between the older unsystematized periods of speculation and collection and the later epoch of the organization of genetically related families. His groupings were those of geographical propinquity, which he invested with historical significance, thus associating Greek and Latin in one closely united family. However, writing when he did, he included Sanskrit among the languages of India, and like Jones before him, pointed to the unmistakable evidence in Sanskrit of its historical connection with the major languages of Europe.[16]

Catherine II's linguistic interests in her Russian dominions resulted in the publication in 1786–9 of comparative word lists from two hundred languages; these were compiled by the German P. S. Pallas, who saw his work in a wider context, since he entitled it *The comparative vocabularies of the languages of the whole world*.[17] Pallas's work was reviewed by C. J. Kraus in 1787, in an essay covering the important fields in which comparative linguistics must look for its advances: phonetics, semantics, grammatical structure, and the geographical location and distribution of languages.[18] By virtue both of its date and of its very real merits, this essay can still be read as an introduction to the study of comparative and historical linguistics.

Much of the gathering of diverse language material that took place in the eighteenth century must appear today rather haphazard and unformed by any comprehensive or directing theory, just as the rather general theories on the origin and development of language put out in the same period, which were noticed in the preceding chapter, seem to be largely empty speculation in the absence of adequate data from actual languages. But both these separate trends take their place in the stream of history, contingently but fortunately occurring in the years just prior to the seminal discovery of the relations between Sanskrit and the major languages of Europe, which in the favourable academic circumstances of the early nineteenth century was the stimulus to the integration of theory and data in an era of continuous progress.

In large part, linguistics in this century was concentrated on the historical study of the Indo-european languages wherein most of the advances and refinements in method and theory took place. This period of linguistics was almost the preserve of German scholarship, and those working in it from other countries were either trained in Germany like the American W. D. Whitney or were German expatriates like Max Müller at Oxford. As was seen above, the European discovery of Sanskrit was the primary source of this development, and a number of the early scholars in historical linguistics were themselves Sanskritists, such as the brothers A. W. and F. Schlegel (1767–1845 and 1772–1829), F. Bopp (1791–1867), and A. F. Pott (1802–87).

In 1808 F. Schlegel published his treatise *On the language and the learning of the Indians*,[19] wherein he stressed the importance of studying the 'inner structures' of languages (i.e. their morphology) for the light that could be shed on their genetic relationships,[20] and it appears that the term *vergleichende Grammatik* ('comparative grammar', still a frequently used title for comparative and historical linguistics) was originated by Schlegel. It was indeed the comparison of the inflexional and derivational morphology of Sanskrit and the other Indo-european languages, especially Latin and Greek, on which the early comparatists concentrated. One may note the title of Bopp's publication of 1816, *On the conjugation system of Sanskrit, in comparison with that of Greek, Latin, Persian, and German*,[21] and more significantly the title of T. Benfey's later account of the first half of the nineteenth century's work, *The history of linguistics and Oriental philology in Germany*.[22] In the high tide of German nationalism, three years after the Prussian needle-gun had defeated the forces of Austria at Königgrätz and two years before the founding of the German Empire after the Franco-Prussian war, Benfey could write that the early workers in this field belonged among 'the brightest stars of the German intellectual heaven', and that the company of distinguished men who had contributed to the development of this branch of learning were almost exclusively the sons of the fatherland.[23]

Admitting the justice of this claim, one should none the less point out that two pioneering attacks on linguistic relationship through the comparative study of inflexions had been made outside Indo-european by non-German scholars at the end of the preceding century. In 1770 J. Sajnovics published his *Proof that the languages of the Hungarians and the Lapps are one and the same*, and in 1799 S. Gyármathi proved the historical kinship of Hungarian and Finnish.[24]

Four of the scholars best known in the linguistic science of the early nineteenth century are the Dane R. Rask (1787–1832) and the Germans J. Grimm (1785–1863), F. Bopp (1791–1867), and W. von Humboldt (1767–1835), and it is with Rask and Grimm that the comparative and historical study of the Indo-european family can be properly said to begin. The term *indogermanisch* (Indogermanic) appears first in 1823 and was used by Pott in 1833; in English *Indo-european* is cited from 1814.

It is often said, and justifiably said, that Rask, Grimm, and Bopp were the founders of scientific historical linguistics. Rask wrote the first systematic grammars of Old Norse and Old English[25]; and Grimm's *Deutsche Grammatik* (*Germanic* rather than *German grammar*)[26] is hailed as the start of Germanic linguistics. The now universal terms *strong* and *weak*, of inflexions (*stark* and *schwach*), *Ablaut* (vowel gradation), and *Umlaut* (vowel change ascribable to earlier environmental conditions) are all technical terms invented by Grimm; and though the existence of different sets of sound changes in the histories of individual languages had been asserted by A. Turgot in his article on etymology in the French *Encyclopaedia* in 1756,[27] it was Rask who first brought order into etymological relationships by setting out systematic comparisons of word forms, matching a sound in one language with a sound in another exemplified in numbers of different words. He wrote: 'If there is found between two languages agreement in the forms of indispensable words to such an extent that rules of letter changes can be discovered for passing from one to the other, then there is a basic relationship between these languages.'[28] The correspondences now known under the title of 'Grimm's law' were in fact first stated and illustrated by Rask in the work just quoted.

'Grimm's law' first appeared in the second edition of his *Deutsche Grammatik* (1822), after he had read Rask's work, in a long section on 'letters' (*von den Buchstaben*). With hindsight we see the importance in history of Grimm's formulation as the first of the sound laws that were to form the structure and support of Indo-european and of other language families. It remains the best known of all sets of sound correspondences within Indo-european, essentially embracing relations between consonant classes of three articulatory places and three types of release in the Germanic languages as compared with other Indo-european languages. These relations were set out by Grimm in Greek, Gothic, and Old High German; they needed later supplementation by Verner's law to account for the differential results of the place of the primitive word accent, and the traditional circularity with which the correspondences are set out, and Grimm's use of *Kreislauf* (rotation) to describe the successive changes from the pre-Germanic stage represented by Greek through Gothic to Old High German depended on the thoroughly unphonetic identification of aspirated plosives such as [pʰ], [tʰ], [kʰ], with the corresponding fricatives [f], [θ], [x] (or [h]), an identification surely only possible when the study of sound change was still undertaken as the study of letters. But though the terminology of 'letter changes' and some of its confusion persisted with Rask and Grimm, their work marks a very definite advance on the hitherto rather indiscriminate assumptions on the possibilities of substituting one sound (letter) for another in the history of languages. Detailed exemplifications from the word forms of specific languages, and the later systematic study of etymology and sound changes such as Pott set out in his *Etymological investigations in the field of the Indogermanic languages*,[29] now gave a solid factual basis for the generalized *a priori* assumptions of eighteenth-century thinkers on the origin and development of language, rather as a century later the descriptions of more and more languages as existing systems of communication were to constitute a necessary observational check and corrective to the speculations of the seventeenth- and eighteenth-century 'universal grammarians'.

One should, however, try to see the work of these early comparative and historical linguists in their contemporary context as well, not merely as they can be fitted into our own subsequent picture of the development of linguistics. The very term 'Grimm's law' is an anachronism; he did not make technical use of the word *law* to describe what he referred to as sound shift (*Lautverschiebung*); and in a much quoted passage he remarked: 'The sound shift is a general tendency; it is not followed in every case'.[30] Grimm and Bopp were very much the children of their own age, inspired by the historicism and nationalism characteristic of the Romantic era in which they lived and with which they were in sympathy. A. W. Schlegel was the German translator of Shakespeare, thereafter regarded as part of German literature ('*unser Shakespeare*') and considered in spirit very much in tune with the *Sturm und Drang* (storm and stress) and Romantic movements in German life and letters. Grimm worked with his brother Wilhelm in collecting the German folktales that formed the basis of 'Grimm's fairy tales', known and loved by children the world over. This work along with Jacob Grimm's Germanic language studies belong to the general upsurge of national pride in the German language that began in the early eighteenth century, when Leibniz proposed the compilation of a dictionary of all the varieties of German,[31] and saw such a remarkable flowering in German literature from then on.

Grimm applied the ideas of Herder (p. 152, above) on the close relationship between a nation and its language to the historical dimension of language, seeing, indeed, in the sound shift to which he gave his name an early assertion of independence on the part of the ancestors of the German peoples,[32] nationalistic interpretations of linguistic phenomena carried still further by W. Scherer two generations later.[33]

Linguistic conceptions of the eighteenth century formed much of the setting for early nineteenth-century work. Rask's *Investigation* was an essay awarded a prize by the Danish Academy of Science for research into the source from which the ancient Scandinavian language could most surely be derived,[34] though he refused to recognize this 'source' in any extant or attested actual language. Bopp saw as the main purpose of his *Conjugation system* the reconstruction of the original grammatical structure of the language whose gradual disintegration had produced the attested languages of the Indo-european family.[35] Linguistic change was conceived as the breakdown of an original integral language state,[36] and Sanskrit was considered at this time to be, not indeed the original language of the family, but the nearest to it in morphological structure. In a striking metaphor Meillet declared that in his quest for the original state of the Indo-european language Bopp was led to discover the principles of comparative grammar as Christopher Columbus discovered America in his search for a new route to India.[37] In his later *Comparative grammar* Bopp declared his aims to be a comparative description of the languages concerned, an investigation of the laws governing them, and the origin of their inflexional forms.[38]

Both the use of comparison as the clue to earlier history and the conception of change as degeneration from primitive integrity were common property of the scientific thought of the time.[39] In analysing the inflexional forms of languages of the Indo-european family Bopp kept alive two other eighteenth-century ideas. He tended to regard inflexions as the result of earlier affixation of formerly separate auxiliary words, a mode of etymologizing already favoured by Horne Tooke (p. 157, above). Thus he analysed the Gothic weak preterites like *sōkidēdun* (they searched) as containing an original verb 'to do', and Latin futures and imperfects in -*b*- (*amābō*, I shall love, *amābam*, I was loving, etc.) as derived from the root *bhū*-, to be (in *fuī*, I was, etc.). As was noticed earlier such processes of word formation do take place, and some of Bopp's etymologies are accepted; but his generalizing of the process to the extent of analysing Latin *amāris*, you are loved, from **amāsis*, as having an element -*s*- cognate with the reflexive pronoun *s(ē)*, and Greek sigmatic aorists and futures like *elūsa* and *lūsō*, I loosed, I shall loose, as containing part of the verb 'to be' (Greek *es*-, Sanskrit *as*-) is pressing *a priori* theory against what the facts warrant. Bopp also, in fact, assumed that formal exponents of root (attribute), copula (predication), and person (subject) would be found in inflected verbal forms as a general rule, citing a plausible Latin example *possum*, I am able, and some untenable examples such as *amāvī*, I loved, in which he identified the -*v*- with the root *bhū*-, to be.[40] While much of his etymology on these lines is impossible, his aim can be seen as that of giving formal expression to the logical analysis of verbs current among the Port Royal grammarians and some others in earlier centuries.[41]

Wilhelm von Humboldt was one of the profoundest thinkers on general linguistic questions in the nineteenth century, and one wonders whether, if his style had been less diffuse and his ideas more worked out and exemplified than they were, and his voluminous works were better known and more widely read, he would not be accorded a position nearer to that given to de Saussure as one of the founders of modern linguistic thought. He was one of the few early nineteenth-century linguists not concentrating predominantly on history. He did not, in fact, sharply distinguish the two aspects of linguistics, synchrony and diachrony, and he drew on his own knowledge and on what he read in Bopp and others to seek answers to the questions he raised of an essentially general linguistic kind.

Humboldt, brother of the geographer and ethnographer A. von Humboldt, played an important part in the public affairs of Prussia, was a widely travelled person, and had a knowledge of a number of languages, western and oriental, together with some acquaintance with a few American-Indian languages. He published a quantity of writings, on language and languages, of which the most important is *The variety of human language structure*, first published posthumously as a lengthy introduction to his description of the ancient Kawi language of Java.[42]

Humboldt's theory of language lays stress on the creative linguistic ability inherent in every speaker's brain or mind. A language is to be identified with the living capability by which speakers produce and understand utterances, not with the observed products of the acts of speaking and writing; in his words it is a creative ability (*energeia*, *Tätigkeit*, *Erzeugung*), not a mere product (*ergon*, *Werk*, *Erzeugtes*).[43] Still less should a language be identified with the dead products of the grammarian's analysis. The capacity for language is an essential part of the human mind; otherwise language could not have originated just environmentally; and by the nature of this capacity languages can be changed and adapted as circumstances require, and only so can the central fact (and mystery!) of language be explained: that speakers can make infinite use of the finite linguistic resources available to them at any time.[44] Therefore no matter how much one analyses and describes a language, something of its essential nature remains unsaid, a point that perhaps linguists of today who look to Humboldt for part of their theory should heed.[45]

Though the capacity for language is universal, Humboldt follows the lines of Herder's thought in asserting the individuality of each different language as a peculiar property of the nation or the group who speak it (here the nineteenth-century nationalist arguments based on linguistic identification are prominent). The articulatory basis of speaking is common to all men, but sound only serves as the passive material for the formal constitution or structure of the language (*innere Sprachform*).[46] Humboldt's *innere Sprachform* is the semantic and grammatical structure of a language, embodying elements, patterns and rules imposed on the raw material of speech. In part it is common to all men, being involved in man's intellectual equipment; but in part also the separate *Sprachform* of each language constitutes its formal identity and difference from all other languages (thus it may be likened in some degree to the *langue* of de Saussure's later *langue-parole* dichotomy). This organizing principle of each language governs its syllable structures, its grammar, and its lexicon, the distinction between the latter two being of paedagogical significance only.[47] The latest potentialities of each language's *innere Sprachform* are the field of its literary artists, and, more important, the language and thought of a people are inseparable. Humboldt carries further Herder's conception of the parallel development of thought and language: 'a people's speech is their spirit, and their spirit is their speech'.[48]

Every language is a product of its past, and some languages show a greater advance than others as instruments and models of thinking. Typically of the time, he declared Sanskrit to be the best developed language of any that were known.[49] Thinking and perception are only made definite and communicable through a language, thought and language being interdependent and inseparable; words are not individual labels or names, but at the same time they both denote something and put it in a distinct category of thought.[50] The words of every language are organized in a systematic whole, so much so that the utterance of a single word presupposes the whole of the language as a semantic and grammatical structure; only loans from foreign languages can constitute extrasystemic isolates.[51] Differences between languages, therefore, turn not merely on the different speech sounds used by them, but involve differences in the speakers' interpretation and understanding of the world they live in (*Weltansicht*).[52]

The influence of this mode of thinking about language was not felt immediately. It has been pointed out that while he cites his contemporaries freely they do not appear to have made great use of his ideas.[53] But a number of lines can be traced from him to later nineteenth- and twentieth-century work. H. Steinthal (his pupil) and W. Wundt drew on him in their development of linguistic psychology and national psychology (*Volkerpsychologie*), and the aesthetic and idealistic school developed his teaching on the individuality, creativity, and artistic potentiality of every language.[54] More recently there have appeared various 'neo-Humboldtian' trends in European linguistics, particularly associated with the work of L. Weisgerber on German, and the relevance of Humboldt's views to Whorfian theories in America needs no elaboration. A direct line has been traced in American linguistics from Humboldt through D. G. Brinton (who translated some of his publications), F. Boas, and E. Sapir to B. L. Whorf, with particular reference to work on the languages of native America.[55]

One may also see how Kantian theory was itself influential in Humboldt's thinking. Kant's theory of perception involved sensations produced by the external world being ordered by categories or 'intuitions' (*Anschauungen*) imposed by the mind, notably those of space, time and causality. This was a universal philosophical theory; Humboldt adapted it relativistically and linguistically by making the *innere Sprachform* of each language responsible for the ordering and categorizing of the data of experience, so that speakers of different languages live partly in different worlds and have different systems of thinking. One notes the use by Humboldt of the three verbal nouns *Anschauen*, *Denken*, and *Fühlen* (perception, thinking, and feeling) in connection with the operation of language.[56]

Possibly Humboldt's best known contribution to linguistic theory is his tripartite language typology, isolating, agglutinative, and flexional, according to the predominant structure of the word as a grammatical unit.[57] This, however, was common ground to a number of contemporaries. F. Schlegel divided languages into those making grammatical use of internal changes of word form and those employing serially ordered elements; commenting on this A. W. Schlegel set up the three classes of isolating, affixing, and inflecting languages, a system presented somewhat differently by Bopp.[58]

Ideas about the typological development of language had been put forward in the eighteenth century (pp. 150-9, above), and Humboldt conceived his scheme as historically relevant, although primarily a matter of synchronic classification. In his *Origin of grammatical forms and their influence on the development of thought* (1822) he traced the passage of languages from bare reference to objects, through the agglutination of auxiliary meaningful elements, to true inflexion as seen in Latin, Greek, and Sanskrit; but in *The variety of human language structure* (1836) the typology is one of description and grading. The two typological poles are Chinese and Sanskrit, the purest analytic or isolating language and the purest flexional language respectively, all others, including the agglutinative languages ('hybrids') being ranged between them.[59]

Humboldt recognized the value and the potentialities of any language structure, but his preference was for flexional languages, those languages whose grammatical word form variations involve either internal root changes or affixes bonded into the word by morphophonemic alternations of the constituent morphemes (to use later terminology) so that the formal unity of the word is reinforced. At the other typological extreme, his attitude to Chinese is peculiar; like so many others at the time (and later) he regarded Chinese as devoid of formal grammatical classes or distinctions, but just for that reason having its own particular excellence as a language. He envisaged the growth and development of inflexions in the formative stage of a language, followed by their gradual decline in favour of a more analytical type of structure such as is seen in English. Chinese, however, had preserved its original isolating structure through its great linguistic conservatism, and Humboldt fancifully pointed out that should a form of Sanskrit have developed devoid of all its former inflexions, it would be quite different in grammatical structure from Chinese which had never had any (in fact, some Sinologists today consider that the state in which Chinese is known to us now is the result of the loss of an earlier inflexional system).[60]

In a separate section Humboldt divided sentence structures into three types also: those, as in Chinese, with no overt grammatical links between words, those like Sanskrit wherein word forms signal grammatical relations, and the type evinced by some American-Indian languages in which the essential structure of the sentence is incorporated into a single word (incorporating or polysynthetic languages). In neither of these typologies, of word form or of sentence form, was any one type wholly exclusive of features appropriate to the others. Confusion results if the two typologies are combined into one, making incorporation a fourth term in the word form typology, where it merely cross-cuts inflexion and agglutination.[61]

In the mid-nineteenth century perhaps the most influential and historically important figure in linguistics was A. Schleicher (1821–68). In his relatively short life he wrote a number of works on historical linguistics and linguistic theory, of which the best known is his *Compendium of the comparative grammar of the Indogermanic languages*.[62] The title is significant; comparative and historical linguistics in the Indo-european field was now considered a fit subject for systematic presentation in a handbook setting out the position so far achieved. Schleicher's own development in the theory of historical linguistics is shown in the subtitle: *Outline of a phonology and morphology of the Indogermanic parent language*. It had been the achievement of the early nineteenth century to work out the conception of historically related families of languages, each containing a definite number of members, derived from an ancestor no longer extant (instead of looking among known languages for the 'oldest' or the 'original'). Schleicher turned his attention to the nature and forms of this hypothetical ancestor and the genetic relationships linking it with its known descendants.

Schleicher had learned a number of European languages in his youth. He made something like a field study of Lithuanian, and his *Handbook of the Lithuanian language* was the first and is still a good scientific description of that language.[63] His interests embraced philosophy (of the Hegelian variety) and natural science, in particular botany, as well as linguistics. The *Stammbaumtheorie* or genealogical tree model, by which he set out the relations between the parent language and the known Indo-european languages, owes something to the methods of botanical classification by species and groups in the Linnaean system, but it may well have been partly inspired by the comparative method of reconstructing the genealogy of manuscripts expounded by F. Ritschl, one of his teachers.[64]

Extant languages were grouped together, by the possession of distinctive shared characteristics (lexical correspondences and the results of sound changes), into subfamilies, Germanic, Italo-celtic, etc., for each of which a parent *Grundsprache* (common language) was assumed (like the known spoken Latin as the parent of the Romance languages), and all of these were traced back to a single *Ursprache* (original language) possessing the characteristics shared by them all. This common ancestor of the Indo-european languages could be reconstructed by the comparison of the attested corresponding forms in the various subfamilies, and the whole system of the languages in their historical relations was set out in the tree diagram.[65] Such reconstructed forms were, of course, different from known forms (and from inferred forms in a partially known language, as in the (different) reconstruction of a fragmentary inscription), and Schleicher initiated the practice of distinguishing them with an asterisk (whence the later term 'starred forms'); but he still felt sufficient confidence in his reconstructions actually to publish a fable composed in the *Ursprache*, just as one might today compose a passage in a dead language, a venture for which later writers have enjoyed criticizing him.[66]

The *Stammbaumtheorie*, as Schleicher's genealogical model is often called, represents an important development in Indo-european historical linguistics, and in historical linguistic theory in general. It provides one means of displaying the members of a linguistic family, and reading from the inferred ancestor downwards one gets some picture of the history and the historical relations of the individual languages. It is, however, open to certain objections, objections which do not require its abandonment but only a sensible interpretation of its inevitably metaphorical representation of the facts. Languages do not sharply split at a given point in time corresponding to the division of a line in the tree; the splitting process begins subdialectally and proceeds through increasing dialectal divergence until the assumption of two or more distinct languages is warranted. This is a lengthy and a gradual process, and the point at which each stage is reached must remain arbitrary. Moreover, as long as geographical contiguity permits linguistic contacts between speakers, different dialects and even different languages can continue to influence one another (in this respect the development of a language family and that of a botanical family are quite different processes, although both can be represented by a tree diagram). This last point was appreciated by Schleicher's successors, including his pupil J. Schmidt, who recognized that certain sets of features were uniquely but differently shared by different groups of languages within Indo-european, thus invalidating the single splits of the *Stammbaumtheorie*. Schmidt supplemented this rather than replaced it, by his *Wellentheorie*, or theory of waves of innovations, linguistic changes, including sound changes, that spread over a given area from dialect to dialect or even from language to language as long as linguistic contacts remained.[67]

Schleicher's model serves best as a literal representation of linguistic history, when language diffusion takes place over distances that involve the near total severance of the speakers, such, for example, as took place in the historical period with the Dutch settlers in South Africa and in certain isolated Spanish-speaking communities in the Latin New World.

The other major objection to a quite literal interpretation of the tree model is that it suggests that dialectal divisions are the most recent feature of linguistic history, since dialects occur at the end points of the tree. Only exceptionally, as in the case of ancient Greek, do we have an adequate knowledge of the dialect situation in dead languages; and the *Ursprache* and intermediate common languages are set up precisely on what is assumed to have been common in each to all the speakers. But all our knowledge of the conditions of language leads us to believe that dialect division was at least as pronounced in early days as it was later (probably more so), and indeed certain sets of correspondences within the Indo-european languages seem to demand the recognition of certain dialectal isoglosses already established within the *Ursprache* during the supposed period of unity. In so far as a strictly literal interpretation can be placed on the model, it should be read upwards as part of the historical linguist's method rather than downward as an accurate picture of historical events.

One important feature of the *Stammbaumtheorie* is that Sanskrit now began to assume its proper position in the family. Schleicher assigned it a place like any other language, in the 'Arian' (Indo-iranian) group, though he assumed that the Sanskrit vowel system /a/, /i/, /u/ (the /e/ and /o/ of classical Sanskrit were later derivatives of diphthongs[68]) was also the original Indo-european vowel system; triadic systems of any kind may have appealed to his Hegelian upbringing. Subsequent study has shown that the Sanskrit language had undergone changes, since the separation of its branch from the original unitary state, at least to the same extent as the other Indo-european languages.

In the form in which Schleicher set them down neither the tree diagram nor the forms of the *Ursprache* have remained unaltered; further study by Indo-european specialists altered both the grouping of languages within the branches of the tree, the forms of the reconstructions, and the phonological inventory ascribed to the *Ursprache*. Even between 1861 and 1891 G. von der Gabelentz could say that this reconstructed language had suffered great changes in its forms,[69] and the twentieth-century discovery of the relatedness of Hittite to the Indo-european languages further altered the picture. These topics and the detailed research into the different groups of languages within

Indo-european that was pursued during this period are matters for the history of Indo-european comparative linguistics rather than for the course of general linguistics as a whole.[70]

Schleicher's theory of linguistic history, whatever its original inspiration may have been, was in line with Darwinian ideas prevalent in the second half of the century. He recognized this, and in 1863 published a short treatise on *Darwinian theory and linguistics*.[71] He regarded himself as a natural scientist and his field, language, as one of the natural organisms of the world, to be treated by the methods of natural science, one moreover that independently of its speakers' will or consciousness has its periods of growth, maturity, and decline.[72] Such ideas were current already, though less elaborated; Bopp had written that languages should be regarded as natural organic objects that grow according to definite laws and, carrying in themselves their own living principle, go through the phases of development and in the end perish.[73] Schleicher maintained that Darwin's theory as worked out for the animal and vegetable kingdoms was broadly appropriate for linguistic history, and that the diffusion of different languages over the earth's surface and their contacts and conflicts could be likened to the struggle for existence in the world of living things, in which the Indo-european languages were victorious![74]

Schleicher's biological approach to language governed both his theory of the *Ursprache* and his treatment of linguistic typology. He regarded the three current language types, isolating, agglutinating, and flexional, as representing historical stages in the growth of languages to their highest point of organization.[75] As has been seen, such historicist ideas go back to eighteenth-century speculation, and something similar had been put forward by Humboldt. Schleicher went rather further, locating the growth period in prehistory as far as the Indo-european family was concerned, with the unitary *Ursprache* as reconstructed by him representing the mature undamaged stage, subsequent historical developments being part of the decline.[76] This could in some degree be supported by the more flexional structure of the ancient classical languages as compared with their later descendants; but one notices from Grimm on a definite admiration for flexional morphology, more especially in its 'purest' manifestation by *Ablaut* as being the best mode of grammatical exponence. National feeling may subconsciously have had some influence; *Ablaut* is an important formative process in Germanic languages, and more fully exploited in German than, for example, in English (cp. the inflexional and derivational use of vowel gradation in such a word series as *sprechen*, to speak, *sprach*, spoke, *gesprochen*, spoken, *sprich*, speak!, *Gespräch*, conversation, *Spruch*, saying, proverb, *Sprüche* (plural)).

Grimm had written earlier of the 'strong' (*Ablaut*-using) inflexions of the Germanic languages as a potent and characteristic feature of this group, though *Ablaut* is, in fact, found in many languages of otherwise quite different composition.[77] As regards historical decline, Schleicher was very hard on English; referring to the changes undergone by the language since its separation from the others, he wrote that they show how quickly the language of a people important in history and in literary history can decline.[78]

The major linguistic controversy in the last quarter of the century was concerned with what is now referred to as the neogrammarian or *Junggrammatiker* doctrine. In treating this as part of the history of linguistics, which one should do, one is already within the bounds of contemporary history. Neogrammarian principles and their implications are, or ought to be, part of any teaching course in general linguistics, and expositions of them are to be found in serious textbooks on the subject.[79]

This, of course, is very far from saying that the neogrammarian standpoint is understood and taught today in the precise way in which its protagonists understood and defined it. As an important and challenging event, its formulation evoked a considerable and an immediate reaction, and, of more significance, stimulated a number of different lines of research and thinking in direct response to what had been said. Much of our linguistic theory, in particular our theory of historical linguistics, would not bear the form it bears today but for its direct dependence on the neogrammarians. In this sense they are part of the contemporary linguistic scene, and 'we are all neogrammarians now'.

In surveying the neogrammarian epoch in a history of linguistics we must endeavour to see it both in its setting when neogrammarian principles were first propounded in a reaction to what had been said and done before, and in its setting as part of subsequent linguistic theory; in other words, we want to understand both how the neogrammarians interpreted their work and how linguists today find it profitable to interpret and use it.

The essence of the neogrammarian theory was summarily set forth in a programmatic article in a journal founded by its two major proponents, H. Osthoff and K. Brugmann, in which the following statements were made: All sound changes, as mechanical processes, take place according to laws that admit no exceptions (*ausnahmslose Lautgesetze*) within the same dialect, and the same sound will in the same environment always develop in the same way; but analogical creations and reformations of specific words as lexical or grammatical entities are equally a universal component of linguistic change at all periods of history and prehistory.[80]

Similar views had been expressed by different scholars in the preceding years; it fell to Osthoff and Brugmann formally to declare them as indispensable to historical linguistics and cheerfully to accept as official the title 'neogrammarian' (*Junggrammatiker*), originally a politically inspired nickname given to a group of young scholars in Leipzig, where they worked.

The conception of the sound law had been late in developing; Grimm had none of it, and mid-century scholars such as Schleicher were not troubled by apparent exceptions to the general run of sound changes in a language. But the years that followed the publication of Schleicher's *Compendium* had seen the results of detailed research in the various branches of the Indo-european family, yielding more material and more evidence of order lying behind the sets of formal correspondences that had either puzzled or escaped the notice of earlier scholars; and it was seen that the existence of comparative and historical linguistics as a science rested on the assumption of regularity of sound change. The history of a language is traced through recorded variations in the forms and meanings of its words, and languages are proved to be related by reason of their possession of words bearing formal and semantic correspondences to each other such as cannot be attributed to mere chance or to recent borrowing. If sound change were not regular, if word forms were subject to random, inexplicable, and unmotivated variation in the course of time, such arguments would lose their validity and linguistic relations could only be established historically by extralinguistic evidence such as is provided in the Romance field of languages descended from Latin.

The advance of scientific work without the explicit formulation of the theory on which its validity rests is no unusual occurrence in the history of science. The implications of nineteenth-century comparative and historical linguistics were stated in 1876 by A. Leskien: 'If one admits optional, contingent, and unconnected changes, one is basically stating that the object of one's research, language, is not amenable to scientific recognition'.[81] Others had spoken to similar effect though less explicitly; Verner, in his exposition of what is now known as 'Verner's law', showed that a large number of apparent exceptions to the Germanic sound shift as formulated by Grimm could be systematically explained by reference to the position of the word accent in the earlier stages of the Indo-european family (e.g. Sanskrit (at the period when the I-E accent survived) *bhrátā*, Gothic *brōþar*, brother, but *pitá̄*, *fadar*, father); significantly he entitled his article 'An exception to the first sound shift', and wrote: 'There must be a rule for exceptions to a rule; the only question is to discover it.'[82] The further implication of the theory was that systematic correspondences between sounds in languages demonstrate their relatedness, not merely the special case of similarity in actual phonetic shape; this was later clearly stated by A. Meillet.[83]

Grimm and his contemporaries lay under the influence of the Romantic movement; Schleicher saw his work within the context of Darwinian theory; the neogrammarians wished to make historical linguistics an exact science with its methods in line with those natural sciences which had made such striking advances in the nineteenth century. Nineteenth-century scientists held strongly to the universality of natural laws, realistically conceived; the uniformity of nature was a current dogma.[84] In this vein Osthoff wrote of sound laws proceeding by blind necessity, independently of the individual's will;[85] nevertheless, language was not a supra-individual organic entity with its own growth and life, as the earlier Humboldt and Schleicher and the later de Saussure (under Durkheimian influence) asserted; it simply had its existence in the individuals composing a speech community, and linguistic changes were changes in individuals' speech habits. In the interests of what they held to be a scientific outlook, the neogrammarians set their faces against the *a priori* and speculative conceptions of such predecessors as Schleicher with his distinction of a prehistoric period of growth and a historic period of decline. Except for the nature of the evidence, they argued that there was no difference between these periods as far as linguistic changes were concerned. Indeed, they drew attention away from the *Ursprache* as a supposed prehistoric reality to the data available in written records and in the spoken dialects of the present day; and from the neogrammarians stems the conception of Indo-european forms as formulae rather than as actual words or morphs. In a rather brutally expressed paragraph, Osthoff and Brugmann attacked any speculation beyond what the facts strictly warranted: 'Only that comparative linguist who forsakes the hypothesis-laden atmosphere of the workshop in which Indogermanic root-forms are forged, and comes out into the clear light of tangible present-day actuality in order to obtain from this source information which vague theory cannot ever afford him, can arrive at a correct presentation of the life and the transformations of linguistic forms.'[86]

Not for the last time in our science were data-orientation and theory-orientation to be brought into personal opposition. The neogrammarians concerned themselves with data and with laws governing the data, drawing on the sciences of physiology (in phonetics) and psychology to cover the domains of sound change and analogical reformation or resistance. Such down-to-earth movements are a continual necessity in a science, but the neogrammarian abandonment of unprofitable speculation in favour of the meticulous attention to detail was bought at the cost of the temporary neglect of much that was fecund in the work of earlier linguists. The structural conception of language suggested by Humboldt, especially in his theory of *innere Sprachform* found no place in their work, and the areas of linguistics lying outside the immediate concern of the neogrammarians were generally treated from a historical point of view. H. Paul's *Principles of the history of language* (1880) exemplifies this (chapter 4), and more strikingly so does M. Bréal's *Essay on semantics* (1897), although he may claim credit in history for introducing into linguistics the now universally used term 'semantics' (*sémantique*).[87] Perhaps it was in reaction to this onesided influence on linguistic studies exercised by the historicism of the period culminating in the neogrammarian school, dominant at the end of the century, that some twentieth-century structuralists and descriptivists have seemed never to tire of contemptuous references to the 'neogrammarian rut' and to 'neogrammarian atomism'.

Certainly the school, despite the opposition it aroused, became dominant, as it deserved to. The books of Bopp and Schleicher were replaced by the formidable *Outline of the comparative grammar of the Indogermanic languages* of Brugmann and Delbrück (Delbrück being responsible for the syntactic sections). Paul's *Principles* expounded neogrammarian theory, declaring that a scientific treatment of language must be a historical treatment, while W. Meyer-Lübke applied the theory to the field of the Romance languages.[88] In England J. Wright, and in France A. Meillet were both trained in neogrammarian linguistics; and so were the founders of American linguistics, F. Boas, E. Sapir, and L. Bloomfield. Bloomfield's work on the comparative and historical study of the Algonkian family of American-Indian languages brilliantly applies the theory and methods, together with Bloomfield's descriptive abilities, to an entirely distinct and remote language family.[89]

As has recently been pointed out,[90] the neogrammarians mark one of the really significant stages in the history of linguistics in the past two centuries. Their influence was threefold: in the encouragement given by their approach to linguistic science, in the immediate reactions of those shocked by them, and in the reactions of later generations.

Two fields that the neogrammarians saw to be very relevant to historical linguistics as they wished it to be pursued were phonetics and dialectology. Descriptive phonetics, whose history in Europe goes back at least to the Renaissance (pp. 117–19, above), had its own line of development in the nineteenth century, which it will be convenient to review in the next chapter. It received powerful reinforcement from the neogrammarian emphasis on living languages and on the inadequacy of the letters of dead languages in giving information on their actual pronunciations. Never again could there be an excuse for confusing written letter with spoken sound. E. Sievers's *Principles of phonetics* (1876) bears the further explanatory title *Introduction to the study of the sounds of the Indogermanic languages.*[91]

The spoken dialects of Europe had been a focus of linguistic attention since the Romantic movement sanctified everything connected with 'the people', but the neogrammarians made them a vital field for scientific investigation in the light they could shed on linguistic change, since they represented the latest stage in the diversification of the Indoeuropean family.[92] Dialect studies, dialect surveys, and the publication of dialect atlases began in earnest during this period, even though some of the strongest opponents of neogrammarian doctrine were found among the dialectologists.

The challenging way in which the neogrammarians propounded their principles, although they were largely the tacit implications of the century's previous work, threw more weight on the study of loan words and on linguistic borrowing as a universal feature of the history of languages, and on analogy as an ever present tendency. Both these factors had been recognized before in linguistics, the existence of loan words since antiquity; and in ancient Greek synchronic grammatical theory, analogy, the regularity of the corresponding forms of grammatical paradigms had been picked out as one of the principles by which language was directed. But they had enjoyed less prominence in historical linguistics hitherto, before the need had been clearly seen of accounting for apparent breaches of sound laws; W. Scherer had stressed the importance of analogical reformation, but his term 'false analogy' showed the secondary place assigned to this aspect of linguistic change.[93]

These developments were all envisaged and intended. But critical and hostile responses were immediate. These were expressed in terms of existing theory and existing knowledge, whereas later reactions resulted from a re-examination of the neogrammarian position in the light of advances made in general linguistic theory and in descriptive techniques.

Criticism took a number of forms. The personal resentment caused among some older scholars by what seemed to them unnecessarily harsh expressions on the part of newcomers (Osthoff and Brugmann had been born in 1847 and 1849, respectively) is understandable and needs no historical discussion (the discourtesy of the young is a recurrent complaint in scholarship as in other fields of life). Some took the line that neogrammarian principles were nothing new, but just a statement of what comparative and historical linguists were doing anyway. This in a sense was fair enough. The neogrammarians were largely drawing out what had been implied by the very practice of the subject and distinguishing it from unnecessary and fallacious assumptions. This in itself was a service, as is any stocktaking in scientific theory and methodology. Moreover, in making explicit the principles on which the science rested, they went a long way towards ensuring that muddled and undisciplined thinking should not accept unsound arguments and false etymological connections.

However, the most important and radical arguments against the neogrammarian position as first set out by Osthoff and Brugmann and their colleagues came from specialists in a branch of linguistics that they had been at pains to encourage, the study of living dialects. The detailed examination of the working of language in relatively small communities closely investigated in the field showed how complex were the phenomena collectively covered by the terms 'dialect split' and 'dialect borrowing'. The more narrowly a language was scrutinized, the more it was seen that geographical dialect divisions are in constant fluctuation and far from clear-cut, as more gross and superficial descriptions imply. The number of relatively coincidental isoglosses required to delimit a dialect must itself be arbitrary, and if one presses differences in detail at all levels, including pronunciation, to their logical limits, then the dialect becomes the idiolect.

Moreover, temporal limits are as hazy as geographical limits. Sound changes, like any other linguistic changes, must begin and cease within some temporal limits as well as extending over certain geographical areas; but the detailed study of actual dialect situations shows that these limits tolerate certain words changing before certain others when the same sounds are involved, and that dialect interpenetration across major isogloss lines may upset the universal application of a sound shift in a particular region. Dialect maps such as the one given in Bloomfield's *Language*, page 328, show the result of catching a linguistic change in progress and descriptively freezing it.

One is not at the end of linguistic variation after pressing geographical divisions down to the idiolect. Most speech communities are cross-cut with social divisions in part manifested in differences of speech habits, as folk-linguistic attitudes to 'correct speech' bear witness; and many individuals carry in their linguistic competence more than one different social and often more than one different regional dialect, to be used in different circumstances; and these differences, in so far as they relate to pronunciation, may be the result of the operation or non-operation of a particular sound change.

Dialect division, rather crudely conceived, and analogical reformation or conservatism were the two factors envisaged by the neogrammarians as apparently running counter to the universality of sound laws. But the minute examination of dialect differences revealed other considerations that were relevant in etymological research, affecting not categories of sounds as such but particular words as individual lexical items. Word forms may be deflected from their expected regular phonetic development by homonymic clash, excessive reduction in length, nearness to or coincidence with taboo-words, popular or false etymologies, loans from a neighbouring dialect for prestige, and by other factors. Such events are necessarily individual and highly variable in their incidence; they are explicable given knowledge of the circumstances (which of course is often not given, especially in earlier periods of a language), but they are not predictable.

It is, therefore, significant that much of the more serious criticism of the neogrammarian assertion of universality came from specialists in dialectology and what has been called linguistic geography. In particular one may cite H. Schuchardt, who included in his works an article 'On sound laws: against the neogrammarians', and J. Gilliéron, responsible for the linguistic atlas of France and numerous studies of individual French etymologies, including his best known *Genealogy of the words for the bee*.[94]

A further development of detailed dialectal research took the form of 'word and thing' (*Wörter und Sachen*) studies, in which the history and geographical distribution of items of material culture (agricultural implements, cultivated plants, etc.) and their associated vocabulary were minutely investigated. Schuchardt was much concerned with this, and so was R. Meringer, responsible for founding in 1909 a journal, *Wörter und Sachen*, expressly devoted to this field.

Gilliéron is to be credited with the doctrine, at first sight utterly opposed to that of the neogrammarians, that 'every word has its own history'. But the two positions are not really so incompatible. Changes in the pronunciation of words involve two things: the transmission from generation to generation of articulatory habits rests on the learning in childhood of sets of sounds heard first in certain words but, once mastered, used without effort in any number of words; but for various reasons, not by any means all understood, changes take place in the course of successive transmission between the generations, and the recurrence of a relatively small number of sounds in the virtually limitless vocabulary of a language makes for the universality of sound changes. But words are also learned as whole lexical units, and any hesitation, individual change, or other peculiarity in the pronunciation of such a unit is also learned, and may be retained and propagated in later generations or within people's speech during their lifetime. Every word has its individual history in its semantics, grammar, and pronunciation. In most cases its phonetic evolution can be described by reference to the phonetic evolution of the sounds occurring in it, but in certain cases its pronounced form must be explained by reference to particular circumstances lying along its own particular history. The neogrammarians stressed phonetic uniformity; Gilliéron and his disciples stressed etymological individuality.

The neogrammarians had said that language had no existence apart from the speakers. A group of linguists known as the idealistic or aesthetic school emphasized the importance of the individual speaker in the origination and diffusion of linguistic change of all kinds. The leader of this group was K. Vossler, of Munich, who drew his ideas on the nature of language from Humboldt and, more immediately, from the Italian philosopher B. Croce, with whom he was in intimate friendship for half a century.

It is interesting to notice that these linguists were just as historically orientated as the dominant neogrammarians; but they conceived the history of languages in a rather different way. Like Humboldt, Vossler stressed the individual and creative aspect of man's linguistic competence. All linguistic change begins with innovations in individual speech habits, and those that are going to give rise to some alteration in the language do so by being imitated by others and thus diffusing themselves. This would probably not be contradicted by the neogrammarians, but the idealists insisted on the conscious role of the individual in the process rather than on 'blind necessity'. Croce laid great importance on aesthetic intuition as a guide in all aspects of man's life, even though one may be unaware of it at the time. The recognized artist only carries further what every human being does all the time.[95]

Language is primarily personal self-expression, the idealists maintained, and linguistic change is the conscious work of individuals perhaps also reflecting national feelings; aesthetic considerations are dominant in the stimulation of innovations. Certain individuals, through their social position or literary reputation, are better placed to initiate changes that others will take up and diffuse through a language, and the importance of great authors in the development of a language, like Dante in Italian, must not be underestimated. In this regard the idealists reproached the neogrammarians for their excessive concentration on the mechanical and pedestrian aspects of language, a charge that L. Spitzer, himself very much in sympathy with Vossler, was later to make against the descriptive linguistics of the Bloomfieldian era.[96] But the idealists, in themselves concentrating on literate languages, overstressed the literary and aesthetic element in the development of languages, and the element of conscious choice in what is for most speakers most of the time simply unreflective social activity learned in childhood and subsequently taken for granted. And in no part of language is its structure and working taken more for granted than in its actual pronunciation, just that aspect on which the neogrammarians focused their attention. Nevertheless the idealistic school did well to remind us of the creative and conscious factors in some areas of linguistic change and of the part the individual can sometimes deliberately play therein.

Certain of the principles of the idealist-aesthetic linguists, combined with detailed dialectological studies, gave rise in Italy to the so-called 'neo-linguistic' school, which has made one of its main concerns the processes by which innovations are diffused over geographical areas (whence the term 'areal linguistics', sometimes used of the work of this school) and the historical inferences that can be drawn from the contrasting developments in central as against peripheral areas, which latter are likely to preserve archaic features the longest.[97]

The neogrammarians stimulated fruitful lines of linguistic research by the shock that the vigorous exposition of their views caused in the learned world of the time. As a result of the reconsideration to which the whole question of historical relationship among languages was subjected, their tenets may be seen today to have been somewhat modified but not at all superseded. Their conception of sound laws operating on languages by 'blind necessity' is as undesirable a reification as were the mythical periods of growth, maturity, and decline favoured by earlier scholars. The exceptionlessness of sound laws should be considered not so much a factual statement (though research has shown that it is borne out by the facts) as a methodological requirement. The linguist sets himself not to accept finally an etymology which appears to break correspondences of sounds established in other words in the language or languages involved, until he is able to explain the seeming deviance in some reasonable manner, whether in relation to the particular etymology alone or, like Verner's law, involving a refinement of the previous formulation of the sound changes. While we certainly will not be able to account for all apparent exceptions and cannot, in the absence of omniscience, absolutely deny the occurrence of 'sporadic sound change', on which the opponents of the neogrammarians laid so much weight, we are bound, as long as comparative and historical linguistics is to remain, in the widest sense of the term, scientific, to reject such etymologies from any arguments in support of historical relations between languages.

The opposition so far surveyed, together with the research and development for which it was partly responsible, sprang from the stage reached by linguistic scholarship at the time of the neogrammarians. Later reactions, from the standpoint of synchronic and structural linguistics, may conveniently be considered in the next chapter. Meanwhile it is worth reflecting on the results of nineteenth-century comparative and historical linguistics. From the isolated and undeveloped, though sometimes inspired, insights of earlier years, scholars in the nineteenth century worked out a theory and a model whereby the history of languages could be presented, and a method whereby research could be conducted. Though largely confined to the Indoeuropean family, which reached a definitive state during this period, their work provided a pattern which, despite some valid criticism, has been fruitfully applied to language families the world over, including some, such as the Algonkian family already mentioned, that had no written records of earlier epochs. By any standards this was a mighty achievement, and one that can be largely attributed to the linguistic scholarship of the German universities, one component of the renown that they rightly enjoyed in this century.

FOR FURTHER CONSULTATION

H. ARENS, *Sprachwissenschaft: der Gang ihrer Entwicklung von der Antike bis zur Gegenwart*, Freiburg/Munich, 1955, 133–402.

T. BENFEY, *Geschichte der Sprachwissenschaft und orientalischen Philologie in Deutschland*, Munich, 1869.

K. BRUGMANN and B. DELBRÜCK, *Grundriss der vergleichenden Grammatik der indogermanischen Sprachen*, Strassburg, 1886–1900.

K. BRUGMANN, *Kurze vergleichende Grammatik der indogermanischen Sprachen*, Strassburg, 1904.

J. GAUDEFROY-DEMOMBYNES, *L'Oeuvre linguistique de Humboldt*, Paris, 1931.

H. M. HOENIGSWALD, 'On the history of the comparative method', *Anthropological linguistics* 5 (1963), 1–11.

W. VON HUMBOLDT, *Über die Verschiedenheit des menschlichen Sprachbaues*, Darmstadt, 1949.

I. IORDAN, *An introduction to Romance linguistics* (tr. J. ORR), London, 1937.

M. IVIĆ, *Trends in linguistics*, The Hague, 1965, chapters 1–12.

O. JESPERSEN, *Language*, London, 1922, chapters 2–4.

L. KUKENHEIM, *Esquisse historique de la linguistique française*, Leiden, 1962.

M. LEROY, *Les grands courants de la linguistique moderne*, Brussels and Paris, 1963, 15–60.

A. MEILLET, *Introduction à l'étude comparative des langues indo-européennes*, Paris, 1922, Appendix 1.

H. PEDERSEN, *Linguistic science in the nineteenth century* (tr. J. W. SPARGO), Cambridge, Mass., 1931 (paperback, *The discovery of language*, Bloomington, 1962).

H. STEINTHAL (ed.), *Die sprachphilosophischen Werke Wilhelm's von Humboldt*, Berlin, 1883.

J. T. WATERMAN, *Perspectives in linguistics*, Chicago, 1963, 18–60.

NOTES

1. JESPERSEN, 1922, 7.
2. Book 1, chapter 9.
3. Book 1, chapter 8.

4. E. BOURCIEZ, *Eléments de linguistique romane*, Paris, 1946, § 320 c.
5. Book 1, chapters 10–16.
6. Book 1, chapter 4.
7. cp. J. C. GREENE, *The death of Adam*, New York, 1961, 62–3, 235.
8. *Origines Antwerpianae*, Antwerp, 1569.
9. 'Matricum vero inter se nulla cognatio est, neque in verbis neque in analogia', *Diatriba de Europaeorum linguis* (*Opscula varia*, Paris, 1610, 119–22).
10. Stockholm, 1671, (glossary) 78–9.
11. *De lingua vetustissima Europae*, Stockholm, 1686.
12. G. W. VON LEIBNIZ, *Neue Abhandlungen*, Frankfurt, 1961, volume 2, 20–1; ARENS, 1955, 77–88.
13. C. I. GERHARDT (ed.), *Die philosophischen Schriften von G. F. Leibniz*, Berlin 1882, volume 5, 263–4.
14. ARENS, 1955, 85–6.
15. Zurich, 1555; Berlin 1806 and 1817 (the last three volumes were edited posthumously by J. S. Vater). Examples of the Lord's Prayer in fifty languages were given in Wilkins's *Essay* (p. 114, above), 435–9.
16. ADELUNG, *Mithridates*, volume 1, 149–50.
17. *Linguarum totius orbis vocabularia comparative*, St. Petersburg, 1786–9.
18. ARENS, 1955, 118–27.
19. *Über die Sprache und Weisheit der Indier*, Heidelberg, 1808.
20. ibid., 28.
21. *Über das Conjugationssystem der Sanskritsprache in Vergleichung mit jenem der griechischen, lateinischen, persischen, und germanischen Sprache*, Frankfurt, 1816.
22. BENFEY, 1869.
23. '... gehören zu den glänzendsten Gestirnen des deutschen Geisteshimmels'; 'Die Genossenschaft ausgezeichneter Männer, welche zur Entwickelung dieser Wissenschaft beigetragen haben, sind fast ausnahmslos Söhne unsres Vaterlandes', BENFEY, op. cit., 15.
24. *Demonstratio idioma ungarorum et Lapponum idem esse*, Copenhagen, 1770; *Affinitas linguae Hungaricae cum linguis Fennicae originis grammatice demonstrata*, Göttingen, 1799.
25. *Vejledning til det islandske eller gamle nordiske sprog*, Copenhagen, 1811; *A grammar of the Anglo-Saxon tongue* (tr. B. THORPE), Copenhagen, 1830.
26. Göttingen, 1819–37.
27. M. E. DAIRE (ed.), *Oeuvres de Turgot*, Paris, 1844, volume 2, 724–52.
28. *Undersøgelse om det gamle nordiske eller islandske sprogs oprindelse*, Copenhagen, 1818 (L. HJELMSLEV, *Ausgewählte Abhandlungen*, Copenhagen, 1932, volume 1, 49–51).

29. A. F. POTT, *Etymologische Forschungen auf dem Gebiete der indogermanischen Sprachen*, Lemgo, 1833–6.

30. 'Die Lautverschiebung erfolgt in der Masse, tut sich aber im einzelnen niemals rein ab', *Deutsche Grammatik* (second edition), Berlin, 1870, volume 1, 503.

31. *Unvorgreifliche Gedanken betreffend die Ausübung und Verbesserung der deutschen Sprache* (*Quellen und Forschungen zur Sprach- und Culturgeschichte* 23 (1877), 44–92).

32. *Geschichte der deutschen Sprache* (fourth edition), Leipzig, 1880, volume 1, 292.

33. W. SCHERER, *Zur Geschichte der deutschen Sprache*, Berlin, 1868.

34. PEDERSEN, 1931, 248–9.

35. *Conjugationssystem*, 8–11.

36. cp. RASK, *Undersøgelse* (HJELMSLEV, *Ausgewählte Abhandlungen*, volume 1, 48–9).

37. MEILLET, 1922, 458.

38. *Vergleichende Grammatik des Sanskrit, Zend, Griechischen, Lateinischen, Litauischen, Gotischen, und Deutschen*, Berlin, 1833, iii.

39. cp. COUNT DE BUFFON (1707–88), *Natural history* (tr. W. SMELLIE), London, 1785, volume 3, 216, volume 8, 62–3; J. F. BLUMENBACH (1752–1840), *A manual of the elements of natural history* (tr. R. T. GORE), London, 1825.

40. *Conjugationssystem*, 96, 151, 99, cp. 148; *Analytic comparison of the Sanskrit, Greek, Latin, and Teutonic languages* (1820, reprinted in *Internationale Zeitschrift für allgemeine Sprachwissenschaft* 4 (1889), 14–60), 23, 46–7, 53–6, 58.

41. cp. P. A. VERBURG, 'The background to the linguistic conceptions of Bopp', *Lingua* 2 (1950), 438–68.

42. HUMBOLDT, 1949.

43. HUMBOLDT, op. cit., 43–4.

44. 'Die Sprache muss von endlichen Mitteln einen unendlichen Gebrauch machen', ibid., 103.

45. cp. N. CHOMSKY, *Current issues in linguistic theory*, The Hague, 1964, 17–21.

46. HUMBOLDT, op. cit., 89–98, 269.

47. ibid., 48.

48. 'Ihre Sprache ist ihr Geist und ihr Geist ihre Sprache', ibid., 41.

49. ibid., 92; 291

50. ibid., 115.

51. *W. von Humboldt's Gesammelte Schriften*, Berlin, volume 4 (1905), 14, volume 3 (1904), 295.

52. HUMBOLDT, 1949, 26.

53. ARENS, 1955, 183–4.

54. W. WUNDT, *Völkerpsychologie*, Leipzig, 1905–6; IORDAN, 1937, chapter 2.

55. L. WEISGERBER, *Von den Kräften der deutschen Sprache*, volumes 1–4, Düsseldorf, 1949–50; id., *Das Menschheitsgesetz der Sprache*, Heidelberg, 1964; H. BASILIUS, 'Neo-Humboldtian ethnolinguistics', *Word* 8 (1952), 95–105; J. B. CARROLL, *Language, thought and reality: select writings of Benjamin Lee Whorf*, New York, 1956; D. HYMES, 'Notes towards a history of linguistic anthropology', *Anthropological linguistics* 5 (1963), 59–103; T. BYNON, 'Leo Weisgerber's four stages in linguistic analysis', *Man* n.s. 1 (1966), 468–83.

56. HUMBOLDT, 1949, 90. Kantian influence is also interestingly seen in some of the more noteworthy synchronic linguistic work of the first half of the nineteenth century, namely the further development of the semantic and grammatical analysis of the category of case in various languages (HJELMSLEV, *La catégorie des cas*, Aarhus, 1935, part 1, 28–32). For continuing Cartesian influences in Humboldt, CHOMSKY, *Cartesian linguistics*, New York, 1966, 19–22.

57. HUMBOLDT, 1949, 114–26.

58. BENFEY, 1869, 366–7; BOPP, *Vergleichende Grammatik*, § 108.

59. HUMBOLDT, *Über das Entstehen der grammatischen Formen und ihren Einfluss auf die Ideenentwickelung*, 1822 (STEINTHAL, 1883, 67–101); HUMBOLDT, 1949, 294, 124.

60. HUMBOLDT, 1822, op. cit., 292–3, 169, 258; B. KARLGREN, 'Le proto-chinois, langue flexionnelle', *Journal asiatique* 15 (1920), 205–32; A. G. HAUDRICOURT, 'Comment reconstruire le chinois archaïque', *Word* 10 (1954), 351–64. As recently as 1937 it was thought worthwhile writing an article under the title 'Has the Chinese language parts of speech?', *TPS* 1937, 99–119 (W. SIMON).

61. cp. C. E. BAZELL, *Linguistic typology*, London, 1958, 17–18.

62. *Compendium der vergleichenden Grammatik der indogermanischen Sprachen; kurzer Abriss einer Laut- und Formenlehre der indogermanischen Ursprache*, Weimar, 1861 (pagination from fourth edition, 1876).

63. *Handbuch der litauischen Sprache*, Prague, 1856–7.

64. HOENIGSWALD, 1963.

65. *Compendium*, 7; fuller version, *Die darwinsche Theorie und die Sprachwissenschaft* (second edition), Weimar, 1873, ad. fin.

66. Text in JESPERSEN, 1922, 81–2.

67. J. SCHMIDT, *Die Verwandschaftsverhältnisse der indogermanischen Sprachen*, Weimar, 1872; cp. L. BLOOMFIELD, *Language*, London, 1935, 314–19.

68. W. S. ALLEN, *Phonetics in ancient India*, London, 1953, 62–4.

69. G. VON DER GABELENTZ, *Die Sprachwissenschaft* (second edition), Leipzig, 1901, 170.

70. Brief details and references in PEDERSEN, 1931, esp. chapter 7.

71. *Die darwinsche Theorie und die Sprachwissenschaft*, Weimar, 1863 (second edition, 1873); J. P. MAYER, 'More on the history of the comparative method: the tradition of Darwinism in August Schleicher's work', *Anthropological linguistics* 8 (1966), 1–12.

72. *Compendium*, 1–3; *Sprachvergleichende Untersuchungen*, Bonn, 1848–1850, volume 2, 21; *Darwinsche Theorie*, 6–7; *Die deutsche Sprache* (second edition), Stuttgart, 1869, 37, 47.

73. *Vocalismus oder Sprachvergleichende Kritiken*, Berlin, 1836, 1; 'Die Sprachen sind als organische Naturkörper anzusehen die nach bestimmten Gesetzen sich bilden, ein inneres Lebensprinzip in sich tragend sich entwickeln, und nach und nach absterben.'

74. 'Das was Darwin für die Arten der Tiere und Pflanzen geltend macht, gilt nun aber auch, wenigstens in seinen hauptsächlichsten Zügen, für die Organismen der Sprachen', *Darwinsche Theorie*, 13; op. cit., 31–2.

75. *Sprachvergleichende Untersuchungen* 2, 15: 'Das Nacheinander der Geschichte in das Nebeneinander des Systems umschlägt'; cp. op. cit., 1,6 and 2,9.

76. *Compendium*, 4; *Sprachvergleichende Untersuchungen*, 2, 10–20.

77. *Deutsches Wörterbuch*, Leipzig, 1919, volume 10.2.1, 876.

78. *Sprachvergleichende Untersuchungen* 2, 231: '... wie schnell die Sprache eines geschichtlich und litterargeschichtlich bedeutenden Volkes herabsinken kann.'

79. e.g. L. BLOOMFIELD, *Language*, London, 1935, chapters 18, 20, 21; L. R. PALMER, *Introduction to modern linguistics*, London, 1936, chapters 3, 4, 7.

80. H. OSTHOFF and K. BRUGMANN, *Morphologische Untersuchungen* 1 (1878), iii–xx.

81. A. LESKIEN, *Declination im Slawisch-Litauischen und Germanischen*, Leipzig, 1876, xxviii: 'Lässt man beliebige, zufällige, unter einander in keinen Zusammenhang zu bringende Abweichungen zu, so erklärt man im Grunde damit, dass das Objekt der Untersuchungen, die Sprache, der wissenschaftlichen Erkenntnis nicht zugänglich ist.'

82. 'Eine Ausnahme der ersten Lautverschiebung', *Zeitschrift für vergleichende Sprachforschung* 23 (1877), 97–130 (101): 'Es muss eine Regel für die Unregelmässigkeit da sein; es gilt nur, diese ausfindig zu machen.'

83. MEILLET, 1922, 470–1.

84. H. W. B. JOSEPH, *An introduction to logic*, Oxford, 1916, chapter 19.

85. *Das Verbum in der Nominalkomposition*, Jena, 1878, 326: 'Die Lautgesetze der Sprachen geradezu blind, mit blinder Naturnotwendigkeit wirken.'

86. *Morphologische Untersuchungen* I, ix–x: 'Nur derjenige vergleichende Sprachforscher, welcher aus dem hypothesentrüben Dunstkreis der Werkstätte in der man die indogermanischen Grundformen schmiedet, einmal heraustritt in die klare Luft der greifbaren Wirklichkeit und Gegenwart, um hier sich Belehrung zu holen über das, was ihn die graue Theorie nimmer erkennen lässt ... nur der kann zu einer richtigen Vorstellung von der Lebens- und Umbildungsweise der Sprachformen gelangen.'

87. H. PAUL, *Principien der Sprachgeschichte* (fifth edition), Halle, 1920 (tr. H. A. STRONG, *Principles of the history of language*, London, 1891), chapter 4; M. BRÉAL, *Essai de semantique*, Paris, 1897 (tr. H. CUST, *Semantics: studies in the science of meaning*, London, 1900).

88. BRUGMANN and DELBRÜCK,1886–1900; PAUL, op. cit., 20–2; W. MEYER-LÜBKE, *Grammatik der romanischen Sprachen*, Leipzig, 1890–1902.

89. C. OSGOOD (ed.), *Linguistic structures of native America*, New York, 1946, 85–129; C. F. HOCKETT, 'Implications of Bloomfield's Algonquian studies', *Language* 24 (1948), 117–31.

90. HOCKETT, 'Sound change', *Language* 41 (1965), 185–204.

91. *Grundzüge der Lautphysiologie: zur Einführung in das Studium der Lautlehre der indogermanischen Sprachen*, Leipzig, 1876.

92. OSTHOFF and BRUGMANN, *Morphologische Untersuchungen* I, viii–ix.

93. *Zur Geschichte der deutschen Sprache*, Berlin, 1868.

94. *Über die Lautgesetze: gegen die Junggrammatiker*, 1885 (reprinted in L. SPITZER (ed.), *Hugo Schuchardt-Brevier*, Halle, 1928, 51–87; *Généalogie des mots qui designent l'abeille*, Paris, 1918.

95. K. VOSSLER, *Positivismus und Idealismus in der Sprachwissenschaft*, Heidelberg, 1904; B. CROCE, *Estetica come scienza dell'espressione e linguistica generale*, 1901 (ninth edition, Bari, 1950), 18: 'Anche niente più che una differenza quantitativa possiamo ammettere nel determinare il significato della parola *genio, genio artistico*, dal non-genio dall'uomo comune'.

96. 'Why does language change?', *Modern language quarterly* 4 (1943). 413–31; reply by BLOOMFIELD, 'Secondary and tertiary responses to language', *Language* 20 (1944), 45–55.

97. M. BARTOLI, *Introduzione alla neolinguistica*, Geneva, 1925; G. BONFANTE, 'The neolinguistic position', *Language* 23 (1947), 344–75.

Eight

Linguistics in the present century

Centuries are a most arbitrary mode of historical periodization. But in cases where certain tendencies are concentrated in given centuries they may have some mnemonic value. Through a number of historical accidents and previous trends in linguistics, the nineteenth century was dominated by historical studies; but in tracing some of the developments that arose directly from the work of the neogrammarians we were led across into the twentieth; and likewise, in following up the genesis of present-day theories and attitudes, we shall be looking back into the nineteenth and preceding centuries, not merely for the antecedents of the scholars involved and the teaching that they received, but for specific movements of thought more closely connected with the present age than with the predominant concerns of the nineteenth century.

The nineteenth-century background, within which the early twentieth-century scholars grew up, has already been considered, and in it at least three major strands can be distinguished: the continuing tradition of grammatical and other linguistic work that had been carried on by European scholars in different ways since antiquity, the progressive appreciation of Indian linguistic scholarship, especially in phonetics and phonology, and the assimilation of linguistic science, specifically as a historically orientated science, to certain general nineteenth-century attitudes, comparatism, evolutionism, and the positivism of the natural sciences.

In attempting to pick out the lines on which linguistics has moved and is moving in the present century, one is dealing with 'contemporary history'. The historical attitude is the same, but the material differs in being more plentiful and less easily formalized. On the one hand, one is concerned with persons and theories already familiar in elementary introductions to linguistics to a greater extent than with some nineteenth-century work and to a far greater extent than with the work of earlier periods; and on the other hand, the very nearness of the scene makes the discernment of definite directions and movements, and of relatively permanent 'schools', more difficult. The traveller, in lifting his eyes to survey the more distant scene whence he has passed, can view the plains, mountains, rivers, and forests that make up and characterize the terrain; but when he looks just about him, hillocks, pebbles, trees, and small streams often present no clearly outstanding picture of how the landscape will appear from a greater distance. Moreover, past scholars and their works are subject to the rough justice, and perhaps sometimes to the rough injustice, of their contemporaries and immediate successors in regard to what is found worthy of mention and development; and not all is preserved, particularly from earlier periods. It has been said that of the world's scientists most are alive today; and this is true of linguistic scientists, in view of the immense and so far unchecked expansion of linguistic studies in the world's universities. Anything like a full account of significant work in linguistics today and in the recent past, even on a scale comparable to that possible in antiquity and the Middle Ages, would be grossly disproportionate in length; and abbreviated mention would come to little more than an exercise in academic name dropping. In this chapter the intention is to survey some of the recent and current linguistic developments in their historical relationship with one another, rather than to give even a summary account of each where this is readily available in textbooks.[1]

The principal and most obvious contrast between the last two centuries has been the rapid rise of descriptive linguistics, as opposed to historical linguistics, to its present position of predominance. This has become the source from which the major developments in contemporary linguistics have sprung; but it must be remembered that before the nineteenth century too, it was the various aspects of synchronic linguistics, as interpreted in the times, that held the forefront.

Significantly, the key figure in the change from nineteenth- to twentieth-century attitudes was the Swiss linguist Ferdinand de Saussure, who first made himself known to scholarship through an important contribution to Indo-european comparative linguistics.[2] Though he published little himself, de Saussure's lectures on linguistics in the early twentieth century so impressed his pupils in Geneva that in 1916 they published his *Cours de linguistique générale* as far as they could reconstruct it from their own and others' lecture notes and such materials as survived in de Saussure's hand.[3] In the history of linguistics, de Saussure is largely known and studied through what his pupils recollected of him.

De Saussure drew on a restricted range of languages, mostly the familiar languages of Europe; but his influence on twentieth-century linguistics, which he could be said to have inaugurated, is unsurpassed. The publication of the *Cours* has been likened to a 'Copernican revolution' in the subject.[4] A number of ideas on language and the study of language very much in sympathy with those of de Saussure had, in fact, been expressed nearly a century before by von Humboldt (pp. 174–7, above); the extent to which de Saussure was directly influenced by Humboldt is uncertain, though a connection has been suggested.[5] Humboldt's general linguistic theory attracted less attention because at the time historical studies were in the ascendant; de Saussure's teaching came in an age when the drive of comparative and historical linguistic theory had temporarily reached an acceptable resting place in the tenets of the neogrammarians.

Historically, de Saussure's ideas may be put under three heads. Firstly, he formalized and made explicit, what earlier linguists had either assumed or ignored, the two fundamental and indispensable dimensions of linguistic study: synchronic, in which languages are treated as self-contained systems of communication at any particular time, and diachronic, in which the changes to which languages are subject in the course of time are treated historically. It was de Saussure's achievement to distinguish these two dimensions or axes of linguistics, synchronic or descriptive, and diachronic or historical, as each involving its own methods and principles and each essential in any adequate course of linguistic study or linguistic instruction (a point that might perhaps be heeded by some latter-day descriptivists).

Secondly, he distinguished the linguistic competence of the speaker and the actual phenomena or data of linguistics (utterances), as *langue* and *parole* (like so many others, these Saussurean terms have passed untranslated into international currency). While *parole* constitutes the immediately accessible data, the linguist's proper object is the *langue* of each community, the lexicon, grammar, and phonology implanted in each individual by his upbringing in society and on the basis of which he speaks and understands his language. Much influenced by the sociological theory of Emile Durkheim, de Saussure perhaps exaggerated the suprapersonal reality of *langue* over and above the individual, more especially as he recognized that changes in *langue* proceed from changes made by individuals in their *parole*, while he yet declared that *langue* is not subject to the individual's power of change.[6]

Thirdly, de Saussure showed that any *langue* must be envisaged and described synchronically as a system of interrelated elements, lexical, grammatical, and phonological, and not as an aggregate of self-sufficient entities (which he compared to a mere nomenclature[7]). Linguistic terms are to be defined relatively to each other, not absolutely. This is the theory expressed in his statement that a *langue* is *forme, non substance*, and illustrated with his well-known metaphors of chessmen and trains, identified and known by their place in the whole system, of the game or the railway network, and not by their actual substantial composition.[8] In a language these interrelations lie on each of the two fundamental dimensions of synchronic linguistic structure, syntagmatic, in line with the succession of utterance, and paradigmatic (associative), in systems of contrastive elements or categories.[9]

This statement of the structural approach to language underlies virtually the whole of modern linguistics, and justifies de Saussure's claim on the independence of linguistics as a subject of study in its own right.[10] Whatever the different interpretations placed on the exact meaning of 'structuralism', few linguists would now disclaim structural thinking in their work.

Hjelmslev's glossematics may be regarded as the Saussurean emphasis on form as against substance in the 'content plane' (semantics and grammar) and in the 'expression plane' (phonology), and on the definition of form as the interrelations of elements, both carried to their logical extremes; that is to say, content analysis must be independent of extra-linguistic existential criteria, and expression analysis (phonology) must be independent of (assumed extra-linguistic) phonetic criteria. Relations between elements, not the elements themselves, are the object of a science, and only by keeping this strictly to the fore can the Saussurean ideal of an autonomous linguistics, not dependent on any other discipline, be realized. The two planes are each regarded as analysable into ultimate constituents (e.g. *mare* into /m/, /ɛ/, /ə/, or *m*, *a*, *r*, *e*, on the plane of expression, and into 'horse', 'female', 'singular', on the plane of content). They are not isomorphous, as no connection can be drawn between the individual phonemes or letters and the minimal elements of content; but both planes are to be analysed in an analogous way, and each is co-ordinate and equivalent in a language system. It is precisely this claim to equivalence between the two planes that others have found difficult to accept, since differences in expression are independently observable in a language and belong to a strictly circumscribed field, whereas differences in semantic content (which is limitless) are only revealed through differences in expression in a language.[11]

Elsewhere in linguistics, the structural study of meanings as depending in part on the co-presence in a language of numbers of related lexical terms in semantic fields represents the working out of ideas brought into prominence by de Saussure.[12]

But the most immediate and historically one of the most important effects of de Saussure's structural theory of language was in the realm of phonology, where it coincided remarkably with the tentative position reached about the same time in phonetics as the result of the work of nineteenth-century phoneticians.

Phonetics, with its allied activities and applications in shorthand, language teaching, and spelling reform, had received considerable attention in England from the Renaissance onwards; and the general stimulus to phonetic studies from the discovery of Indian phonetic work at the end of the eighteenth century has been mentioned in chapter 6. Sir William Jones himself expressed and aroused great interest in the problems of the phonetic transcription of languages such as Sanskrit, Persian, and Arabic, which had a long tradition of literacy in systems of writing other than roman letters. His 'Dissertation on the orthography of Asiatick words in roman letters'[13] praised the phonological appropriateness of the Devanagari syllabary and of the Arabic script to the disadvantage of English alphabetic spelling. Unlike most of his contemporaries he clearly distinguished between letter and sound, and he vigorously protested against the paedagogical reference to 'five vowels' in English.[14]

Sir William Jones's phonetic work was studied carefully in England by A. J. Ellis, who collaborated with Sir Isaac Pitman on alphabetic reform; and English interest in the physiology of speech led to the publication of C. R. Lepsius's *Standard alphabet*,[15] a cooperative product of English and continental scholarship, setting out the possible vowel and consonant sound types classified by their articulation, represented by distinctive symbols, and illustrated from a number of different languages. This was followed in 1877 by Sweet's 'broad romic', and in 1889 by the revised International Phonetic Alphabet of what was later designated the International Phonetic Association.

Through the emigration of the remarkable Bell family, this same interest resulted in the invention of the telephone in the United States, where the name of the youngest Bell (Alexander Graham, 1847–1922) is commemorated in the Bell Telephone Company of America. He, like his father, Alexander Melville (1819–1905) and his grandfather, Alexander (1790–1865), worked on speech training and remedial applications of phonetics. A. M. Bell was the inventor of a system of 'visible speech', on the lines of earlier attempts (p. 119, above), wherein each separate process of articulation received its own graphic notation. This system was adopted, with some corrections and modifications by Sweet in his *Primer of phonetics*.[16]

Henry Sweet (1845–1912) was one of the leaders in the study of phonetics and of Old, Middle, and New (modern) English in Great Britain in the second half of the nineteenth century. He was temperamentally inclined towards the synchronic, descriptive aspects of linguistics, in part by his rather intense nationalism and his hostility towards the dominant historical linguistic scholarship which he rightly associated with Germany. As it happened, in the perversity of human affairs, recognition for being the outstanding scholar that he was came more readily abroad, and notably in Germany, than in this country, where his outspokenly critical bearing, suspiciousness, and, in later years, his justified resentment prevented him from ever attaining professorial rank in a British university.[17]

During the nineteenth century, phonetic work drew on the progress of the allied fields of physiology and acoustics, and experimental investigations were an accepted part of phonetic research by the end of the century. The applications of phonetics in spelling reform and in language teaching were regarded as playing a major part in current efforts towards the extension of education and the cause of social progress in general.[18]

Up to the time of Sweet, phoneticians had concerned themselves with spelling reform, including the devising of additional alphabetic symbols, and with universal phonetic symbol systems. In the latter half of the century it became evident that with the increase in phonetic sophistication every orthography, however much it was reformed, would omit great numbers of observable phonetic differences, and that any narrow transcriptional representation that came anywhere near the unattainable goal of 'one sound, one symbol' would be too hopelessly complicated for practical use in the writing of a language. The approach to this dilemma can be seen in Sweet's early writing. In his *Handbook of phonetics* (1877) he drew the distinction between sounds whose differences depend in the language on their phonetic environment and are therefore non-distinctive, and sounds which may by themselves establish two words as lexically separate items. Virtually the same phonetic difference may be distinctive in one language and non-distinctive in another; and only the distinctive sound differences need separate notation in a broad transcription system for a particular language.[19]

Sweet did not use the term *phoneme*, though the concept clearly underlies his work. The explicit terminological distinction between sound or phone and phoneme was the work of a Polish scholar teaching in Russia, Baudouin de Courtenay, who made technical use of the Russian word *fonema*. His theory of the phoneme was published in 1894, but he had probably arrived at it rather earlier, around the same time as Sweet, though there was no contact between them then.[20]

It was not, however, before the second decade of the twentieth century, after the teaching of de Saussure had begun to make its impact, that the term *phoneme* gained wide currency, soon thereafter to become a linguistic universal. De Saussure had used the French word *phonème*, though generally in the sense of speech sound as a phonetic occurrence; but his structural theory of language in its application to phonology quite clearly formulated the concept of phonemic distinctiveness as its centrepiece.

Daniel Jones made it the basis of 'broad' versus 'narrow' transcription (terms previously used by Sweet) in his *Outline of English phonetics*, first published in 1914. During the twenties its status as a linguistic unit, or as a class of sounds, was debated and it was variously held to be a psychological entity, a physiological entity, a transcendental entity, and just a mere descriptive invention.[21] But the first really significant development in the evolution of the theory of the phoneme was the work of the Prague school in the twenties and thirties.

The Prague school, as it is known, was constituted by a group of Czech and other scholars doctrinally centred round Prince Nikolai Trubetzkoy, a professor in Vienna 1923–39, which held regular meetings and published the *Travaux du cercle linguistique de Prague*. Their main interest lay in phonological theory, and the most important work associated with the school was Trubetzkoy's *Grundzüge der Phonologie* (principles of phonology), completed just before the end of his life.[22]

Trubetzkoy and the Prague phonologists applied Saussurean theory to the elaboration of the phoneme concept. Speech sounds belonged to *parole*, the phoneme belonged to *langue*. In studying languages as systems of internally related elements, Prague scholars did not treat the phoneme as a mere class of sounds or as a transcriptional device, but as a complex phonological unit realized by the sounds of speech. The relation of realization (representation or implementation) between units at one level and those at another level is fundamental to Prague theory. Each phoneme was composed by a number of separate distinctive or 'pertinent' features, which alone characterized it as a linguistic entity; and each distinctive feature stood in a definite opposition to its absence or to another feature in at least one other phoneme in the language. Phonological systems were classed in various ways according to the features distinguishing their component phonemes; thus English /p/, /b/, /t/, /d/, and /k/, /g/ formed oppositions of voicelessness and voice at each articulatory position, while ancient Greek had a three term plosive system

$$\begin{array}{ccc} /\text{p}/ & /\text{t}/ & /\text{k}/ \\ /\text{p}^\text{h}/ \quad /\text{b}/ & /\text{t}^\text{h}/ \quad /\text{d}/ & /\text{k}^\text{h}/ \quad /\text{g}/ \end{array}$$

involving the oppositions of voice and its absence and aspiration and its absence.[23]

The analysis of speech sounds into their component articulation features was not new, but the analysis of the unitary phonemes of the phonological level that were realized by speech sounds into ordered sets of specific contrasts between a smaller number of distinctive features was a definite advance in phonological theory and descriptive method.

Moreover this analysis below the phoneme revealed the complexity of phonological systems. Phonemes were seen not to be all members of one undifferentiated set of contrastive units in a language, but to enter into different systems of relations in different positions. /p/, /b/, /t/, /d/, and /k/, /g/ contrast as voiceless and voiced initially, medially, and finally in English words, but after initial /s/ the voice-voiceless contrast is non-operative or 'neutralized', as only one plosive can occur at each point of articulation. The same contrast is neutralized in German in word final position, where only voiceless plosives in the plosive class are found. This more refined analysis of phonological contrast was expressed by setting up 'archiphonemes', comprising just the features still distinctive in these positions of neutralization (i.e. bilabiality, etc. and plosion).[24]

Similar processes of analysis were applied to features other than the consonant and vowel segments with which phonological theory had begun, the so-called prosodic (non-segmental) features of syllables, such as length, stress, and pitch (including intonation), an extension of descriptive phonology having important implications for the future. An equally significant move included in phonological analysis the syntagmatic functions of certain sound units and sound features as demarcators of syllable and word boundaries in addition to their paradigmatic function in constituting distinct phonemes. In this syntagmatic, demarcative role they were referred to as *Grenzsignale* or *signes oristiques* (boundary markers).[25]

The phoneme concept had originated in the search for the theory of broad transcription. As the result of the work of the Prague school it became one of the fundamental elements of linguistic theory as a whole, and of the scientific description and analysis of languages.

While the main efforts of the Prague school were directed to the explication of the phoneme concept and the development of phonological theory, its members made a number of contributions to other areas of linguistics, including the more peripheral topics such as stylistics. Several syntactic studies were published, and the comparative syntactic typology of Czech and other Slavic languages is strongly represented in the work of Czech linguists since 1945. In morphology, Jakobson's study of the Russian case system and his attempt to abstract from it a basic semantic content for each case represents an application of the same analytic procedures as were being applied in phonology to the description of grammatical categories.[26]

Soon after the publications of de Saussure's *Cours*, other books were published in Europe dealing wholly or principally with synchronic linguistics, for example, O. Jespersen's *Language*, A. Gardiner's *Theory of speech and language*, K. Bühler's *Sprachtheorie*, and two important books written by Hjelmslev before the full working out of his glossematic theory, *Principes de grammaire générale* and *La catégorie des cas*.[27] At the same time certain trends in philosophical thought were bringing logicians into closer contact with the problems of linguistic analysis.[28] The inauguration of a series of international congresses of linguists in 1928 is further illustration of the growth of interest in synchronic linguistic research.

However, it was in America that linguistics, and in particular descriptive linguistics, received most recognition in universities during the 1920s; and the genesis and course of American linguistics in the interwar decades exercised a profound and lasting effect on the development of linguistic studies and linguistic thinking throughout the world. In

1924 the Linguistic Society of America was constituted, with the periodical *Language* as its annual publication.

Three outstanding scholars set American linguistics on its course, Franz Boas, Edward Sapir, and Leonard Bloomfield. Boas was the eldest and he taught several American linguists of the next generation. Bloomfield is quoted as referring to him as 'the teacher in one or another sense of us all', and he paid generous tribute to his work for American linguistics in his obituary.[29]

These three men were not detached from their antecedents. Boas and Sapir were born in Europe, and Bloomfield studied neogrammarian historical linguistics under Leskien and Brugmann (1913–14). They were familiar with the work of the earlier American historical linguist and Sanskritist W. D. Whitney, himself much influenced by nineteenth-century European thought. Boas's and Sapir's basic attitude to language in its intimate bonds with the whole way of life and way of thought of its speakers can in great part be traced back to Humboldtian ideas (p. 176, above). Noticeably in his writing on phonemic theory and procedure, Sapir espoused the psychological view of the phoneme, stressing the correspondence between the linguist's abstraction and the native speaker's reactions and intuitions on his language.[30]

In their work we can see represented the major influences on American linguistics at this formative time. American theory was conditioned by the rigorous positivism of the behaviourist or mechanist psychologists. This influence was especially strong in Bloomfield, who drastically revised his first book on linguistics, *An introduction to linguistic science* (London and New York, 1914), to bring its theoretical basis in line with the mechanist outlook of such behaviourists as A. P. Weiss, wherein statements about human activity and experience must be wholly expressed in terms relating, at least potentially, to phenomena observable in space and time by any and every observer. Bloomfield's 'talking to oneself or thinking' and 'mental images, feelings, and the like are merely popular terms for various bodily movements' are typical of this attitude.[31]

On the practical side, the anthropological interest of Boas and Sapir were reflected in the close collaboration and association of anthropology and linguistics in American universities. Anthropologists and linguists faced a joint challenge in the vast field of the almost wholly preliterate American-Indian languages, scattered, often in small and dwindling communities, over so much of the United States and Canada. Since colonial days, missionaries, traders, and enthusiastic amateurs had compiled dictionaries and grammars of a number of these languages, and in 1891 J. W. Powell published the first full-scale classification of them.[32] Boas concentrated his work on these languages, and in addition to several descriptive studies he edited and in part wrote the *Handbook of American-Indian languages*.[33] Its *Introduction*, by Boas, is still an excellent introduction to descriptive linguistics.

Some American linguists made these languages their prime concern, extending their scope to include the languages of Central and South America (where Spanish and Portuguese missionaries and others had done work in earlier centuries); and many others prepared a descriptive account of one native American language in the course of their career, often as a doctoral thesis. The languages chosen had in most cases had little previous scholarship expended on them, and the field worker was learning the language at the same time as he was analysing it, a situation quite unlike that prevailing in earlier studies of most European languages. He was cast upon his own resources, and had himself to decide on and justify every statement and classification he made. This was, and still is, a most valuable part of a training in linguistics, but it may also have been partly responsible for the heavy emphasis in American linguistic work of the succeeding decades on 'discovery procedures', so that linguistic theory was virtually required to specify the operations by which a language was actually to be analysed as well as providing the framework for the analytic statement.

Sapir and Bloomfield stood in contrast, and they complemented each other in their approaches to their subject. Bloomfield was rigorously scientific, in the light of his own, mechanist, interpretation of science, concentrating on methodology and on formal analysis. His *Language*, published in 1933, remains unsurpassed as an introduction to linguistics after more than thirty years. While it is unjust to say that Bloomfield was not interested in the study of meaning, his demand for the strictly mechanistic statement of all meanings and his consequently rather pessimistic attitude towards semantics must have contributed to the relative neglect of this aspect of linguistics during the 1930s and 1940s on the part of more orthodox American linguists.[34]

Sapir, by contrast, ranged widely through and around his subject, exploring its relations with literature, music, anthropology, and psychology, and expressing views on language, like those of Boas, that were both reminiscent of Humboldt and anticipatory of Whorf in their insistence on the pervasive influence of language on every department of human life. A glance through his *Selected writings* shows how wide was the scope of his scholarship, and a comparison of his *Language* with Bloomfield's *Language* gives a fair picture of the differences in their approaches to their subject.[35]

Because of the status of his book *Language* as a students' textbook (though it is much more than that) and his deliberate concentration on methodology, Bloomfield's interpretation of linguistics predominated in the attitude and outlook of most American linguists during the thirties and forties. Much of the work done in these years was conceived by the scholars involved in it as the articulation or development of some of the ideas or suggestions expressed by Bloomfield; and the ensuing period has now come to be known as the 'Bloomfieldian era', although it cannot be said that every one of its characteristics can be directly traced back to Bloomfield's teaching.

Every scholar is an individual, and 'schools' and 'periods' are abstractions doing doubtful justice to the work and the workers actually comprised in them. But in a survey as this, 'Bloomfieldian linguistics' can reasonably be treated as a unity; and because, during this period (1933–57), linguistics as an autonomous discipline became more firmly established and more widely represented in universities of the United States than elsewhere, Bloomfieldian influences were felt over the whole learned world in linguistic studies.

American linguists concentrated their attention on formal analysis by means of objectively describable operations and concepts, as Bloomfield had insisted that one should. The two fundamental units of description were the phoneme, successively extended to include all phonologically distinctive phonetic phenomena (p. 216, below), and the morpheme, the minimal unit of grammatical structure. The distinction between speech sound and phoneme was generally interpreted as that between member and class, with *phone* and *allophone* used to denote speech sounds. Grammatical analysis modelled itself on the already established phonological method, using *morph*, *allomorph*, and *morpheme* in the same way.[36]

Though Bloomfield had devoted some attention to the formal definition of the word as a grammatical unit, later American linguists placed less weight on it in grammatical description. Sentence structure was set out in terms of immediate constituent analysis, in which the morphemes were linked together in trees, representing constructions of ascending size and complexity (such an analysis was implicit in the 'parsing and analysis' of traditional paedagogy, and was partially involved in Jespersen's theory of ranks). Bloomfield made a basic distinction between endocentric and exocentric constructions, according to whether the construction was or was not itself broadly similar syntactically to any of its own immediate constituents, and later generations formalized a preference for binary divisions within constituents.[37]

The generally favoured model of statement, in phonology and in grammar, was that of distribution. Some linguists of the period were characterized as 'distributionalists', and linguistic description was held by them to be the statement of the distributional relations of phonemes in phoneme sequences and of morphemes in morpheme groups and constituents. Thus Z. S. Harris, whose *Methods in structural linguistics* may be regarded as the development of certain aspects of Bloomfieldianism to their extremes, could write that linguistic procedures were directed at a 'twice-made application of two major steps: the setting up of elements, and the statement of the distribution of these elements relative to each other'.[38]

In such procedures the traditional distinction between syntax and morphology tended to be somewhat downgraded in importance; and also, in the interests of purely distributional statement, 'process' terminology (wherein forms are said to be related in terms of processes such as vowel change (*Ablaut*) or consonant alternation) was as far as possible avoided. Quite illegitimately, descriptive process was sometimes allegedly confounded with historical process, and therefore disliked in synchronic linguistics.[39]

The relation of the two levels, grammar (morphemics) and phonology (phonemics) was the province of morphophonemics, the link between the two principal aspects of formal linguistic analysis (Prague linguists had used *morphophonology* in a similar sense). It was first conceived as a relation of composition; morphemes were said to be composed or to consist of phonemes. This relationship is hard to maintain in the face of allomorphic variation in which different, and sometimes wholly different, phoneme sequences are morphemically equivalent, and later writers generally interpreted the relation between phoneme and morpheme as one of representation: phonemes compose morphs, and thereby represent the morpheme as a class.[40]

The two levels were considered to be hierarchically ordered in that morphemic analysis presupposed phonemic analysis, but not *vice versa*. The doctrine of the 'separation of levels', though not found as such in Bloomfield, was pressed by some linguists, G. L. Trager, for example, to such lengths that no grammatical statement of any kind could be legitimately used in phonemic analysis, and, conversely, grammatical analysis could only begin when phonemic analysis had been completed in a language. The deliberate abandonment of such 'grammatical prerequisites' as grammatical word boundaries laid a great, and some would say an intolerable, weight on the juncture phonemes delimiting phonemic words (wordlike sequences of phonemes juncturally definable).[41] A phonemic transcription, given the statement of the allophones of all the phonemes of a language, must, on this view, be unambiguously and directly readable (excepting only for free variation among allophones), and, conversely, any uttered text must have one, and only one, phonemic transcription. This theoretical demand was later referred to as the requirement of 'biuniqueness'. D. Jones's limitation of phonemic analysis to phonetic phenomena within word boundaries was criticized as inadequate just because of its lack of biuniqueness.[42]

Grammatical statement in purely distributional terms, framed comparably to sequential phonemic statement, put a premium, in terms of ease of analysis, on languages and parts of languages in which successive morphemes could be matched in one-to-one relations with successive phonemes or phoneme groups, and the less allomorphic variation among the bound forms (internal *sandhi*) the better. In English, words like *baked* and *cats* were more easily analysable morphemically than *took* and *mice*, and sometimes zero morphs were set up to provide a theoretical sequence when the overt word shape did not provide one: *took* was analysed as /tuk+Ø, /tuk/ being an allomorph of /teik/, and Ø being an allomorph of the past tense suffix, like /-d/, /-t/, /-id/, etc.; and *mice* was analysed as /mais/+Ø, /mais/ being an allomorph of /maws/ and Ø an allomorph of the plural suffix, like /-s/, /-z/, /-iz/, /-n/, etc.[43] Distributionalist typological evaluation would therefore seem to rate highest the agglutinative languages rather than the flexional languages, which involve much internal *sandhi*, *Ablaut*, and similar formations, so prized by nineteenth-century typologists (pp. 177, 181–2, above).

'Bloomfieldian' linguistics as it ultimately developed is presented in a number of textbooks produced towards the end of this period in the history of the subject: C. F. Hockett's *Course in modern linguistics*, H. A. Gleason's *Introduction to descriptive linguistics*, and A. A. Hill's *Introduction to linguistic structures*.[44] The period is surveyed historically through selected texts in M. Joos's *Readings in linguistics*, and various aspects of it are covered in some of the contributions to *Trends in European and American linguistics 1930–1960*.[45]

In recent years a somewhat divergent development of Bloomfieldian immediate constituent analysis in grammar has been developed by K. L. Pike and his associates; it has mostly been exemplified in studies of Central and South American languages, in which these linguists have become predominantly interested. This system of analysis, which grew out of a more general theory of human behaviour suggested by Pike,[46] is known as tagmemics, since the tagmeme is its fundamental grammatical unit. The tagmeme unites in a single unit a function in a larger structure and a class of items fulfilling that function; it is defined as 'the correlation of a grammatical function or slot with a class of mutually substitutable items occurring in that slot'.[47] 'Subject manifested or filled by noun', 'predicate manifested or filled by verb', and 'object manifested or filled by noun phrase' are all tagmemes. Such tagmemes compose larger structures like clauses and sentences, and sentences are analysed, not into successions of (usually binary) immediate constituents, but into strings of collateral constituents (whence the title 'string constituent analysis' is also used of this approach). The subject and object nouns or noun phrases are related equipollently to the verb in many tagmemic analyses, whereas by the usual immediate constituent analysis the division is

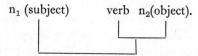

In identifying tagmemes, semantic function as well as syntactic function is taken into account, as long as an identifiable class meaning can be associated with a definite class of formal items as 'fillers', so that 'subject', 'location', 'time', 'qualifier', and the like may all constitute tagmemic slots or functions. In thus employing semantics diagnostically, and in severely modifying immediate constituent structures in syntax, tagmemics marks its major divergences from 'Bloomfieldian' grammatical analysis. Its positing of a unit comprising both function (slot) and class of items (filler) performing that function seems to be most useful in dealing with languages in which a diversity of formally different classes may perform the same function (e.g. where the morphologically different classes of noun, adjective and verb can all be predicates), or, conversely, in which the same class may perform diverse functions in the sentence (e.g. nouns as subjects, modifiers, or objects). Where a single class of items fills a single slot, there is redundancy in expressing this by means of a complex unit.[48]

Synchronic linguistic studies in Great Britain were initially concentrated on phonetics and phonology. Sweet's teaching was taken up and extended by D. Jones, whose *Outline of English phonetics*, first published in 1914, and *English pronouncing dictionary*, first published in 1917, are known and used all over the world, having carried the study and practice of 'received pronunciation' (R.P.) far beyond the relatively narrow geographical and social confines in which it characterizes the pronunciation of a native dialect.

More general linguistic questions were treated in Gardiner's *Theory of speech and language* (1932); but distinctive linguistic theory and the recognition of general linguistics as an academic subject in Great Britain owe most to J. R. Firth, Professor of General Linguistics in the University of London from 1944 to 1956, the first holder of a title in linguistics in this country. Firth devoted much of his attention to phonology, in which he put forward the theory of prosodic analysis (pp. 217–19, below). This was conceived within his general theory, which may be called the contextual theory of language.

Like American linguists, Firth drew on the work and thought of anthropologists, in his case particularly that of B. Malinowski, who, faced with the task of translating native words and sentences in ethnographic texts from the Trobriand Islands into comprehensible English, developed his theory of context of situation, whereby the meanings of utterances (taken as the primary data) and their component words and phrases were referred to their various functions in the particular situational contexts in which they were used.[49]

Firth extended this approach to language by treating all linguistic description as the statement of meaning, thereby stretching the application of the equation 'meaning is function in context' to cover grammatical and phonological analysis. The statement, for example, of the syntactic uses of a case form in a language such as Latin is the statement of its function in various grammatical contexts, and the statement of the phonological contrasts and the sequential possibilities of a consonant such as [b] or [n] in English is the statement of its function in various phonological contexts and in the context of the phonological system of the language.[50]

Meaning in the ordinary sense of the relation between language and the world of experience was handled in terms of the semantic functions of words, phrases, and sentences in different contexts of situation, of a more abstract nature than Malinowski's actual observed particulars, and providing a framework of categories, including reference and denotation,[51] by which utterances and their parts could be related to the relevant features and events in the external world. Firth stressed the parallelism between the internal, formal, contexts of grammar and phonology and the external contexts of situation, thus justifying his otherwise paradoxical extension of the use of the term *meaning*. It may be said that the basic differences between formal and semantic analysis were underestimated by Firth,[52] but the move in semantics away from the entification of meanings simply as what is 'stood for' or referred to (since with many words no such referent is readily available), towards the interpretation of meaning as function (how words and combinations of words are used) was a most valuable one.

In the analysis of linguistic form itself, Firth, like most British linguists of his time, was much more concerned with phonology than with grammar. Linguistic form was envisaged by him as sets of abstractions, at the lexical, grammatical, and phonological levels, referable to actual features and occurrences of phonic data serving as their several exponents. At each level the elements and categories abstracted were related to each other along the two Saussurean dimensions in syntagmatic structures and paradigmatic systems (Firth specialized the terms *structure* and *system* to refer respectively to these two dimensions of intralinguistic relationship); consonant-vowel-consonant and preposition-noun were typical structures, while the syllable initial plosives of a language or its nominal cases constituted systems of contrasting elements or categories. The levels were weakly hierarchic, in that phonological abstractions could themselves serve mediately as exponents of grammatical abstractions while themselves having phonetic exponents in the phonic data, though exponency could also be taken directly as the relation between grammatical or lexical abstractions and the phonic data; this rather loose arrangement has been made more rigid by the neo-Firthians, p. 220, below.[53]

The most distinctive aspect of Firth's linguistic work was prosodic phonology, the outlines of which were first presented programmatically in 1948, and developed in applications to a number of languages in the decade following.[54]

Firth's prosodic phonology should be considered along with other systems of phonology that were evolved in the 1940s as responses to the challenge that phonology, as a part of descriptive linguistics, faced during the 1930s. This challenge may be likened to something of a scientific crisis, in that observational data were proving too much for existing theory, the early phoneme theory, and at the same time this theory was itself being shaken by the phonological insights and developments of the Prague phonologists.

Phonetics, an observational and descriptive science, aided by more and more sophisticated instruments ('experimental phonetics'), was now capable of distinguishing and recording phonetic phenomena involved in speech with a greater degree of accuracy than hitherto, and was bringing into the field of its precision features such as stress and the pitch levels and movements involved in intonation, together with the sound differences and their associated articulations that related to the transitions between syllables, words, and other stretches within whole utterances. Such phonetic phenomena had been noticed by Sweet, under the title of 'synthesis' (as contrasted with 'analysis', the description of consonants and vowels considered as separate sequential segments),[55] but in the interval they had been somewhat neglected in phonological theory. In part they provided the material for the *Grenzsignale* of the Prague school (p. 206, above).

The classical phoneme theory, developed almost exclusively within accepted word boundaries and focused in the first place on consonant and vowel segments and such features as the tones of tone languages, functioning very similarly, was incapable, as it stood at the time, of dealing adequately with this mass of newly described material, whose relevance to phonological analysis was becoming ever more apparent. Simultaneously the Prague analysis of the phoneme concept itself into its component distinctive features, showed that to regard it as an indivisible unit, whose status was simply one of contrastiveness, the theoretical counterpart of the broad transcription symbol, failed to express the linguistic facts on which the very theory rested.

This crisis in phonology was met in three ways, by different scholars or groups of scholars. The most conservative solution was the one adopted by D. Jones, who maintained that the phoneme as a phonological concept should not be extended radically beyond the limits tacitly accepted hitherto. Existing practice was thus formalized in explicit theory. Intonation, and stress as a feature whose location characterizes words as whole units, fell outside the range of phonemic interpretation; and accepted grammatical word boundaries, so far from being illegitimate considerations in phonemic analysis, as some 'Bloomfieldians' taught, were quite explicitly declared by Jones to be essential to a satisfactory phonemic analysis and phonemic transcription.[56] Jones's mature theory of phonological analysis is expounded in *The phoneme: its nature and use* (1950); his contributions to phonetic description and to phonological analysis show how the limits he placed on the extension of the phoneme concept in no way restricted his linguistic work. He simply operated within a thought system different from that adopted either by post-Bloomfieldian linguists in America or by Firth and those associated with him in Britain.

An alternative solution was taken up by American linguists working within the Bloomfieldian tradition. Faced with the inadequacy of the existing, largely segmental, phoneme concept to compass all the relevant phonetic features employed in languages, these linguists responded to the challenge by a logical extension of the theory of the phoneme, so that every phonologically relevant feature could be assigned to some phoneme and represented by some symbol in the phonemic transcription. New classes of phonemes were created, covering distinctions other than those directedly assignable to consonant and vowel segments; hence the generic term *suprasegmental phoneme* applied to them.

The suprasegmental phonemes included phonemes of stress, length, and pitch, which extended over or could extend over more than a single consonant or vowel segment. Intonation was sometimes treated as a single phoneme extending over several syllables, but more generally the intonation tunes were analysed into series of distinctive pitch phonemes, American English being treated in terms of four contrasting levels.[57]

Another class of suprasegmental phonemes was constituted by the juncture phonemes. These were set up to analyse the distinctive differences found at sentence final position, in breaks between stretches of speech within a sentence, and in audibly contrastive word transitions like *a notion* and *an ocean* in English, where the actual segmental phoneme sequences were the same. Juncture phonemes assumed very considerable importance when phonemic analysis was taken across word boundaries (which Jones had refused to do), and when the demands for the strict 'separation of levels' ruled out any use of grammatical factors in phonemic analysis or in the symbols of phonemic transcriptions. (Word divisions, unless they could be shown to correlate with juncturally marked divisions, were inadmissible.)[58]

American juncture phonemes covered much of the ground of the Prague *Grenzsignale* (the first reference to 'juncture phoneme' in E. P. Hamp's *Glossary* comes from the year 1941, two years after the publication of Trubetzkoy's *Grundzüge*)[59]; but American theory integrated these demarcative phenomena into their phonemics, whereas Trubetzkoy had left them assigned partly to phonemic and partly to non-phonemic status. We owe to the 'Bloomfieldian' distributionalist era much of our proper awareness of the nature and importance of junctural phenomena in speech.

The suprasegmental phonemes of pitch, length, and stress, involved American phonemics in a break with seriality in the conception of phonemes and their representation in transcriptions. But the origin of the phoneme in transcriptional requirements maintained a strong hold on this advanced phonemic theory. Juncture phonemes, though they might be suprasegmental in terms of the phonetic features involved, were allocated a serial place between segmental phonemes in transcriptions, sometimes disjoined from the maximally prominent feature associated with them, as when Swahili stress was phonemicized as an interword juncture located after the syllable following the stressed syllable.[60] The demand for biuniqueness, noticed above, sprang from transcriptional practice, and so did the overall monosystemic interpretation of the theory, whereby the contrasts between phonemes found in positions of maximal contrast were generalized for all other positions ('once a phoneme, always a phoneme'). The different contrast systems operative at different places in a language, made explicit by Prague theory and dealt with there by the concepts of neutralization and the archiphoneme (p. 205, above), were covered, less elegantly perhaps, by statements of the different distribution of different phonemes, after the sounds occurring in positions of neutralization had been, sometimes arbitrarily, assigned to one or another of the phonemes set up for the positions of maximal contrast (thus the second consonant sounds of English words like *span*, *stitch*, and *sketch* were regarded, following the orthographic tradition, as allophones of /p/, /t/, and /k/, although they shared some features (e.g. non-aspiration) with /b/, /d/, and /g/).[61]

Such transcriptional influences may have been tacit rather than explicit, but the reluctance with which the 'vertical' analysis of segmental phonemes into their distinctive features or components ('componential analysis') was pressed during the thirties and forties was openly attributed to its transcriptional inconvenience.[62]

In this last respect, prosodic theory made the most radical break with existing theory. Firth insisted on the separation of the requirements of transcription from the structure of an adequate phonological theory. Twaddell had, indeed, suggested such a divorce earlier, but with little effect on the phonological theory of the time. For Firth the phoneme as a theoretical unit had its value in the devising and justifying of economical broad transcriptions; the full display of the functional inter-relations of sound features in utterance required a different set of terms and a different mode of analysis.[63] Since Firth was a strong adherent of the view that analytic concepts exist only within the descriptive system of the linguist and not in the language itself, such a coexistence of separate conceptual systems serving different purposes presented no difficulties for him.

Prosodic analysis involves two types of basic element: phonematic units and prosodies. Each of these is set up in relation to some phonetic feature (or group of features) serving as its exponent in the actual uttered speech material. Phonematic units are consonants and vowels, and are serially ordered as segments; but any phonological structure (e.g. syllable, or syllable group) may include one or more prosodies. Prosodies are assigned to definite structures, not to places between phonematic units, and are set up to handle syntagmatic relations between certain phonetic features. Broadly, phonetic features are allotted to prosodies rather than to phonematic units, if they either extend over the whole or the major part of a structure, or are positionally restricted in it and thus serve to delimit or demarcate it. As examples, the tones in Siamese (Thai) are treated as syllable prosodies by the first criterion, and plosion in this language, being confined to syllable initial position, is regarded as a syllable (part) prosody by the second criterion.[64] Comparable examples of prosodies of words, as phonological units, are vowel harmony restrictions (usually accompanied by related differences in the consonantal articulations) in languages like Turkish and Hungarian, and stress confined to a fixed place in the word and thus serving to delimit its boundaries.

It will be seen that Firth's prosodies, and the prosodies of analyses that followed this theory, in part deal with the same phenomena as the *Grenzsignale* of Prague and the suprasegmental phonemes of the American phonemicists. There are, however, a number of differences. Any type of phonetic feature that can be shown to be syntagmatically involved with more than a single segment can be treated as the exponent of a prosody; American suprasegmental phonemes, other than junctures, were generally limited to stress, length, and pitch, features not involving a basic difference in the shape of the sound waves.[65] In prosodic analysis no such restrictions apply, and some phonetic material that in other systems of analysis would be part of some consonant or vowel phonemes may be assigned to prosodies (e.g. retroflexion in Sanskrit and some modern Indian languages, and palatal and non-palatal articulation in some varieties of Chinese[66]), and for the same reason the exponents of some phonematic units may comprise fewer phonetic features than would belong to the nearest corresponding phonemes in a phonemic analysis.

With transcriptional needs no longer a relevant consideration, a monosystemic set of analytic elements is not necessary. Prosodic analysis is prepared to set up different systems of phonematic units and prosodies at different places in structures where this facilitates the analysis. Thus syllable initial consonants may well form a different system from syllable final consonants, with no identification of the members of one system with the members of another, even though certain phonetic features (exponents) may be shared between them. Moreover, unlike the 'Bloomfieldians', but somewhat like the later transformational-generative linguists (p. 229, below), prosodic phonologists see phonology as the link between grammar and the actual utterance, or, more abstractly, between grammar and phonetics; and grammatical categories and structures are properly relevant to phonological statement wherever a phonetic feature or phonetic features can be associated with them as exponents. From this come the recognition of word and sentence prosodies, as well as syllable prosodies, and also the possibility of phonological systems different in certain respects for words of one class in a language and words of another class.[67] The last two respects in which prosodic analysis differs from transcriptionally orientated phonemic analysis gave rise to the term *polysystemic* with reference to prosodic phonology. The outcome of a prosodic analysis is not a readable transcription, but a diagrammatic representation of the interrelations of elements and features in a stretch of utterance, that can be put into connection with its grammatical structure.[68]

It is important to consider these three responses to the challenge faced by phonology in the 1930s not so much as rivals contending for the recognition of superiority, but rather as solutions each meeting certain requirements. Jones's phonology is economical and easily understood; 'Bloomfieldian' phonemics is rigorous and exhaustive, and it claims to fit all the relevant phonetic features into a transcriptional representation and a complete phonemic inventory; prosodic analysis, at the price of some complexity, is able to bring out more explicitly the phonological functions of the various phonetic features in a language and to link these to a grammatical analysis. Some valuable, though only partial, contrastive treatments of the same language material by prosodic and by phonemic analysis at the hands of a single writer have been published.[69] Such studies are more significant, at any rate in a historical survey, than the more intemperate assertions by devotees on the supremacy of one particular approach to phonological analysis.

It may fairly be said that phonology was the pace-maker in the Bloomfieldian era, as far as descriptive theory and methodology were concerned. By far the strongest impulse to a revision of theory and of its associated concepts came from progress in phonetic observation and phonological analysis. The Prague school and the earlier Firthians devoted most of their attention to the phonological level of language; Jones concerned himself wholly with phonology and phonetics; and in America phonemic theory advanced further in its chosen direction than grammatical theory, and the grammatical theory of the time, with its especial interest in morphemic analysis, followed in the wake of progress made in phonemics. In a comment on Hockett's *Manual of phonology* (1955), published towards the end of the period, one can read the well justified remark that a comparable manual of grammar could not as yet be envisaged.[70]

Developments that have taken place after the 'Bloomfieldian' era, for all their differences, show an equal concern for all levels of language; phonology no longer determines the course of linguistic theory and linguistic method, and semantics is no longer regarded, as Bloomfield had unwittingly led many of his contemporaries to regard it, as somehow beyond the purview and the competence of linguistic science.

Significantly the recent British development of Firthian linguistics lays no special weight on prosodic phonology, but is primarily an articulation of his general theory of language. Firth's conception of context of situation as the means of making statements of meaning and of phonology as the link between grammar and phonetics, are formalized in the following schematic diagram of descriptive linguistics:[71]

phonetics				
	linguistics			
substance	↔	form	↔	situation
phonic substance	phono-logy	grammar (closed system)	context	extralinguistic features
graphic substance	ortho-graphy	lexis (open system)		

Neo-Firthian theory involves four fundamental categories: unit, structure, class, and system, and three scales: rank, exponence, and delicacy (hence the designation 'scale and category linguistics', that is also used of this development).

Units, for example sentences, have structures, in which units lower in rank (e.g. clauses and words) occur, and units below the highest in rank are grouped into classes by reference to their function in structures: and the members of classes are grouped into systems.

At either the phonological or the grammatical level, relative size falls along the scale of rank. In grammar, sentence, clause, phrase, word, and morpheme are in descending rank scale; in phonology, syllable group, syllable, and segment are likewise.

The scale of exponence relates abstractions at either level to the actual data, and by moving towards the data within abstractions one is considered to be moving down the scale of exponence (in passing, for example, from grammatical unit in clause structure to noun, and then to *man* as an instance or exponent of the class 'noun', and ultimately of the category 'unit').[72]

The scale of delicacy relates to the subdivision of classes and structures in order to take account of more detail. 'Intransitive verb' and 'concessive clause' are more delicate than 'verb' and 'subordinate clause'.

In distinguishing level, rank, and exponence, neo-Firthian linguistics brings to bear on linguistic analysis certain precisions not always maintained in 'Bloomfieldian linguistics'.[73] The theory has been set out in M. A. K. Halliday's *Categories of the theory of grammar*, and more popularly in M. A. K. Halliday, A. McIntosh, and P. Strevens, *The linguistic sciences and language teaching*.[74] In the first mentioned reference, liberal citations from Firth's writings appear and attention is drawn to the way in which the theory may be said to derive from his linguistic scholarship. The degree to which, in fact, neo-Firthian linguistics represents a continuation or a divergence from Firth's theoretical position is disputed, but as Firth's exposition on several points in his theory was often allusive and fragmentary rather than explicit and articulated, such a question must remain in part undecided.

The linguistic theory worked out, with phonological analysis principally in mind, by Trubetzkoy and his associates of the Prague school led to a number of developments. The essence of Prague phonology, the analysis of phonemes into their component distinctive features, is seen in the studies of 'componential analysis', in both phonology and grammar, by American scholars, in which phonemes and morphemes are analysed 'vertically' as unitary compounds of distinctive components or categories, though without the further refinement of the Prague concept of neutralization.[75] This type of analysis has been extended to semantics, in the hope that it may help to formalize the apparently limitless range of semantic functions or meanings carried by lexical items in languages. Obvious places for its application are restricted lexical sub-systems of terms in culturally delimited areas, such as kinship vocabularies. In English, for example, 'aunt' can be analysed into 'kin' 'first degree ascending generation' 'first degree collaterality' and 'female', contrasting with 'uncle' by the feature of sex difference. Several attempts have been made to extend this sort of componential schematization to other and wider areas of the lexicons of languages, but it seems unlikely that it will prove possible to analyse all lexical meanings along these lines.[76]

In phonetics and phonology, distinctive feature analysis made striking advances in alliance with instrumental and acoustic studies of speech transmission. This development has been particularly associated with R. Jakobson, one of the original Prague circle, who relatively early in his career decided that more light would be shed on some phonological questions by considering the distinctive features composing phonemes from the acoustic and from the hearer's point of view rather than from the articulatory or the speaker's position. In this approach, Jakobson drew on the findings of earlier acousticians such an H. von Helmholtz and C. Stumpf for the basic triangles

$$/i/ \qquad /u/ \qquad\qquad /t/ \qquad /p/$$
$$\text{and}$$
$$/a/ \qquad\qquad\qquad /k/$$

wherein acuteness and gravity are contrasted horizontally, and diffuseness and compactness are contrasted vertically, as acoustic features resulting from differences in the configurations of the vocal tract.[77]

Under pressure of war Jakobson moved to the United States, and in collaboration with scholars working with such equipment as the sound spectrograph he has analysed the inherent distinctiveness of the phonemes of all languages into combinations of up to twelve binary contrasts of acoustic features, defined in terms of the distribution of energy at different frequencies ('formants') in their sound waves, rather than directly in relation to their articulations.[78] In this type of analysis, phonological systems are set out on a matrix of feature oppositions, the phonemes participating in more than one binary contrast in relation to the other phonemes of the language. This is displayed in Jakobson's and Lotz's diagram of the phonemic system of French. Feature analysis, in which segmental units are taken theoretically as no more than sets of simultaneous distinctive features, has provided one mode of stating the phonological link between the output of the syntactic component and the transcribed utterance in transformational-generative grammar (p. 229, below), though in this case the stage of phonemic transcription is often by-passed.[79]

In historical linguistics, the phoneme theory, especially in its Prague interpretation, led to a significant modification of the neogrammarian position (pp. 182–3, above). The neogrammarian achievement had been to formalize and to make explicit the concept of the sound law, and it was with sounds as individual phonetic segments that they were concerned. When sound change was reconsidered in the light of the phoneme theory, by which the sounds of languages were understood as forming interrelated systems of contrasts, attention was paid to the evolution of phonological systems rather than to the changes of individual and supposedly independent sounds. This approach could be and was made from two different directions. Firstly, the end product of a sound change was a different phonological system, unless the change related merely to phonetic difference within the limits of an existing set of contrasts. In an eight vowel system with four front and four back vowel phonemes, the merger of two back vowels (say [ɔ] > [o]) entails the loss of the contrast of /ɔ/ and /o/, and an asymmetrical system of four front and three back vowel phonemes results. Jakobson traces the sequence in Latvian of /k/ and /g/ developing fronted allophones before the front vowels /i/ and /e/ ([ts] and [dž]), and these becoming separate phonemes, /ts/ and /dž/, contrasting with /k/ and /g/, after /ai/ had been monophthongized to /i/; Fourquet has re-examined and reinterpreted the Germanic sound changes comprising 'Grimm's Law' in terms of the evolution of systems rather than of the changes of particular sounds, and has explained the historical phenomena as the maintenance of phonological oppositions under the pressure of successive general changes in the force of articulation on the part of speakers.[80]

Secondly, sound change can be considered not as regards its systemic effect, but from the viewpoint of its systemic causation. The neogrammarians had played very safe over the question of the causes of sound change, and Bloomfield followed them in declaring: 'The causes of sound-change are unknown'.[81] The occasion for sound change has always been seen in the conditions in which speech is transmitted as a socially learned capability from one generation to another; but quite certainly the causes are multiple and complex. External factors such as language contacts, bilingualism, the effects of substrates in the super-imposition of an alien language upon a speech community, and the influence of writing systems must all be acknowledged; and perhaps genetic influence, though this is still very speculative, cannot be ruled out.[82] But a significant cause of sound changes is to be found within the phonological systems of languages themselves.

Strangely enough, de Saussure, for all his emphasis on the importance of the structural conception of language in synchronic linguistics, went so far as to deny explicitly any diachronic relevance of structure.[83] But two factors are constantly at work within phonological systems. The economy of effort produced by the multiple use of each feature contrast that has been once mastered tends towards the maintenance and the generation of symmetry in phoneme systems (/p/, /t/, /k/, /d/, /g/ requires as many contrasting articulation features as the fuller and more symmetrical system /p/, /t/, /k/, /b/, /d/, /g/); but the physiological asymmetry of the vocal tract interferes with the achievement of perma-nent symmetry (for example, in the matter of distinctive degrees of tongue height in vowel phonemes, there is more latitude for keeping the front vowels apart than for the back vowels). A. Martinet cites as an illustration the fronting of /u/ in Azores Portuguese, whereby the exploitation of the front-back contrast (acoustically acute-grave) in the close rounded vowel phoneme releases more space for the ready main-tenance of phonemic contrast between the remaining back vowels, /a/, /ɔ/, and /o/.[84]

Researches on these lines, and the broadening of the theory of his-torical linguistics to embrace their results do not invalidate the neo-grammarian insistence on the regularity of sound change as the basis of historical linguistics; but they do bring to historical linguistics further important insights and more powerful means of investigation.

During the nineteenth century, Russian linguists were in touch with general European developments, and the phoneme concept was appa-rently arrived at independently by eastern and western scholars at about the same time (p. 204, above). Trubetzkoy was Russian by birth and education, and had worked on some of the vernacular languages of the Russian empire before leaving the country after the first world war. The Bolshevik revolution brought with it a sharp break with the linguistic scholarship of the rest of the world, and during the twenties, thirties, and forties, although phonological work went on and with it the

study of the phoneme theory, Soviet linguistics was dominated by the
eccentric dogmatisms of N. J. Marr (1864–1934).

Marr, himself half Georgian by birth and from his early youth gifted
with remarkable language learning ability, turned his attention first,
like some other Russian scholars, to Georgian and the rest of the Caucasian languages. In investigating the history of the Caucasian languages
he gradually evolved his own theory (or theories) of linguistic history.
Rejecting the accepted Indo-european theory, he drew his ideas from
eighteenth-century beliefs in the gestural origin of language and from
middle nineteenth-century opinion on linguistic typology as an indication of stages of progressive linguistic development. The 'Japhetic'
languages, a term he used to cover the languages of the Caucasus,
represented a stage in the evolution of language through which some
other languages had already passed. Languages were historically related, not in linguistic families, but by the different evolutionary 'layers'
of structure deposited from continual mixtures and combinations.
Languages were not national, but class phenomena, and were part of
the superstructure whose changes corresponded to changes in the
economic base of the speakers' social organization; here he claimed the
theoretical alliance of Marrism and Marxism.

Claiming to explain not only linguistic history but also linguistic
prehistory by his theory, Marr soon transcended merely observational
statements, and declared that the words of all languages could be
traced back to four primitive elements: [sal], [ber], [jon], and [roʃ].
Such unsupported theorizing enjoyed official patronage, and several
other Russian scholars found it prudent to uphold and even eulogize
Marr's pronouncements, until 1950 when suddenly Stalin ordained the
rejection of the whole Marrist edifice, pointing out, among other things,
that language was not dependent on economic organization since the
same Russian language served both pre-revolutionary capitalism and
post-revolutionary communism, a statement of the obvious not apparently made before. Stalin's intervention both ended the long reign of
Marrist theory and drew the world's attention to it.[85]. Since then, and
especially since the rather more liberal phase of Soviet rule, Russian
linguists have started to work in closer collaboration with those of the
rest of western Europe and America, and current western developments
are being keenly and fruitfully debated. In general linguistics particular
attention is paid to lexicography, which is accorded the status of a
component of linguistics along with phonology and grammar, rather
than being merely a part of the description of languages. In comparative

and historical linguistics, Slavic studies, suppressed under the eccentricities of Marr, have seen very considerable development.[86] There is good hope that this kindlier atmosphere will continue, and that Marrism will be remembered only as a sterile aberration, an awful warning of the extent to which modern tyranny can keep fantasy enthroned in defiance of fact.

A general theory of linguistic analysis that derives some of its characteristics from Prague theory is 'stratificational grammar', propounded by S. M. Lamb (*grammar* being used in its widest sense to cover formal analysis as a whole, as in transformational usage, pp. 228-9, below).[87] Four levels or strata are posited within language structure for the analysis of sentences: sememic, wherein the distinctive meaning units of the language are set out in a network of relations (e.g. 'tiger', 'catch', 'male', 'human', 'agent', 'goal', and 'past'); lexemic, wherein the distinctive lexical units *man, catch, -ed, tiger*, etc. are linked together in a sentence structure; morphemic, wherein morphemes appear in a successive string; and phonemic, wherein simultaneous bundles of distinctive features make up a string of phonemic units (*the man caught the tiger*).

The levels are hierarchically related and linked together by the relation of representation or realization, in that the lexemic level represents the sememic and is represented by the morphemic, which in turn is represented by the distinctive features of the lowest structural level, the phonemic. The nature of representation varies from simple, when one unit of a higher level is represented by one unit at the next lower level, to such complex representations as neutralization (two or more units not structurally distinguished in representation), composite representation (one unit represented by more than one lower level unit, as in multiple allomorphic representation of a morpheme), zero representation, portmanteau representation, etc.

This theory reacts against the dominant linearity of 'Bloomfieldian' distributionalism, by displaying the different types of structural relation that may be involved in linguistic analysis, and the number of different ways in which a structure at one level may be related to (realized in, or represented by) a structure at another.

What is probably the most radical and important change in direction in descriptive linguistics and in linguistic theory that has taken place in recent years may be located in 1957, when Chomsky's *Syntactic structures* was published, inaugurating the transformational-generative phase of linguistics, so named from the principal distinctive method and orientation of the work taken in hand. It has already been stressed that the assignment of changes in the history of a subject to particular years is arbitrary and somewhat artificial; work on Praguean, Firthian, and Bloomfieldian lines went on after 1957 and still does go on. What can and should be said of transformational grammar (as it is usually designated) is that it is in a state of rapid development and has become the focus of attention of some of the most energetic and able linguistic scholars of the present day, especially in the United States. It seems certain that its effects on the whole of linguistic theory and practice will be deep and lasting.

So rapid, indeed, are the changes in some of the theoretical concepts and methods of transformational grammar, that a definite statement of its present position would be inadequate and certainly dated within a few years. In a historical survey, the main outlines of transformational grammar can most readily be seen in the first statement of this approach to the description of languages, *Syntactic structures*, supplemented where necessary by references to later contributions.

The aim set by transformationalists to their work is higher than that explicitly set by any previous group of linguists. It amounts to nothing less than presenting in a description of a language everything that is implied by the linguistic competence of a native speaker. Thus Katz and Postal, who include a theory of semantics partly based on componential analysis within their exposition of a transformational-generative theory, write: 'A linguistic description of a natural language is an attempt to reveal the nature of a fluent speaker's mastery of that language.'[88] Further appeals to linguistic intuitions or practical knowledge of the language are, ideally, unnecessary and illegitimate, because all such intuitions and performative knowledge should have been made explicit and incorporated into the description of the language; correspondingly, transformationalists attach more importance than did linguists of the Bloomfieldian period to the agreement of their descriptions with the intuitions of native speakers, and linguistic theory must be adequate for this purpose, with resources to explain and justify such descriptions.[89] But transformationalists reject the demand that their theory (or any theory of linguistic description) should itself provide the means of working out the analysis or of specifying discovery procedures.

The objects of the transformationalists are to be attained by framing linguistic descriptions in terms of rules that embody the creative capacity of a native speaker to generate or produce and to understand an infinite number of sentences (all and only the grammatical sentences of the language), most of which he has never uttered or heard before. A contrast is drawn between the 'grammar of lists' of recurrent items, explicitly defined, in distributional relations with one another, and the 'grammar of rules'. The former is associated with 'Bloomfieldian' distributionalist and 'taxonomic' linguistics, and the static conception of de Saussure's *langue*, the latter with transformational work and the creative ideas of Humboldt on language as *energeia* (pp. 174–5, above).[90]

The rules of a transformational-generative grammar fall into three sets, or components. Firstly, rules of phrase structure successively expand the sentence (S), as a prime, into constituents, through the successive representations of it in strings whose elements are dominated by other elements (nodes) at a preceding (higher) representation. This produces trees with labelled bracketings, in a manner somewhat similar to the immediate constituent analysis of Bloomfieldian linguistics:

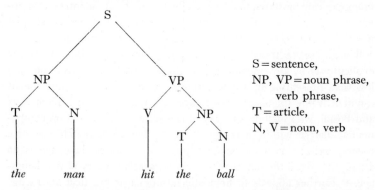

S = sentence,
NP, VP = noun phrase,
     verb phrase,
T = article,
N, V = noun, verb

These elements, though they share the same names with many of those used in Bloomfieldian analyses, are not explicitly defined, but they have their definitions arising from the rules by which they are introduced and the lexical items assigned to them in the rules.[91]

The second component applies specific transformations, some obligatory, some optional, to the final output strings of phrase structure rules, involving such operations as deletions, additions, and changes of order. *Syntactic structures* distinguishes kernel sentences produced by applying only obligatory transformations to the phrase structure strings (e.g. the transformation of affix + verb into verb + affix in the present tense, *hit-s*, etc.), and non-kernel sentences that involve optional transformations in addition, such as active to passive (*the ball was hit by the man*); but later interpretations of the theory have made less use of this distinction, stressing rather the distinction between the underlying 'deep structures' of a sentence and its 'surface structure', that it exhibits after the transformations involved in it have been applied.[92] Further transformations serve to link two or more simple sentences into one complex one by coordination or subordination (or 'embedding').

The lexicon, in the form of lexical rules ('N → *man, boy, ball, game*, etc.*) is introduced at some point before the phonological rules take over; in *Syntactic structures* they form part of the phrase structure rules, but later transformational writings have varied this, as they have also varied the allocation of grammatical material between phrase structure and transformational rules.[93]

Finally, the output of the phrase structure and transformational components, which includes word division, is converted into utterance, or into the narrow transcription of an utterance, by the phonological or morphophonemic component, whose rules convert the elements of the syntactic level (phrase structure and transformations) into sounds, or into symbolization of sounds, either letters of the phonetic alphabet or sets of distinctive features such as were developed by Jakobson and others from the articulatory distinctive features of the Prague school. Transformationalists, like Firthians, regard phonology as the link between grammar (narrowly considered) and utterance (or phonetics), and like them they reject an independent phonemic representation in a linguistic analysis as at best unnecessary, and perhaps objectionable, since certain phonetic differences may be distinctive in one environment, where they must be symbolized, and non-distinctive in another, where they should not be (in the interests of economy).[94]

Rules are ordered in the descriptive statement so that later rules take account of the results of prior rules. In this way an economy of descriptive apparatus, such as was a prime objective of Pāṇini, is achieved. Thus the irregular English strong past tense formations (*take, took*, etc.) are given before the regular weak forms (/-d/, /-t/, /-id/), so that these can have a clear run through the rest of the verbs.[95]

Transformationalists claim that their system of linguistic description is inherently more powerful than others, and, in particular, more powerful than 'Bloomfieldian' descriptivism, dominated by the concept of immediate constituency. Of course it needs to be, if it is to achieve the objectives that the transformationalists have set themselves. Certainly a number of statements that linguists ought to be able to make can be made more easily in transformational descriptions than in some others; and the conception of grammar as a succession of rules allows for the limitless recursiveness of language (sentences may be indefinitely prolonged), by providing for the reintroduction of an earlier rule at a later stage (just as NP appears twice in the generation of the phrase structure expansion shown above). The intuitive associations of active sentences with passive sentences, and of declaratives with interrogatives are formalized by the transformational rules that derive one from another, or both from a common source; and intuited structural distinctions, such as that between *the wine was drunk by midnight* and *the wine was drunk by John*, which have the same immediate constituent analysis, are shown to have resulted from formally different transformations.

Transformational linguistics was immediately hailed by American reviewers as a decisive break with the Bloomfieldian taxonomic descriptive tradition.[96] This was certainly the case. The integration of lexicon, grammar, and phonology into sets of rules, the reversal of the hierarchic relationship of grammar (syntax and morphology) and phonology, the rejection of the separation of levels and the requirement of biuniqueness for phonemic transcriptions, and indeed the denial of a place in the description of a language to the phoneme as an independent linguistic unit, were all violent changes in the course that linguistics had followed in America for the preceding twenty-five years. Transformations had no place in Bloomfieldian descriptions, and the starting point of transformational grammar was the opposite of that assumed in 'Bloomfieldian' work. The transformationalists devise rules by which the production of grammatical sentences can be described and explicated in detail, stressing the generative aspect of linguistic science.

In previous American descriptive linguistics, the stress had been on its analytical function; linguists had made texts, actual utterances, recorded or elicited data, their starting point, and had aimed at devising a theory and a method for subjecting these to a progressive analysis down to the fundamental units, the phonemes and the morphemes, although actual expositions often began from these smallest units and worked up to the sentence or utterance.[97] It is, however, noteworthy that the concept of a conversion relation or a transformation between two or more actual sentences in texts had been outlined by Harris, Chomsky's teacher, as one means of extending the descriptive analysis of texts beyond and across sentence boundaries.[98]

In a wider geographical and temporal context, transformational linguistics did not constitute anything like so sharp a break. European reviewers noticed that in contrast to its opposition to much of its immediate American past, transformationalism formalized, made explicit, and carried further ideas and methods implicitly accepted in traditional European language teaching and incorporated into some earlier European linguistic theory.[99] While its aims and assumptions look back in some respects to Humboldt, certain transformational relations were anticipated by the rationalist Port Royal grammarians (for example the embedding or subordinating transformations involved in relative clauses, p. 125, above), and traditional Latin paedagogy has for long made use of transformational techniques in working from the grammar of direct speech to the grammar of indirect speech, while all teachers of languages have assumed the close association of active and passive and of declarative and interrogative, whose formal relations are stated in ordered series of rules in transformational grammars.

Such antecedents to transformational grammar are acknowledged and emphasized by Chomsky, in a protesting reply to critics who have ascribed his linguistic theory, doubtless because of the extensive use of mathematical and logical symbols and the overtly 'scientific' style in which discussions between transformationalists are carried on, to such immediate antecedents as machine translation and the application of computers to language analysis.[100]

One may also consider the rather different contexts of language study in America during the Bloomfieldian era and in the years following the second world war. The challenge of the American-Indian languages provided a good part of the stimulus for synchronic linguistics in America during the 1920s and after, with the consequential emphasis on procedure and methodology. In this field, for the most part the linguist learned the language and worked out his descriptive analysis at the same time. During the war, hastily devised language teaching programmes which were aimed at meeting actual or expected operational requirements also involved several American linguists in the study of hitherto rather neglected languages. All this fell within the period characterized as 'Bloomfieldian', and one may observe that while discovery procedures are largely ignored or deliberately excluded in most post-'Bloomfieldian' linguistics, one of the most recent books specifically devoted to this aspect of linguistic work comes from a member of the tagmemic group, whose interests still centre on the description and analysis of native American languages.[101]

Over much of the world in post-war years, in which the expounders of transformational linguistics received their training and began their work, the teaching of well-established European languages, and especially the teaching of English, has for various reasons become a dominant theme in what is called 'applied linguistics'; and in America, as in Britain, probably more effort is devoted to English teaching methods, courses, and projects, than to any other single application of linguistic science. Correspondingly one sees that whereas in the pre-war years and during the war the so called 'exotic' languages and particularly the American-Indian languages were freely cited in theoretical and procedural publications, transformational-generative theory has in large part been worked out, developed, and illustrated with reference to English, and some other European languages, whose grammar and phonology are already 'known' in some sense by the linguist before he begins his work, however many gaps in our explicit knowledge may be revealed, as they have been revealed, by transformational analyses.

Of course there are exceptions on both sides of this division. C. C. Fries's *Structure of English* sets out 'Bloomfieldian' discovery procedures in arriving at a formal descriptive analysis of English, and some transformational work has been exemplified in American-Indian language material;[102] but the difference in the environments in which linguistics is studied is certainly marked, and is very probably of historical relevance in this change of direction.

Transformational linguistics has been chosen as the point at which this brief account of the history of the subject comes to its end. This is not because transformational-generative theory is likely to supersede all other approaches to language (despite the claims made by some adherents on its behalf), but because it is both one of the most recent developments and one that is certainly destined to make progress and to exert great influence on linguistic work, theoretical and practical, in the future. The historian must leave his narrative when he reaches the contemporary situation, but history does not thereupon stand still. He tries to understand and to interpret the past, and to see the present as its product; but his efforts do not justify him in setting himself up as a prophet. However, some comprehension and appreciation of the history of linguistic science will enable him to study future movements and controversies with a greater sympathy, tolerance, and insight. To relate one's immediate interests to the trials and the achievements of fellow workers in past ages should lead to more balanced judgments and less intemperate enthusiasms. This may further justify the selection of the transformationalist school to close a survey of the history of linguistics, since several of its members look both to the new discoveries that their theory enables them to make and to the links that it has with the linguistic enquiries of earlier generations. Language is perhaps the most specifically human of mankind's faculties. In striving towards the understanding and knowledge of language, man has throughout his intellectual history been seeking more fully to attain self-knowledge, and to obey the injunction that faced the visitor to Apollo's temple at Delphi,[103] the centre of the ancient Greek world, where our civilization finds its source:

ΓΝΩΘΙ ΣΕΑΥΤΟΝ.

FOR FURTHER CONSULTATION

H. ARENS, *Sprachwissenschaft: der Gang ihrer Entwicklung von der Antike bis zur Gegenwart*, Freiburg/Munich, 1955, 388–525.

E. BACH, *Introduction to transformational grammars*, New York, 1964.

L. BLOOMFIELD, *Language*, London, 1935.

N. CHOMSKY, *Syntactic structures*, The Hague, 1957.

——, *Current issues in linguistic theory*, The Hague, 1964.

——, *Aspects of the theory of syntax*, Cambridge, Mass., 1965.

J. R. FIRTH, 'The English school of phonetics', *TPS* 1946, 92–132.

——, *Papers in linguistics 1934–1951*, Oxford, 1957.

M. A. K. HALLIDAY, 'Categories of the theory of grammar', *Word* 17 (1961), 241–92.

Z. S. HARRIS, *Methods in structural linguistics*, Chicago, 1951.

L. HJELMSLEV, *Prolegomena to a theory of language* (tr. F. J. WHITFIELD), Baltimore, 1953 (first published in Danish, 1943).

M. IVIĆ, *Trends in linguistics*, The Hague, 1965, 69–242.

R. JAKOBSON, *Selected writings I: phonological studies*, The Hague, 1962.

D. JONES, *An outline of English phonetics* (sixth edition), London, 1947.

——, *The phoneme: its nature and use*, Cambridge, 1950.

——, 'History and meaning of the term "phoneme"', *Maître phonétique* July to December 1951, supplement.

M. JOOS (ed.), *Readings in linguistics*, New York, 1958.

A. KOUTSOUDAS, *Writing transformational grammars*, New York, 1966.

M. LEROY, *Les grands courants de la linguistique moderne*, Brussels and Paris, 1963, 61–178.

B. MALMBERG, *New trends in linguistics* (tr. E. CARNEY), Stockholm, 1964.

C. MOHRMANN, A. SOMMERFELT, and J. WHATMOUGH (ed.), *Trends in European and American linguistics 1930–1960*, Utrecht, 1961.

C. MOHMANN, F. NORMAN, and A. SOMMERFELT (ed.), *Trends in modern linguistics*, Utrecht, 1963.

E. SAPIR, *Language*, New York, 1921.

——, *Selected writings* (ed. D. G. MANDELBAUM), Berkeley, 1951.

F. DE SAUSSURE, *Cours de linguistique générale* (fourth edition), Paris, 1949.

16—S.H.L.

N. S. TRUBETZKOY, *Grundzüge der Phonologie*, *TCLP* 7 (1939), translated by J. CANTINEAU, *Principes de Phonologie*, Paris, 1949.

J. VACHEK, *The linguistic school of Prague*, Bloomington, 1966.

J. T. WATERMAN, *Perspectives in linguistics*, Chicago, 1963, 61–98.

C. L. WRENN, 'Henry Sweet', *TPS* 1946, 177–201.

Studies in linguistic analysis (various authors), special volume of the Philological Society, Oxford, 1957.

History of linguistics (articles by various authors), *Anthropological linguistics* 5.1 (1963).

NOTES

1. Further details on prominent scholars and their work may be found in IVIĆ, 1965, LEROY, 1963, MALMBERG, 1964, and WATERMAN, 1963, which are devoted to nineteenth- and twentieth-century linguistics, surveyed from a historical point of view.

2. *Memoire sur le système primitif des voyelles dans les langues indo-européenes*, Leipzig, 1879.

3. DE SAUSSURE, 1949, preface to first edition: for more details, R. GODEL, *Les sources manuscrites du Cours de linguistique générale de F. de Saussure*, Paris, 1957.

4. P. A. VERBURG, *Lingua* 2 (1950), 441.

5. WATERMAN, 1963, 67.

6. E. DURKHEIM, *Les règles de la méthode sociologique* (eleventh edition), Paris, 1950; DE SAUSSURE, 1949, 31, 37, 138; cp. the judicious comments of SAPIR, 'Do we need a superorganic?', *American anthropologist* n.s. 19 (1917), 441–7.

7. DE SAUSSURE, 1949, 34, 97.

8. ibid., 151–4, 157, 169.

9. ibid., part 2, chapter 5; de Saussure used the term *associatif*, but since it was first suggested by Hjelmslev (*Acts of the fourth international congress of linguists*, Copenhagen, 1936, 140–51), *paradigmatic* has become the more generally current word.

10. DE SAUSSURE, 1949, 317.

11. HJELMSLEV, 1953; id., 'Structural linguistics', *Studia linguistica* 1 (1947), 69–78; H. SPANG-HANSSEN, 'Glossematics', MOHRMANN, SOMMERFELT, and WHATMOUGH, 1961, 128–64. Criticism of some aspects of glossematic theory in E. FISCHER-JØRGENSEN, 'Remarques sur les principes de l'analyse phonémique', *TCLC* 5 (1949), 214–234; B. SIERTSEMA, *A study of glossematics*, The Hague, 1955.

12. See further S. ULLMANN, *Principles of semantics*, Glasgow and Oxford, 1957, 152–70; S. ÖHMAN, 'Theories of the "linguistic field"', *Word* 9 (1953), 123–34; cp. pp. 176–7, above.

13. *Works*, volume 3, London, 1807, 253–318.

14. *Works*, volume 3, London, 1807, 264.
15. London, 1855.
16. A. M. BELL, *Visible speech: the science of alphabetics*, London, 1867; SWEET, *Primer of phonetics*, Oxford, 1890; cp. Sweet's general discussion of 'Sound notation', *TPS* 1880–1, 177–235.
17. WRENN, 1946.
18. cp. Sweet's Presidential Address to the Philological Society, *TPS* 1877–9, 1–16.
19. SWEET, *Handbook*, 100–8, 182–3.
20. R. JAKOBSON, 'Henry Sweet's paths toward phonemics', *In memory of J. R. Firth* (ed. C. E. BAZELL, J. CATFORD, M. A. K. HALLIDAY, and R. H. ROBINS), London, 1966, 242–54; B. DE COURTENAY, *Versuch einer Theorie phonetischer Alternationen* (German translation), Strassburg, 1895; JONES, 1951.
21. SWEET, *Handbook*, 105; JONES, 1950, chapter 29; W. F. TWADDELL, *On defining the phoneme*, Baltimore, 1935, and further references therein.
22. TRUBETZKOY, 1939 (page references are taken from the French translation).
23. ibid., 3, 33–46, 68–93; VACHEK, 1966, chapter 3. Like Hjelmslev, Trubetzkoy was greatly influenced by the structural and relational theory of de Saussure, but this did not lead him to reject phonetic criteria in phonological analysis.
24. TRUBETZKOY, 1939, 80–7; id., 'Die Aufhebung der phonologischen Gegensätze', *TCLP* 6 (1936), 29–45.
25. TRUBETZKOY, 1939, 196–246, 290–314; id., *Anleitung zu phonologischen Beschreibungen*, Brno, 1935.
26. 'Beitrag zur allgemeinen Kasuslehre', *TCLP* 6 (1936), 240–288; VACHEK, 1966.
27. London, 1922; Oxford, 1932; Jena, 1934; Copenhagen, 1928; Aarhus, 1935.
28. cp. E. CASSIRER, *Philosophie der symbolischen Formen*, Berlin, 1923–1929; BLOOMFIELD, 'Language or ideas?', *Language* 12 (1936), 89–95.
29. C. C. FRIES in MOHRMANN, SOMMERFELT, and WHATMOUGH, 1961, 218; *Language* 19 (1943), 198.
30. 'Sound patterns in language', *Language* 1 (1925), 37–51; 'La réalité psychologique des phonèmes', *Journal de psychologie normale et pathologique* 30 (1933), 247–65 (in English in SAPIR, 1951, 46–60).
31. WEISS, *Theoretical basis of human behavior*, Columbus, 1929, chapter 13; BLOOMFIELD, 1935, preface, 28, 142; id., obituary of A. P. Weiss, *Language* 7 (1931), 219–21.
32. *Indian linguistic families of America north of Mexico* (seventh annual report of the Bureau of Ethnology), Washington, 1891.

33. Washington 1911 (parts 1 and 2), New York 1938 (part 3).

34. BLOOMFIELD, 1935, 140; FRIES in MOHRMANN, SOMMERFELT and WHATMOUGH, 1961, 212–17.

35. SAPIR, 1921 and 1951; id., 'The status of linguistics as a science', *Language* 5 (1929), 207–14; S. NEWMAN, *IJAL* 17 (1951), 180–6; J. B. CARROLL (ed.), *Language, thought, and reality: selected writings of Benjamin Lee Whorf*, New York, 1956.

36. Critics were able to point out that the actual uses of these two types of unit were not as parallel as the theory suggested (C. E. BAZELL, 'Phonemic and morphemic analysis', *Word* 8 (1952), 33–8); the development of American linguistic methods during this period can be traced in JOOS, 1958.

37. BLOOMFIELD, 1935, 178–89, 167, 194–7; O. JESPERSEN, *The philosophy of grammar*, London, 1924, chapter 7; R. S. WELLS, 'Immediate constituents', *Language* 23 (1947), 81–117.

38. HARRIS, 1951, 6.

39. C. F. HOCKETT, 'Two models of grammatical description', *Word* 10 (1954), 210–34.

40. BLOOMFIELD, 1935, 161; HOCKETT, *Manual of phonology* (*IJAL* 21.4, part 1, 1955), 14–17.

41. G. L. TRAGER and H. L. SMITH, *Outline of English structure* (Studies in linguistics occasional papers 1, 1951); HOCKETT, 'A system of descriptive phonology', *Language* 18 (1942), 3–21. The term *grammatical prerequisite* is from K. L. Pike, who never accepted this restriction on phonemic analysis ('Grammatical prerequisites to phonemic analysis', *Word* 3 (1947), 155–72; 'More on grammatical prerequisites', *Word* 8 (1952), 106–21). On the separation of levels, TRAGER and SMITH, op. cit., 50, 53–4.

42. CHOMSKY, 1964, 80; H. L. SMITH, *Language* 28 (1952), 144–9 (see pp. 215–16, above).

43. So B. BLOCH, 'English verbal inflection', *Language* 23 (1947), 399–418.

44. New York, 1958; New York, 1955; New York, 1958.

45. JOOS, 1958; MOHRMANN, SOMMERFELT, and WHATMOUGH, 1961.

46. *Language in relation to a unified theory of the structure of human behavior*, Glendale, 1954–60.

47. B. ELSON and V. PICKETT, *An introduction to morphology and syntax*, Santa Ana, 1962, 57.

48. V. WATERHOUSE, 'The grammatical structure of Oaxaca Chontal', *IJAL* 28.2 (1962), part 2. See further R. E. LONGACRE, 'String constituent analysis', *Language* 36 (1960), 63–88; V. PICKETT, *The grammatical hierarchy of Isthmus Zapotec* (*Language* 36.1, part 2, 1960); ELSON and PICKETT, op. cit.

49. MALINOWSKI, 'An ethnographic theory of language', *Coral gardens and their magic*, London, 1935, volume 2, chapter 1; FIRTH, 'Ethnographic analysis and language with reference to Malinowski's views', *Man and culture* (ed. R. W. FIRTH), London, 1957, 93–118.

50. FIRTH, 'The technique of semantics', *TPS* 1935, 36–72.

51. The inclusion of reference and denotation within the relations comprised by a Firthian context of situation is disputed by J. LYONS, 'Firth's theory of "meaning"', *In memory of J. F. Firth*, 288–302; but it seems both compatible with his theory and, indeed, necessary, if the theory is to be sustainable.

52. F. R. PALMER, 'Linguistic hierarchy', *Lingua* 7 (1958), 225–41.

53. FIRTH, 'Synopsis of linguistic theory', *Studies in linguistic analysis*, 1953, 1–32; ROBINS, 'General linguistics in Great Britain 1930–60', C. MOHRMANN, F. NORMAN, and A. SOMMERFELT, 1963, 11–37.

54. FIRTH, 'Sounds and prosodies', *TPS* 1948, 127–52; ROBINS, 'Aspects of prosodic analysis', *Proceedings of the University of Durham Philosophical Society*, series B (Arts), 1 (1957), 1–12; *History of linguistics*, 1957.

55. SWEET, *Primer*, 41.

56. JONES, 1950, §§ 34, 463–9, 688–9; id., 'Some thoughts on the phoneme', *TPS* 1944, 119–35.

57. BLOOMFIELD, 1935, 90–2; M. R. HAAS, *Tunica*, New York, 1941, 19–20; WELLS, 'The pitch phonemes of English', *Language* 21 (1945), 27–39; PIKE, *The intonation of American English*, Ann Arbor, 1946.

58. HARRIS, 1951, chapter 8; HOCKETT, *Manual of phonology*, 167–72; GLEASON, *Introduction to descriptive linguistics* (second edition), New York, 1961, 43.

59. E. P. HAMP, *A glossary of American technical linguistic usage 1925–1950*, Utrecht, 1958.

60. HARRIS, 1951, 82–3.

61. TWADDELL, *On defining the phoneme*.

62. HARRIS, 'Simultaneous components in phonology', *Language* 20 (1944), 181–205; HOCKETT, 'Componential analysis of Sierra Popoluca', *IJAL* 13 (1947), 258–67.

63. TWADDELL, op. cit.; J. T. BENDOR-SAMUEL, *The verbal piece in Jebero* (*Word* 17, supplement, 1961), chapters 2 and 3.

64. E. J. A. HENDERSON, 'Prosodies in Siamese', *Asia major* n.s. 1 (1949), 189–215.

65. PIKE, *Phonemics*, Ann Arbor, 1947, 63.

66. W. S. ALLEN, 'Some prosodic aspects of retroflexion and aspiration in Sanskrit', *BSOAS* 13 (1951), 939–46; N. C. SCOTT, 'A phonological analysis of the Szechuanese monosyllable', *BSOAS* 18 (1956), 556–60.

67. F. R. PALMER, 'The verb in Bilin', *BSOAS* 19 (1957), 131–59.

68. HENDERSON, op. cit., further references in ROBINS, 'General linguistics in Great Britain 1930–1960'.

69. e.g. BENDOR-SAMUEL, 'Some problems of segmentation in the phonological analysis of Tereno', *Word* 16 (1960), 348–55; LYONS, 'Phonemic and non-phonemic phonology: some typological reflections', *IJAL* 28 (1962), 127–33.

70. LONGACRE, *Language* 32 (1956), 301.

71. Based on HALLIDAY, 1961, 244; a somewhat different diagram appears in M. A. K. HALLIDAY, A. MCINTOSH, and P. STREVENS, *The linguistic sciences and language teaching*, London, 1964, 18.

72. HALLIDAY, 1961, 271; HALLIDAY, MCINTOSH, and STREVENS, op. cit., 24–5.

73. HALLIDAY, 1961, 280–92.

74. See note 71.

75. e.g. HOCKETT, 'Componential analysis of Sierra Popoluca'; HARRIS, 'Componential analysis of a Hebrew paradigm', *Language* 24 (1948), 87–91.

76. A. F. C. WALLACE and J. ATKINS, 'The meaning of kinship terms', *American anthropologist* n.s. 62 (1960), 58–80; E. A. HAMMEL (ed.), 'Formal semantic analysis', *American anthropologist* 67.5 (1965), part 2, special publication. This mode of semantic analysis bears some resemblances to the semantic field theories of European scholars; but componential analysis is primarily concerned with the analysis of the terms by reference to their semantic features, while field theory is concerned with the division of a semantic field among the terms (cp. p. 202, above).

77. JAKOBSON, 1962.

78. R. JAKOBSON and M. HALLE, *Fundamentals of language*, The Hague, 1956, 28–32.

79. R. JAKOBSON and J. LOTZ, 'Notes on the French phonemic pattern', *Word* 5 (1949), 151–8; CHOMSKY, 1964, 65–75.

80. JAKOBSON, 'Principes de phonologie historique', in TRUBETZKOY, 1939 (tr. CANTINEAU), 315–36, and in JAKOBSON, 1962, 202–20; J. FOURQUET, *Les mutations consonantiques en germanique*, Paris, 1948; cp. WATERMAN, 1963, 77–81.

81. BLOOMFIELD, 1935, 385.

82. L. F. BROSNAHAN, *The sounds of language*, Cambridge, 1961.

83. DE SAUSSURE, 1949, 124.

84. A. MARTINET, 'Structure, function, and sound change', *Word* 8 (1952), 1–32; A. G. HAUDRICOURT and A. G. JUILLAND, *Essai pour une histoire structurale du phonétisme français*, Paris, 1949.

85. E. J. SIMMONS (ed.), *The Soviet linguistic controversy*, New York,

1951; L. C. THOMAS, *The linguistic theories of N. J. Marr, UCPL* 14 (1957); summary account in IVIĆ, 1965, 102–7.

86. T. A. SEBEOK (ed.), *Current trends in linguistics I : Soviet and East European linguistics*, The Hague, 1963.

87. S. M. LAMB, 'The sememic approach to structural semantics', *American anthropologist* 66.3 (1964), part 2, 57–78; id., 'On alternation, transformation, realization, and stratification', *Monograph series on languages and linguistics* (Georgetown) 17 (1964), 105–22; id., *Outline of stratificational grammar*, Washington, 1966. The connection between stratificational linguistics and Prague theory is pointed out in VACHEK, 1966.

88. J. J. KATZ and P. M. POSTAL, *An integrated theory of linguistic descriptions*, Cambridge, Mass., 1964, 1.

89. CHOMSKY, 1964, chapter 2; id., 1965, chapter 1. This demand has been characterized as one of 'total accountability' by HOCKETT, 'Sound change', *Language* 41 (1965), 185–204.

90. CHOMSKY, 1964, 23; W. O. DINGWALL, 'Transformational grammar: form and theory', *Lingua* 12 (1963), 233–75. Hockett, for example, wrote in 1942 (*Language* 18, 3): 'Linguistics is a classificatory science'.

91. CHOMSKY, 1957, 27, 46; BACH, 1964, 28–9, 152.

92. CHOMSKY, 1957, 39, 45; id., 1965, 17–18; P. SCHACHTER, 'Kernel and non-kernel sentences in transformational grammar', *Proceedings of the ninth international congress of linguists*, Cambridge, Mass., 1962, 692–6.

93. In *Syntactic structures* the lexicon appears as part of the phrase structure rules. cp. DINGWALL, op. cit. 266–7. It should be pointed out that the theory presented in CHOMSKY, 1965, and in some other recent writers, already differs in some important respects from earlier versions, in its modes of analysis, but not in its aims and objectives. Indeed, it is hoped that these aims will be more effectively attained. In particular, the lexical rules have been remodelled to carry more grammatical information and specification, and the phrase structure (or base) component has been expanded to include more rules, some covering ground hitherto wholly covered by certain transformation rules, and has, strictly speaking, gone beyond the range of simple phrase structure generation (op. cit., 88). Thus such categories as negative, imperative, and passive are represented in phrase structure by specific elements or markers, and recursiveness and embedding are allowed for, e.g., by the optional introduction of S (sentence) as itself a component of a sentence structure. The role of transformation rules is now to convert these phrase structures to the terminal strings (surface structures) underlying actual sentences. So far, the bulk of exemplification and

application has been couched in terms of earlier versions of the theory; but the warning on page 227, above, is emphasized by these recent developments. See further, w. o. DINGWALL, 'Recent developments in transformational-generative grammar', *Lingua* 16 (1966), 292–316; CHOMSKY, *Topics in the theory of generative grammar*, The Hague, 1966.

94. CHOMSKY, 1964, 66, 88–9; BACH, 1964, 127–32.
95. CHOMSKY, 1957, 32; BACH, 1964, 24–6.
96. R. B. LEES, reviewing CHOMSKY, *Syntactic structures, Language* 33 (1957), 375–408.
97. HARRIS, 'From morpheme to utterance', *Language* 22 (1946), 161–173.
98. HARRIS, 'Discourse analysis', *Language* 28 (1952), 1–30; id., 'Co-occurrence and transformation in linguistic structure', *Language* 33 (1957), 283–340. On the relation between Harris's and Chomsky's use of transformation, CHOMSKY, 1964, 62–3 (note 2).
99. cp. W. HAAS, reviewing CHOMSKY, *Syntactic structures, Archivum linguisticum* 10 (1958), 50–4.
100. CHOMSKY, 1964, 25: 'It should be obvious that its roots are firmly in traditional linguistics'.
101. CHOMSKY, 1957, chapter 6; HALLIDAY, 1961, 246; LONGACRE, *Grammar discovery procedures*, The Hague, 1964. On some relations between tagmemics and transformational grammar, W. A. COOK, *On tagmemes and transforms*, Washington, 1964.
102. C. C. FRIES, *The structure of English*, New York, 1952; P. M. POSTAL, 'Mohawk prefix generation', *Proceedings of the ninth international congress of linguists*, Cambridge, Mass., 1962, 346–55; G. H. MATTHEWS, *Hidatsa syntax*, The Hague, 1965.
103. *Gnôthi seautón* (know thyself), PAUSANIAS 10.24.1; JUVENAL 11.27; cp. BLOOMFIELD, *An introduction to linguistic science*, New York, 1914, 325: 'Linguistic science is a step in the self-realization of man'.

Index